Anticipations

Utopianism and Communitarianism
Lyman Tower Sargent and Gregory Claeys
Series Editors

Utopianism and Communitarianism
Lyman Tower Sargent and Gregory Claeys, Series Editors

This series offers historical and contemporary analyses of utopian literature, communal studies, utopian social theory, broad themes such as the treatment of women in these traditions, and new editions of fictional works of lasting value for both a general and scholarly audience.
Other titles in the series include:

Anticipations

*Essays on Early Science Fiction
and its Precursors*

EDITED BY
DAVID SEED

SYRACUSE UNIVERSITY PRESS

First published 1995 by
LIVERPOOL UNIVERSITY PRESS
PO Box 147, Liverpool, L69 3BX
United Kingdom
All rights reserved.

Copyright © 1995 by
Liverpool University Press

Syracuse University Press Edition 1995
95 96 97 98 99 00   6 5 4 3 2 1

Library of Congress Cataloging-in-Publication Data
Anticipations: essays on early science fiction and its
precursors / edited by David Seed
    p.   cm.—(Utopianism and communitarianism)
ISBN 0-8156-2632-0 (cl).—ISBN 0-8156-2640-1 (pb)
    1. Science fiction, English—History and criticism.
    2. Science fiction, American—History and criticism.
    3. Science fiction, French—History and criticism.
    4. Utopias in literature. 5. Voyages, Imaginary.
6. Literary form. I. Seed, David. II. Series.
PR830.S35A58   1995
823'.0876209—dc20   94-43054

Printed and bound in the European Community

Contents

Contributors

PAUL BAINES is a member of the English Department at Liverpool University. He is a specialist on eighteenth-century literature and is currently working on a study of forgery in that period.

TONY BARLEY is a member of the English Department at Liverpool University. He is the author of *Taking Sides: The Fiction of John Le Carré* and *Myths of the Slave Power*.

STEPHEN R. L. CLARK is Professor of Philosophy at Liverpool University. His most recent publications include *How to Think about the Earth* and the three-volume *Limits and Renewals*. He regularly incorporates science fiction references in his writings on philosophy and has also contributed a paper on Olaf Stapledon to the *Interdisciplinary Science Reviews*.

SIMON DENTITH is Reader in the English Department at Cheltenham and Gloucester College of Higher Education. He has written a study of George Eliot and *The Rhetoric of the Real*, which includes sections on William Morris and Edward Carpenter. He is currently completing an introduction to Mikhail Bakhtin.

VAL GOUGH is a member of the English Department at Liverpool University. Her current research interests include Sally Miller Gearhart and a study of utopian mysticism in Virginia Woolf and Hélène Cixous. She is co-organizer of the Charlotte Perkins Gilman Conference which will take place in Liverpool in 1995.

M. HAMMERTON is Emeritus Professor of Psychology at the University of Newcastle. He has written on Wells and contributed to *Twentieth Century Science-Fiction Writers* (3rd edition). His essay on Verne is part of a work in progress on technological prediction.

EDWARD JAMES has been the editor of the science fiction journal *Foundation* since 1986 and is Director of the Centre for Medieval Studies at the University of York. He is the author of *Science Fiction in the Twentieth Century*.

BRIAN NELLIST is a member of the English Department at Liverpool University. He has edited an edition of Milton's *Comus* and has published essays on a wide variety of literary topics ranging from Shakespeare to Byron and Scott.

PATRICK PARRINDER is Professor of English at Reading University. He has published a seminal study, *Science Fiction: Its Criticism and Teaching*, and has written extensively on H.G. Wells among other topics, editing *H.G. Wells: The Critical Heritage* and co-editing *H.G. Wells's Literary Criticism*. He is currently compiling a study of Wells to be called *The Prophetic Habit of Mind*.

DAVID SEED is a member of the English Department at Liverpool University. He has published books on Thomas Pynchon, Joseph Heller, Rudolph Wurlitzer and James Joyce. He is currently working on a study of American science fiction of the Cold War.

BRIAN STABLEFORD is one of the most prolific critics of science fiction in Britain as well as a novelist in his own right. He has written, among other works, *Masters of Science Fiction, Future Man,* and *The Sociology of Science Fiction* as well as his classic study *The Scientific Romance in Britain.*

Note

All the essays in this volume appear in print for the first time with the following three exceptions. Chapters 3, 7, and 9 were originally published in *Interzone, Foundation,* and *Renaissance and Modern Studies* respectively.

Preface

DAVID SEED

The house of fiction, Henry James insisted, had many windows and a similar pluralistic open-mindedness is necessary when approaching science fiction, especially in its early phase. Disputes continue about the origins of this genre which have been traced as far back as Lucian and Plato; and it is even debatable whether it should be thought of as a single genre rather than as a series of subgenres which gradually converged on each other during the nineteenth century: the fantastic voyage, the utopia, the tale of the future and so on. In a brave attempt to define this fiction Brian Aldiss draws on the figure of the quest: 'Science fiction is the search for a definition of mankind and his status in the universe which will stand in our advanced but confused state of knowledge (Science), and is characteristically cast in the Gothic or post-Gothic mode'.[1] Aldiss puts his main emphasis on this fiction as a mode of inquiry moving towards 'science' in its etymological sense of non-specialized knowledge. It is a definition, therefore, which stands as quite congenial, for example, to W.V. Harcourt's inaugural address to the British Association for the Advancement of Science in 1831. 'The chief Interpreters of nature', he declaimed, 'have always been those who grasped the widest field of inquiry, who have listened with the most universal curiosity to all information'.[2] As early as the turn of the eighteenth century this Enlightenment conviction was being viewed with misgiving by novelists. The American writer Charles Brockden Brown declared in 1788 that 'the world of conjecture is without limits. To speculate on the possible and the future, is no ineligible occupation.'[3] But his novels and those of William Godwin and Mary Shelley as often as not traced out the horrendous and unpredictable consequences of curiosity as a main-spring of human inquiry. To speculate or, as Brian Aldiss would say, to search runs the risk of releasing forces, of setting off a train of events which turn out to be as ungovernable as Frankenstein's monster.

It reflects the now secure status of science fiction that the second edition of the *OED* should favour it with a definition which runs as follows: 'Imaginative fiction based on postulated scientific discoveries of spectacular environmental changes, frequently set in the future or on other planets and involving space or time travel'. It is helpful to highlight the twin parameters of space and time since these play a crucial role in articulating the speculative thrust of this fiction. As long as there were unexplored areas of the globe the fantastic voyage subgenre could figure the expansion of knowledge as a journey. The opening essay of this volume surveys examples from the seventeenth and eighteenth centuries of fantasy voyages to the moon and elsewhere. The goals of these voyages represent symbolic outside points from which to view the writer's home culture. A major motif running through this collection is the interplay between the familiar and the strangely new. To modify Darko Suvin's proposition that science fiction revolves around cognitive estrangement, we could say that the imaginary voyage literally distances the traveller from the familiar, cueing in the bewildered comparisons of cultures that follow once she has reached the new world. The traveller's return then takes on a special importance, since questions now arise over whether readjustment is possible or not. Gulliver's disgusted rejection of his family in favour of their horses is an extreme but by no means unique case. The fantasy voyage offered writers, as Paul Baines shows, a means of depicting their worlds under satirical or transmogrified perspectives, and of setting up, through the interaction between traveller and 'natives', a dialogue between actuality and potential. This could involve the nature of reality itself. Edwin A. Abbott's *Flatland* (1884), for instance, repeats Gulliver's experiences in Brobdingnag when he dreams that he has left his familiar world of two dimensions (the narrator is named A. Square) and entered one of a single dimension where he tries to convince the monarch of his errors. Then the relative roles of sceptic and rationalizer are reversed when the narrator himself is visited by an inhabitant of the third dimension and subsequently taken there. It is unusual for fantasy journeys to be described in such abstract terms but Abbott follows Swift's practice of reversing perspective so as to implicate the reader in recognizing the relative nature of cultural perception. As the globe was progressively mapped out towards the end of the century, the concept of space had more and more to be extended outwards to the planets so that by 1898 H.G. Wells situated his alien intelligences on Mars. The famous opening lines of *The War of the Worlds* point an implicit moral of humans being blinded by their species' arrogance: 'No one would have believed in the last years of the nineteenth century that this world was being watched keenly and closely by intelligences greater than man's and yet as mortal as his own'. The Martians' observation of the Earth is an inversion of the contemporary fascination with the red planet and their invasion confronts earthlings with possible future versions of themselves, hence the irony of defeat coming about by means of superior military technology.

None of the voyages discussed in these pages is either disinterested or truly innocent. It has become a commonplace in Defoe criticism to point out the political implications of the technological aids to Robinson Crusoe's survival, his creation of a miniature kingdom, and so on. Similarly, voyages carry implications of future trade routes or demonstrate through their very means a technological supremacy. Jules Verne's *From the Earth to the Moon* centres on the members of the Baltimore Gun Club who discuss—only half-jokingly—taking over European countries like Britain. The novel describes the project of firing a cannon ball at the moon as a physical demonstration of America's unrivalled position in arms manufacture. The specific details of the project might be scientifically vulnerable (cf. the Verne essay in this volume), or they might offer a preliminary 'effect of the real' which, for Robert M. Philmus, characterizes science fiction as a whole, namely supplying a 'scientific rationale to get the reader to suspend disbelief in a fantastic state of affairs'.[4] Even more pointedly, the massive cannon aimed at the moon is named the 'Columbiad' after Joel Barlow's epic poem celebrating the history of the United States.

Where Verne explicitly aligns national military prowess with the moon project in his novel, *Frankenstein* juxtaposes three distinct but analogous kinds of exploration in its main male characters. Walton has been led by his 'love for the marvellous' to stray beyond the conventional track of human endeavour in his search for the pole; Clerval has developed philanthropic ambitions from his reading of romances which he aims to realize by becoming an orientalist; and between them Frankenstein sees himself as would-be explorer and deity: 'Life and earth appeared to me ideal bounds, which I should first break through, and pour a torrent of light into our dark world. A new species would bless

me as its creator and source . . .'[5] Brian Stableford argues here
that the novel could fit into a number of different possible genres
and one reason may lie in its analogies. Walton could be read as a
would-be Frankenstein and Clerval as the latter's potential better
self. One kind of enterprise is repeatedly shading into another:
physical exploration into intellectual inquiry, and so on. Even
the language becomes ambiguous, as where Walton dreams of
acquiring 'dominion' over the 'elemental foes of our race' where
scientific mastery is expressed in the discourse of triumphalism,
and Frankenstein's metaphor of enlightenment looks forward to
the light/dark antithesis of imperial fiction at the end of the
century.

In his discussion of Western writings on the Orient Edward Said
proposes a related antithesis between two broad categories: 'ours'
as against 'theirs'. This opposition was stark and extended its
polarities, he argues, so that the East was encoded as the alien
Other, confirming presumptions about Western cultural supremacy
and solidarity. Inevitably, Kipling figures in Said's discussion as
the promoter of a stereotyped white man whose quality remained
essentially unchanging from work to work.[6] The real situation
in Kipling's oeuvre, Stephen Clark proposes here, is rather more
complex and varied. Kipling shared Dickens' fascination with
exploring unfamiliar areas of city life and transposed such reports,
refracted through James Thomson's Gothic poem *The City of
Dreadful Night*, on to nineteenth-century Calcutta. Here the risk
was of the subject turning into sheer spectacle before the European
gaze but Kipling constantly insisted on the necessity of reading
all the cultural differences within the Indian scene, reserving his
sharpest ironies for those newcomers from Britain who were
unprepared to accommodate to the new culture. The imperial
theme is simpler and therefore the ironies all the more stark in
Charlotte Perkins Gilman's *Herland*, where the impulse to explore
is heavily tinged with a sexual frisson by reports filtering out of
the interior of a 'terrible woman land'. Val Gough shows that
the male explorers' penetration of this interior is a quasi-sexual
act (still accelerated by the commercial consideration that they
might discover a precious commodity like cinnabar). The title
of Gilman's novel shrewdly counters the explorers' presumption
that the land is available for appropriation and once they meet its
inhabitants Gilman sets up an extended dialogue, where their
preconceptions of gender and culture are challenged with greater
and greater force.

If space is one major parameter of science fiction, time has occupied at least as prominent a place in this mode. The *OED* definition alludes to a speculative model based on extrapolation. Stephen Toulmin and June Goodfield have summarized a crucial premise to the theorizing of natural history which applies equally well to science fiction if we substitute 'future' for 'past' in the following: 'We must treat the past as continuous with the present, and interpret the traces left by earlier events in terms of the same laws and principles as apply in the present era'.[7] The leading historian of British tales of the future, I.F. Clarke, finds a first example of the genre as early as 1644, but these works really begin to proliferate towards the end of the eighteenth century. 'These versions of the life-to-be are the cosmogonies of the new industrial societies', Clarke states. 'They are both explicative and communicative—acts of mediation between the better self in any society and for a better state of things in time-to-come.'[8] A heightened consciousness of time as such seems to have been one consequence of the Industrial Revolution, so much so that John Stuart Mill, making one of the many attempts to define his age which will recur right through the century, gives the following priority: 'The first of the leading peculiarities of the present age is that it is an age of transition'.[9]

The awareness of change in the works discussed here results in complex time-schemes which often overlay one period on another, present the march of time as a rerun of the Middle Ages (an anticipation of such twentieth-century classics as Walter M. Miller's *A Canticle for Leibowitz*), or describe a future following a catastrophe or historical lacuna. Mary Griffith's 1836 utopia *Three Hundred Years Hence*, for instance, cannot describe the new sanitary efficiency of Philadelphia without referring to its earlier civic label, the 'Athens of America, as it was called three centuries back'.[10] The gaze into the future, in other words, frequently reverses and so it is no paradox that a predictive work should be called *Looking Backward* or that Butler's Erewhonians should say 'that we are drawn through life backwards'. The greatness of Philadelphia, Griffith implies, can only be understood in relation to alternative cities, whether of the past or future. Brian Nellist demonstrates in these pages that our sense of periodicity is itself timebound and, just as fantasy locations are used to approach so as to view one's own culture differently, so utopian and futuristic science fiction repeatedly looks forward so as to look back. William Morris's 1887 lecture 'The Society of the Future' cautiously hedges about how desired change might come about (although *News from Nowhere* is unusual in showing the process of social transformation towards utopia) and deliberately refuses to specify what the end state might involve beyond generalities about freedom. On the other hand, Morris railed against the ways in which luxury had defaced the English landscape: 'It has covered the merry green fields with the hovels of slaves, and blighted the flowers and trees with poisonous gases, and turned the rivers into sewers'.[11] Morris's desired change implicitly requires a reversal of this process, the recapturing of a lost pre-industrial idyll. Anxieties about urban development came charged with class fears as much as misgiving fears about scale, sanitation, and so on, and were repeatedly focused on London and the home counties. In 1882 Frederic Harrison countered the millenarian confidence of 'civil engineers and railway kings' with a vision of the Thames Valley transformed out of all recognition: 'To bury Middlesex and Surrey under miles of flimsy houses, crowd into them millions and millions of over-worked, underfed, half-taught, and often squalid men and women; to turn the silver Thames into the biggest sewer recorded in history . . . this is surely not the last word in civilisation'.[12] Harrison parodies the quantification of urban sprawl as an erasure of known beauty and turns the criterion of size on its head qualitatively in order to give an unrelievedly negative picture of the future.

The processes of change dealt with in this fiction have themselves been put forward as an identifying characteristic of the genre which has recently been defined as a 'popular modern branch of prose fiction that explores the probable consequences of some improbable or impossible transformation of the basic conditions of human . . . existence'.[13] The mechanism of such a transformation might be supplied by natural upheaval. Grant Allen's 'The Thames Valley Catastrophe', for example, transposes a geological eruption more familiar to Colorado on to a 'black lake of basalt'.[14] The catastrophe functions as a kind of social test under which the English perform none too favourably since they plunge into a Zolaesque orgy of dissipation. More usually, change occurs so gradually that the registering consciousness needs a rapid transition into the future in order to identify the transformations that have taken place. In his contextualization of Mary Shelley's *The Last Man*, Patrick Parrinder rightly stresses the special nature of catastrophe as a sudden and violent disruption, sometimes on the scale of a secular apocalypse.

It should already have become evident from these remarks that science fiction is deeply embedded in the historical processes of technological and political change. Technology ambiguously offered the means of progress and disturbing possible transformations of social life. Hence Matthew Arnold's 1869 complaint that 'faith in machinery is . . . our besetting danger'.[15] Arnold felt to be witnessing a usurpation of the domain of belief by a technologically driven materialism, and the site for such change is usually the metropolis. In the same decade Samuel Butler complained in one of the articles that was to form the germ of *Erewhon*: 'Day by day . . . the machines are gaining ground upon us; day by day we are becoming more subservient to them; more men are daily bound as slaves to tend them, more men are daily devoting the energies of their whole lives to the development of mechanical life'.[16] In these words Butler sums up a concern which developed into a major area of science fiction: that dealing with robots, computers or (as in a work like Vonnegut's *Player Piano*) business combines which have mushroomed into an entire state apparatus. Although Butler addresses an anxiety arising out of technological development, while Edward Bulwer-Lytton's *The Coming Race* (1877) envisages a new species of humanity similar to that dreamt of by Frankenstein, both writers underpin their narratives with bearings from Darwin. Just before the publication of his novel Lytton wrote to the publisher John Forster: 'The only important point is to keep in view the Darwinian proposition that a coming race is destined to supplant our races, that such a race would be very gradually formed, and be indeed a new species developing itself out of our old one . . .'[17]

This preoccupation with supersession recurs at the turn of the century in Joseph Conrad and Ford Madox Ford's *The Inheritors* (1901) and much more prominently in the fiction of H.G. Wells. Indeed it was Wells who pulled together the different themes of technology, social planning or gender relations. Looking back on his career Wells saw *Anticipations* (1901), whose title is shamelessly borrowed for the present volume, as the 'first attempt to forecast the human future as a whole and to estimate the relative power of this and that great system of influence'.[18] By contrast, the writers before us deal in what Wells called 'partial forecasts and forebodings'.

NOTES

1. Brian Aldiss with David Wingrove, *Trillion Year Spree: The History of Science Fiction* (London, 1986), p.25.

2. George Basalla, William Coleman and Robert H. Kargon (eds), *Victorian Science* (Garden City, N.Y., 1970), p.33.

3. Charles Brockden Brown, *The Rhapsodist and Other Uncollected Writings*, ed. Harry R. Warfel (Delmar, N.Y., 1977), p.46.

4. Robert M. Philmus, *Into the Unknown: The Evolution of Science Fiction from Francis Godwin to H.G. Wells* (Berkeley, 1970), p.vii.

5. Mary Shelley, *Frankenstein* (London, 1960), p.47.

6. Edward W. Said, *Orientalism* (Harmondsworth, 1991), pp.226–28.

7. Stephen Toulmin and June Goodfield, *The Discovery of Time* (Harmondsworth, 1967), p.299.

8. I.F. Clarke, *The Pattern of Expectation 1644–2001* (London, 1979), p.22.

9. John Stuart Mill, 'The Spirit of the Age' (1831), in *Mill's Essays on Literature and Society*, ed. J.B. Schneewind (New York, 1965), p.30.

10. Mary Griffith, *Three Hundred Years Hence* (Boston, 1975), p.60. This narrative originally appeared as part of a longer work entitled *Camperdown*.

11. *Political Writings of William Morris*, ed. A.L. Morton (London, 1973), p.193.

12. Frederic Harrison, 'A Few Words about the Nineteenth Century', *The Victorian Sages. An Anthology of Prose*, ed. Alan W. Bellringer and C.B. Jones (London and Totowa, NJ, 1975), p.98.

13. Chris Baldick, *Concise Oxford Dictionary of Literary Terms* (Oxford, 1991), p.200.

14. Collected in *The Best Science Fiction of the 19th Century*, ed. Isaac Asimov, Martin H. Greenberg and Charles C. Waugh (New York, 1981).

15. Matthew Arnold, *Culture and Anarchy* (London, 1924), p.11.

16. 'Darwin among the Machines' (1863), in *The Notebooks of Samuel Butler* (London, 1915), p.46.

17. *The Life of Edward Bulwer-Lytton, First Lord Lytton* by his Grandson (London, 1913), vol.2, p.465.

18. H.G. Wells, *Experiment in Autobiography, Discoveries and Conclusions of a Very Ordinary Brain (Since 1886)* (Boston, 1962), p.551.

'Able Mechanick': *The Life and Adventures of* Peter Wilkins *and the Eighteenth-Century Fantastic Voyage*

PAUL BAINES

I

In 1724 William Hogarth published an engraving called 'Some of the Principal Inhabitants of ye Moon: Royalty, Episcopacy and Law'. It depicts, as if through the lens of a telescope, a king whose face has been replaced by a coin, a lawyer with a mallet instead of a head, and, at the centre, a bishop with a Jew's harp for a face, operating a machine for coining money. Various subsidiary characters also appear, again constructed out of metallic objects. Like Pope's 'bodies chang'd to various forms by Spleen', these are satiric concretizations; distorted, surreal, but recognizable: the telescope is actually a mirror. By the light of the moon one perceives a world whose dominant figures have been transfigured into the commodities they fetishized.[1] As a fantastic voyage, Hogarth's engraving uses technology to discover the mutations and deformations of a material mind-set, and gives us a neat emblem of the kind of issue raised in early travel fantasies. I will begin my account of these tales with a brief look at the extraterrestrial theme, before moving on to the image of technology in sublunar travel fictions.

Many of the moon voyages of the seventeenth and eighteenth centuries engender a recognition like that encountered in Hogarth's telescopic mirror.[2] The moon is the earth. From the character book *The Man in the Moone telling Strange Fortunes* (1609) to Blake's unfinished satire *An Island in the Moon* (c.1784) with its open 'affinity to England', runs a series of transparent encounters with aliens who act as projections or extensions of human types. Indeed, the earliest surviving moon voyages in Western literature, the *True History* and the *Icaromenippus* of Lucian, are comic in character, and the device of the 'Man in the Moon' commenting on contemporary political events survives into the nineteenth century.[3] The moon becomes a satiric haven for things which cannot be seen truly on earth; in Book 34 of Ariosto's *Orlando Furioso* (1532), Astolfo discovers a valley full of things lost on earth (including Orlando's wits): an empty bladder (representing Power), a bellows (representing Promises), and so on. Cyrano de Bergerac's *Comical History of the States and Empires of the World of the Moon* (1656) bears out its title partly with satiric reference; Aphra Behn's *The Emperor of the Moon* (1687) contrives some hasty social comparisons and Thomas D'Urfey's *Wonders in the Sun* (1706) both reflects and inverts contemporary social mores in its 'high-flying' and 'low-flying' kingdom of the birds. In Defoe's *Consolidator* (1705) the flying machine becomes a metaphor for parliament and the journey the 'vehicle' for economic comment.[4] Such voyages fed into Swift's *Gulliver's Travels* (1726), which in turn stimulated Gulliverian moon-voyages such as *Cacklogallinia* (1727), in which 'Captain Samuel Brunt' is hoisted to the moon by some huge chicken-like birds in search of gold (the reference is to the financial crash of 1720 known as the South Sea Bubble).[5] Brunt actually finds an Edenic world of virtuous human spirits, as well as temporary illusions of earth characters enacting dreams and nightmares on a psychological holiday from earth. Murtagh McDermot's *Trip to the Moon* (1728) facilitates discussions of politics, tea and the theatre which need little translation. *A Trip to the Moon: Containing an Account of the Island of Noibla*, by 'Sir Humphrey Lunatic' (1764), requires even less deciphering, being simply a series of anagrammatic (Noibla/Albion) comments on human bad habits, compared with the inimitable civic virtue of the Utopian moon. When Uranus was discovered in 1781 and named 'Georgium Sidus' after George III, another writer took the opportunity to 'discover' this new planet rather closer to home than the astronomers imagined: its inhabitants are literally two-faced.[6]

For the connection with science, and what we now call science fiction, we have to look at a brief period in the early seventeenth century.[7] Johannes Kepler's *Somnium* (published 1634) subordinates description of lunar inhabitants to promulgation of a Copernican world-view from a usefully non-terrocentric perspective; it also has 'satiric shafts', but these seem designed more to disguise an heretical science as conventional satire.[8] In 1640 Bishop John Wilkins argued seriously for the possibility of plural worlds, and for the likelihood that future ages would find means to travel to the moon; he was in part apparently influenced by the fictions of another Bishop, Francis Godwin, who in 1638 published (anonymously) *The Man in the Moone: or a Discourse of A Voyage Thither.*[9] This records a passage from picaresque to fantasy literature in the person of a Spaniard, Domingo Gonsales, who after the customary seaborne adventures trains some special birds called 'Gansas' to bear his weight in a special carriage, and flies to the moon. This turns out to be a Christian Utopia (no lawyers, doctors, liars and so on) as well as a perfect place to explore the science of gravity, light and speed. It is also a fantasy of magic: Gonsales returns bearing stones which retain heat forever, or give off unquenchable light, or help you fly. Another extra-terrestrial voyage, Margaret Cavendish's *The Description of a New World, Called The Blazing World*, was originally published together with her *Observations Upon Experimental Philosophy* (1666) and takes the opportunity of a voyage to a parallel planet to speculate on a number of chemical and physical questions (though there is also satirical comment).

However, the 'science' in other tales more often borders on comedy; Cyrano is drawn into the air by the action of the sun on vials of dew he has attached to his belt and he finally gets to the moon by being accidentally blown up by gunpowder and sucked the rest of the way by the action of the moon on the bone marrow he has applied to bruises sustained in a previous attempt. In spite of Cyrano's evident concern to combat the intellectual repression of French society, this fiction is not much more serious than Sir Humphrey Lunatic's supposition that his passage to the moon is eased by his possession of 'lunar' literature (Methodist sermons and economic theory).[10] *Cacklogallinia* makes some play with magnetism, and McDermot with physiology; the latter's most interesting idea is a submersible craft with windows of transparent steel.[11] But perhaps the only fully-fledged scientific fantasy of the later period is *The Life and Astonishing Transactions of John Daniel* (1751), in which the machine which flies to the moon is powered by a hand-operated pump; this narrative also makes an attempt to imagine non-allegorical Selenites of an extreme difference. But the moment is slight, and the travellers do not even realize they have been to the moon until they have left it.

Many of the satires have little interest in other worlds as such, in the science of their apprehension or in the technical aspects of flight. Comedy prevails, and often there is outright hostility to the aspirations of technology. Lucian's *True History* contains a moon voyage as one of a series of absurd traveller's tales, and the *Icaromenippus* invents a 'true' voyage of access to divine secrets to pour scorn on philosophical theories of astronomy; these works were first translated into English in 1634, at the same period as the more serious works by Godwin and Wilkins, and enjoyed a parallel vogue. Samuel Butler's 'An Elephant in the Moon' describes the fantasticated theories of power-mad Royal Society astronomers who discover through a telescope a world in the moon, a world at war, with an enormous elephant on the rampage. It turns out that a mouse is trapped in the telescope.[12] In Behn's *Emperor of the Moon* a learned doctor is cured of his obsession with the world in the moon by the elaborate fiction of a visit from its emperor, accompanied by Kepler and Galileo; the 'ridiculous inventions' of scientists are parodied in extreme form as the sublunary lovers outwit the aged philosopher. Hogarth, and Blake (with his satiric characters 'Inflammable Gass' and 'Obtuse Angle') also take an antagonistic pose towards mechanical science.

Fantasy here is of a non-scientific kind. Behn's illusion of a visit from the Emperor of the Moon is actually presented with a solemn extravagance which must impress the theatre spectator as well as the deceived doctor on stage; and Settle's *The World in the Moon* (1697) sets a genuine 'Masque of Cynthia' within a comic romance, investing hugely in a barely-framed operatic grandeur. D'Urfey makes the tale of Gonsales visible: his flying machine *moves* in the theatre. Comic descriptions of the moon often have a surreal life of their own, and invented languages and nonsense verses a disturbing charm. The allegorical mode does have a kind of celestial claim: Spenser's account of a moon voyage in the 'Mutabilitie' cantos casts history in astronomical terms, while Astolfo's trip in Orlando Furioso is divinely-inspired: his guide is the evangelist John. Drayton's *Endimion and Phoebe* (1595) and *The Man in the Moone* (1606), and Lyly's *Endimion, the Man in the Moone* (1591) in their various ways use the moon to envisage an 'ideal' universe. Even in satire there is often the desire for celestial vision: the 'eagle eye' with which Lucian's Menippus is equipped in order to spy the real activities of philosophers, before reaching an audience with Zeus; the eagle which Jove sends to raise the dreamer in Chaucer's *House of Fame* to a higher plane of perception; the celestial eye of Defoe's *Consolidator*—these represent a fantasy of superior insight. Many moon-dwellers are described as huge in stature, in a kind of fantastic replenishment of lost power or parental security.[13] Many moon-voyagers are shown round by semi-divine attendants in distant memory of the mental voyage of Dante; Sir Humphrey Lunatic witnesses a series of dialogues of the dead between historic figures, again distantly calling on the underworld testimonies of Homer and Virgil, as well as Chaucer's poem and Gulliver's summoning of authentic spirits in Part Three of the Travels to reveal an unassailable truth beyond the corruptions of history.[14] The dominant imagining is one of intellectual rather than technological power.

II

Something similar could be argued of earth-bound imaginary voyages of the period. These have naturally less need of scientific formulae in the construction of new territories, though Bacon's *New Atlantis* (1627) exists only to promote the inner secret of Solomon's house as a vast research unit, offering a fantastic plenitude of experimental knowledge in metallurgy, aviation, genetics, ballistics and alchemy. More's *Utopia* (1516) is driven more by social theories than scientific speculation, though it sees God as a kind of hyper-industrialist and admits the necessity of iron technology (it also has a cautionary tale to tell of over-reliance on magnetic navigational methods).[15] In Henry Neville's *The Isle of Pines* (1668), a prototypical shipwreck romance, the survivors bear with them only the Promethean technology of fire, and a few tools cast up by 'the working of the sea', a phrase which suggests that actually there is little to labour at in this idle and libidinous retreat.

In Defoe's *The Life and Strange Surprizing Adventures of Robinson Crusoe, of York* (1719), the technology of survival is a much harder affair.[16] Crusoe's father had warned of 'the labour and sufferings of the mechanick part of mankind' (p.28), and in his disobedience Crusoe condemns himself to a state where becoming a 'compleat natural mechanick' (p.89) is all that can save him. To begin with, Crusoe knows only the cerebral techniques of navigation by compass; after his enslavement by pirates he discovers dexterity at fishing and learns to skin lions in an admired stone-age fashion. His last act before shipwreck is to receive a huge store of 'tools, iron-work, and utensils' for his Brazilian plantation (p.57). It is a salutary gesture, for after the shipwreck on a tropical island Crusoe's immediate concern is to retrieve as much of the material technology of his own culture as he can. The decaying ship becomes a quarry of material, the tools and iron representing the construction kit or template with which Crusoe must replicate his social identity. Again and again Crusoe stresses the enormous revaluation of the most ordinary utensil in this alien and non-economic zone: he recoups a knife, saws, an axe, a hammer; cables, mastwood and iron; and navigational instruments. Everything is amassed into 'the biggest maggazin [sic] of all kinds now that ever were laid up, I believe, for one man'.[17] The carpenter's chest alone is 'much more valuable than a ship loading of gold would have been at that time'; Crusoe reflects on the hugely-enhanced value of this rescue equipment.[18]

Raw materials become transformed in a primitive (but to Crusoe, alchemical) industry: Crusoe *makes* a pick-axe, spade and hod, a grindstone, a sickle, earthenware pots, a pestle and mortar and a sort of oven, an umbrella, an anchor. He learns to make, and improve, a raft, a table and chair, clothes, and charcoal. He learns from scratch all the skills needed to grow, harvest and process corn, and 'improved my self . . . in all the mechanick exercises' (p.153). Apart from wickerwork, which he remembers from boyhood, every craft has to be re-invented *ab initio*. He moralizes on the great increase of his power:

> as reason is the substance and original of the mathematicks, so by stating and squaring every thing by reason, and by making the most rational judgement of things, every man may be in time master of every mechanick art. I had never handled a tool in my life, and yet in time, by labour, application, and contrivance, I found at last that I wanted nothing but I could have made it, especially if I had had tools . . . (p.85)

However, the note of triumphalism is muted; there is actually much that cannot be done. Crusoe cannot reinvent the wheel, nor can he make a barrel. His first boat, the product of 'infinite labour', is too big to drag to the shore (pp.138–39). His spade requires far more labour than a real one and his anchor is inefficient. Everything is extremely laborious compared with the wonders of systematic technology: 'I was two and forty days making me a board for a long shelf . . . whereas two sawyers, with their tools and a saw-pit, would have cut six of them out of the same tree in half a day'.[19] Home-brew technology is power, but it is not magic. Skill is rediscovered, the utensil is revalued, and yet real (and now magicalized) power remains in the hands of economic teams.

Nonetheless, the tool-bag suffices to turn the alien island into something recognizably European. Starting out as a hunter-gatherer, Crusoe begins to enclose the island, taming goats and planting crops—Crusoe's barley crop may seem bizarre to us, but to him it forms a providential reassurance. In exploration Crusoe finds only a few plants that he can use, such as some wild ('imperfect') sugar cane; the only Arcadian indulgence this tropical island affords are commodities already familiar, such as melons, grapes (which he makes into raisins) and 'wild creatures which I called hares' (pp.112–13, 128). The rest, though they 'might perhaps have vertues of their own', Crusoe does not recognize, and ignores (p. 112). Abundance occurs only in comparison with known models: with his 'living magazine' of goats, his pigeons, turtles and grapes, 'Leaden-hall Market could not have furnished a table better than I' (p.122). Crusoe dines off commodities deemed rare in England, and which are thus established in a familiar system of demand.[20]

Crusoe also flies the flag of domestication by treating his cave as a house with a cellar and kitchen; later establishments allow him in 'fancy' to think of 'my country-house, and my sea-coast-house' (p.115), with dogs for his 'domesticks' (p.124). A fantasy of dominion develops: 'I was lord of the whole manor; or if I pleased, I might call my self king or emperor over the whole country which I had possession of' (p.139). To begin with this 'absolute command' is comic, and Crusoe smiles at his treatment of his parrot as a sort of court favourite, alone permitted to speak to 'my majesty the prince and lord of the whole island' (p.157). But the fantasy 'little kingdom' (p.147) becomes an economic reality when peopled by those Crusoe rescues from cannibals, and later by a mutinous crew: 'the whole country was my own meer property; so that I had undoubted right of dominion' (pp.240–41). Crusoe parades a fictional governmental system before the mutineers, referring to 'the governour, the garrison, the castle, and the like' in order to subdue them to his actual authority (pp.254–67). Leaving them as colonial occupiers, Crusoe escapes to place his island on the economic map, sending back the necessary tools for full exploitation.

The real 'alien' culture against which this colonial crusade reacts is that of the stone-age cannibals who occasionally use the island as a barbecue site. Crusoe's fear of the cannibal savage begins before his shipwreck, and his elaborate fortifications on the island bespeak an internalization of that fear. The lone footprint on the sand, if it cannot be accommodated to Crusoe's own trace, must be that of the devil; the sickening discovery of cannibal practice, though partly mediated through an ad hoc cultural relativism, eventually leads to a dual conquest: the taming of Friday, and the destruction of the cannibal parties. It is here that Crusoe's rescued technology shows its true symbolic force; for Crusoe has a gun. Again, this has already shown its worth in the pre-shipwreck era: in his escape from slavery he stores gunpowder and uses several guns to kill a lion; the gun also helps to scare and subjugate savages. On the island, Crusoe is conscious that his is 'the first gun that had been fired there since the creation of the world' (p.72). His fort is lined with guns in an elaborate parade of artillery, and guns facilitate the exultant victory over the cannibals. But most of all, the gun represents European magic, a technology which can kill at a distance with a huge sound but no apparent physical touch. This ordinary weapon terrifies the savage and mystifies Crusoe as a god: Friday 'thought that there must be some wonderful fund of death and destruction in that thing . . . he would have worshipped me and my gun' (pp.213–14). Crusoe lets Friday 'into the mystery, for such it was to him' and extends his military machine through the other subordinates (p. 223), as well as using powder against wolves on the mainland; but its primary function is to render him supernatural. The cannibals take him and Friday for 'two heavenly spirits or furies, come down to destroy them . . . they believed whoever went to that enchanted island would be destroyed with fire from the gods' (p.242). One recalls that in *The New Atlantis*, where weapons far outstrip those in the known world, the inventor of gunpowder is one of the worthies honoured.

III

Crusoe's experience, then, renders 'mechanick arts' newly valuable; the colonial voyage into alien culture actually serves to revalue one's own. The ordinary becomes strange and rare, the familiar weapon a devastating Promethean device; science is re-imagined as fantasy. In many ways this recalls Defoe the enthusiastic 'projector' of money-making schemes, the artificer who reports on the state of industry in Britain.[21] A quite contrary account of these matters occurs in Swift's *Travels into Several Remote Nations of the World* (1726), commonly known as *Gulliver's Travels*.[22] This book is dominated by a severe agrarian and anti-industrial ethos and a deep scepticism of scientific exploration as proposed by Bacon and practised by the Royal Society (established in 1662); the science and the fantasy in the book do not really combine. The unsettlingly exact verisimilitude can be taken as a critique of the naive empiricism of the 'Robinsonade', and the primal fantastic quality is, as in the moon voyages on which *Gulliver* is partly based, limited by satiric reference. The projections of tiny and huge human figures, and the direct access to the truths of the past through the raising of the spirits of the dead among the magicians at Glubbdubdrib, prove a distorting but exact mirror of European society; Terry Eagleton is right to argue that the real territory of exploration is Gulliver, himself 'an area traversed and devastated by intolerable contradiction' (though *Crusoe*, for all its secular grittiness, can also be read subversively as a study in solipsism).[23] Gulliver's standard humanity is repeatedly brought into question by his arrival in states with a different model of humanity. There is no question of the re-invention of the self, conquering the alien to advance the economic individual; Defoe's subject-centred fantasy is converted to a parable of alienation. Gulliver is himself the curiosity, the show, the *lusus naturae*, the disoriented alien who drops from the moon, whose desperate attempts to assimilate himself to local mores render him eccentric everywhere.[24]

Implicit in Gulliver's fall is his representation of man the toolmaker; he is the apostle of science and technology. He describes himself as having 'a Head mechanically turned' (I.107), a phrase which ominously recalls Swift's *Mechanical Operation of the Spirit* and *Tale of a Tub* (1704), in which the body becomes a system of aberrant and malfunctioning hydrostatic forces over-powering reason; Gulliver's head is 'turned' both in the sense of having a machine origin and of being wildly off-course.[25] The Lilliputians do not recognize Gulliver's watch, but conclude it to be his God, because he will do nothing without consulting it; they are partly right, as are those Brobdingnagians who take him to be clockwork. Gulliver is a physician and mathematician by training, and therefore has a mind constituted by dealing in terms of physical calculation: his is truly a 'Mechanical Genius' (II.103).

The basic technology of survival, with which Crusoe begins, is never at issue; rather, Gulliver meets with varying technological mores implicit in everyday life. His own contrivances and dexterity cause much comment and praise. In the first two parts, they are mainly devoted to bridging the enormous size gaps in each direction: in Lilliput, a stage for the king's cavalry to display skill, stools to give access to the court, and a table and chair of appropriate size (this last recalling Crusoe's needs); in Brobdingnag, another chair and a comb. Gulliver declares that the Brobdingnagians' voices actually sound to him like watermills and looms; his own compulsive measuring and anatomical dissections are met halfway by local scientific theory. He is appreciative of Lilliputian mathematics and contrivances on his behalf and allows himself to be measured by a quadrant and subjected to various calculations relating to his diet and dress. In Brobdingnag he is again analysed scientifically, and again the craftsmen are summoned to accommodate him appropriately; often Gulliver himself directs the 'ingenious Workman' (II.89).

This cosy *rapprochement* between technological cultures begins to break down in the third part. Again the mutual curiosity leads to a formal quantification of Gulliver by the Laputans and Gulliver's 'philosophical' account of the flying island and its technological base, the huge magnet.[26] But their assessment of him is inaccurate, because science here has flown away from any practical responsibilities; Gulliver's earth-bound geometry is treated with scorn. The Laputans clothe themselves in mathematical signs and their food is cut to geometric shape in a travesty of scientific application; their science is wholly speculative, and secretly driven by a neurotic astrology. Gulliver, in his customary attempt at acculturation, attempts to see some value in the obviously futile and self-destructive experiments taking place in the Academy at Lagado (Swift's assassination attempt against not only the Royal Society but also Bacon's lavish research institute in *New Atlantis*). The episode at Glubbdubdrib, where Gulliver is magically granted access to the spirits of the dead, allows Cartesian cosmology to be authoritatively demolished, while the encounter with the Struldbruggs, whom Gulliver naively proposed as keepers of fantastic long-term experiments, proves a sobering rebuff to hopes of scientific improvement. Lord Munodi's superb (traditional) agricultural economy is on the verge of being ruined by the entropic machinations of scientific 'projectors', and even Gulliver, who 'had myself been a sort of Projector in my younger Days', cannot miss the devastation.[27]

In the final part there is almost no technology at all: contrary to More's assertion of the basic necessity of iron in *Utopia*, the Houyhnhnms have no knowledge of metals, though they can use flint. They use their hooves with surprising dexterity, but simply wait for trees to fall down and then build without cutting the trunks. As a consequence, Gulliver has to explain the most fundamental industrial processes and products: boats, horseshoes, clothes. Increasingly, this renders them not simply strange, re-invented in a conceptual version of Crusoe's practical discoveries; but fatuous, irrelevant, empty. Technology is devalued; not power, but rather the weak art of those who cannot live by nature alone, and do not even have the natural strength of the Yahoos. All the more poignant, then (especially after Crusoe's example) that the converted Gulliver is condemned (with the aid of a lower-grade Houyhnhnm) to transport himself out of the land in a canoe of his own making.

This is the culmination of a long process, and one motif links the stages: as in *Crusoe*, the highest emblem of technology is the gun. Here Swift oddly recalls Milton: for it was not Roger Bacon but Satan's devils, those metallurgists and bridge-builders, who invented the cannon which (temporarily) split the Spirit. Milton's description is put in the mouth of Raphael, an innocent angel relating to the pre-technological Adam the first appearance of something 'new and strange', a terrible weapon they can only describe in terms of 'pillars', thunderbolts and 'iron globes'. To the future victims of what Raphael calls 'devilish machinations' (the 'Argument' to Book VI calls them 'engines') this takes no decoding, but the sense of contrivance, the possibility of having, naturally, no concept of the gun, forces one to question one's casual acceptance of technological sophistication.[28] Swift has learned from this. The Lilliputians discover a number of things which they do not recognize in Gulliver's pockets, and provide the Emperor with long physical and analytical descriptions of them which act as successful defamiliarizations: the reader soon recognizes the object, but must mentally re-imagine it as 'new and strange'. Apart from the watch, which we have already mentioned, they find his snuff-box, money, razors and pistols ('a hollow pillar of iron, about the length of a man, fastened to a strong piece of timber . . . ' (I.39), together with powder and shot. All these are made imaginatively new. In Brobdingnag, Gulliver, who has already functioned as a secret weapon for the Lilliputians by dragging away the enemy fleet, offers the horrified King the secret of gunpowder as a miracle weapon in a larger and more explicit version of this estranged description:

> I told him . . . That, a proper quantity of this Powder rammed into an hollow Tube of Brass or Iron . . . would drive a Ball of Iron or Lead with such Violence and speed as nothing was able to sustain its Force. That the largest Balls thus discharged, would not only destroy whole Ranks of an Army at once, but batter the strongest Walls to the Ground, sink down Ships with a thousand Men in each, to the bottom of the Sea; and when linked together by a Chain, would cut through Masts and Rigging, divide hundreds of Bodies in the middle, and lay all waste before them. That we often put this Powder into large hollow Balls of Iron, and dis-charged them by an Engine into some City we were besieging, which would rip up the Pavements, tear the Houses to Pieces, burst and throw Splinters on every side, dashing out the Brains of all who came near. That I knew the Ingredients very well, which were cheap, and common; I understood the manner of compounding them, and could direct his Workmen how to make those Tubes of a Size proportionable to all other Things in his Majesty's Kingdom, and the largest need not be above an hundred Foot long; twenty or thirty of which Tubes charged with the proper quantity of Powder and Balls, would batter down the Walls of the strongest Town in his Dominions in a few Hours, or destroy the whole Metropolis, if ever it should pretend to dispute his absolute Commands. (II.125–26)

The experience in Laputa, where the fantastic flying island can crush any terrestrial resistance by simply adjusting its magnetic mechanism and landing on top of it (though one possible form of counter-technology is recorded), reinforces the impression that state science is likely to be oppressive, and when in part four Gulliver again undertakes the description of gunpowder, it is similar in detail but transformed in kind; from being the pinnacle of rational technology it has now become all too obviously its defining curse (IV.124–26). The converted Gulliver later imagines what war against the Houyhnhnms, as strangers to 'missive weapons' would be like; but celebrates his guess that their natural power would overcome all opposition (IV.190–91).

IV

Robinson Crusoe and *Gulliver's Travels* were the dominant imaginary voyages of the eighteenth century, and were much imitated. The first reviewer of Robert Paltock's anonymously-published *The Life and Adventures of Peter Wilkins* (1750) found it 'very strange': 'It seems to be the illegitimate offspring of no very natural conjunction betwixt *Gulliver's* travels [sic] and *Robinson Crusoe*'.[29] To cross-breed such ideologically-opposed works as these seems an unlikely possibility. The reviewer went on to give some praise to the author for 'the invention of wings for mankind to fly with'; this made him 'an able mechanick' in the novel trade, and I will be arguing that Paltock is mostly of Crusoe's (and the Devil's) party as far as technology is concerned. Yet the presentation of a race of winged humanoids, discovered in a secret world, also takes the novel beyond Defoe's technological graft into a realm of magic and fantasy not altogether removed from the initial premise of *Gulliver's Travels*.[30] Indeed, the suggestion of miscegenation between Crusoe and Gulliver (the 'Arabian Nights' are also mentioned as part of the lineage; moon voyages might have been) points to the very sign of fantasy in the book: the 'marriage' between Wilkins, the ordinary man, and the beautifully exotic, and winged, Youwarkee. Their progeny constitute a genetic trace of the cross-breeding: some have the full 'graundee' (the membrane which facilitates flight), some have a partial version, some none at all, in an exact permutation of species variation. Nowhere else in the fantasy voyage up to 1750 does this happen. Crusoe seems deeply sexless, marrying and being widowed at the end of the book in the space of a sentence and apparently oblivious to sexual need on the island itself (though in the sequel he delivers 'wives' to his colonists); the suggestion of inter-breeding between Gulliver and his aliens is either comic (in the first two parts) or horrific (his status as Yahoo is finally proved by the desire of a female).[31] In *The Isle of Pines* the narrator is stranded with four women, one of them a negress whom he clearly imagines to be of a different species: his copulation with her is in the nature of an experiment. But the main point of that fantasy is simply polygamy, and the exponential population growth just the sign of complete sexual freedom.[32] In *Peter Wilkins*, sexual union marks the literal entry into a fantasy zone, the 'graundee' a seductive veil of magic finally penetrated.

It is not hard to see 'fantasy' as the determining concept of the book. As in Godwin's *Man in the Moone* (and *Crusoe*) the main fantasy is preceded by a picaresque section. This early narrative strips Peter of everything, but the fantasy section restores it all in hugely-augmented form. The son of a rebel executed for his part in Monmouth's rebellion of 1685, Wilkins becomes Kingmaker and empire-builder for the monarch of the 'Country of Glums and Gawrys, or Men and Women that fly'; deprived of his patrimony, he carves out a new dominion and reinvents money for that kingdom. An orphan, separated from his dysfunctional family (he has never seen his two children), he acquires a new family: his flying wife is an angelic and transfigured version of his wife Patty; he is also regarded as a 'father' to his new country. Enslaved, he escapes to abolish slavery; bred to no skill or trade, he becomes a technological Messiah to a stone-age people; and as a poor scholar he reveals the magic of writing to a priestly caste and translates the Bible into their language.[33]

As in Mary Shelley's *Frankenstein* (1818), the narrative is presented as a tale told on shipboard by a man rescued from icy waters, and like the later novel, there is very little to show that the whole narrative is not mere psychological projection: Peter has brought no 'evidence' in the manner of Crusoe or Gulliver. It is a voyage in interior space, an *infraterrestrial* realm of semi-darkness into which Peter is symbolically reborn by a 'wonderful Passage through a subterraneous Cavern'.[34] But this is no oneiric Hades, revealing to Peter supernatural truths; it is a realm of authentic natural life. The fantasy is not framed, as with Gulliver: it is the substance of the book, which also has six plates to give a visual account of the flying people. Though a satiric reading is possible, it is hard work; it is much easier to accept the individual fantasy as equivalent to the narrative fantasy.[35]

I have suggested that the picaresque beginning to the novel has an important proleptic function in rendering the new world desirable. The interplay between technology and magic, or more loosely between art and nature, is established once again in the marine sphere, through conventional travel. Escaping from his slavery in Africa with the native Glanlepze, Peter must learn to survive in the wild; but to Glanlepze, the wild is home. He shows

Peter unfamiliar fruits, acts as a doctor, demonstrates the correct technique for killing a monstrous alligator (which Peter has naively mistaken for a tree-trunk) and constructs a raft to convey Peter, who cannot swim, across a river. Glanlepze's reunion with his faithful wife is poignantly described as a contrast to Peter's own domestic chaos. Here, in a reversal of the Crusoe-Friday relationship, is a domesticated and natural technology which Peter can only admire.[36] When finally bereft of all human help, in shipwreck, Peter begins to show a more experimental dexterity. His ship crashes into a huge rock at great speed, and Peter finds iron bars flying around it: a suggestion of bedevilment which he soon learns to ascribe to the natural (though still wondrous) power of magnetism in the rock. He establishes himself as 'master' of the ship, purifies water, repairs the boat, makes fishing lines and experiments on the fish he catches: the store of food and tools establishes the situation as 'domestic'.

In an amplification of this, following his accidental passage through the rock to the 'new world' beneath (again, he is the victim of an irresistible natural force but is saved by his lamp, the flame of his technology) Peter establishes a camp in a 'grotto' which quickly becomes, as with Crusoe, a domestic house with a chimney and ante-chamber, and then the capital of a dominion or kingdom with him as 'absolute and sole Lord' (p.84). His rescued tools are the template of civilization, a simple kettle proving 'the most useful Piece of Furniture I had' (p.80). He is able to make ropes, plaster, a spade (made with much less labour than Crusoe's) and a cart: he can reinvent the wheel, thanks to his use of fire to mould and transform a now useless metal key into a spindle, so rendering a principal device of the old society into a fundamental component of his new technological world. The fruit is all unfamiliar, but experiment sorts out the good from the bad, and Peter contrives versions of treacle, cream cheese and vinegar, as well as bottles and packthread from natural materials; the packthread is then woven into a fishing net which undergoes several trials and improvements. Hollow gourds, after some adjustments, make fine utensils. Even a monstrous 'beast-fish' turns out to have a use as a source for oil and clothing. Technology renders the alien land much more Arcadian than Crusoe's island: labour is conspicuously easier for Peter.[37]

With the arrival of Youwarkee, the Gawry injured on a pleasure flight from her home territory whom Peter rescues and marries, labour becomes easier still, especially once there are children to help. The continuing domestication is figured by the taming of various chicken-like fowl (a technique remembered from his mother), the production of salt, the contrivance of 'spectacles' (sunglasses) to help Youwarkee bear the daylight to which she is unused; and 'ordinary' joinery (a table and chair constructed out of bits of the ruined ship by Peter and his family). He has now 'become a tolerable Mechanic' (p.171). Peter instructs Youwarkee in the true domestic art of needlework, and the pupil soon develops skill beyond her master; she also learns, from small hints from Peter, how to melt pitch and caulk a boat, and we are treated to her long technical account of the process: again, normality is reinvented as strange and new. In fact, Youwarkee is a huge bonus to Peter as a labourer because of her ability to fly: she can get back to his ship, which is beyond a high cliff and inaccessible to Peter, with ease, and sends back down the tunnel cask after cask of tools and worldly goods. In childbirth she has 'as favourable a Labour as could be' (p.128) and her 'labour' for Peter is effortless, since flight is as easy as a flight of the imagination: she tells him, 'if you had but the Graundee, flying would rest you, after the greatest Labour' (p.134). Peter envies his family 'this Exercise, which they seemed to perform with more Ease than I could only shake my Leg, or stir an Arm' (p.161). The principal fantastic element in the novel thus grants the representative of technological man a huge access of extra power: primitive nature marries sophisticated art.

Peter first becomes aware of the presence of aliens through a mysterious semiotic trace, like Crusoe's footprint; he hears voices at night which he takes to be those of spirits. His dream that his wife Patty has been transfigured into an angel (and is therefore dead) precedes Youwarkee's dream-like arrival and angelic appearance, providing both a fictional transmigration and a deeply fantastic erotic challenge.[38] Following the literal and metaphorical penetration of her graundee, we are given the kind of extended scientific account of 'the most amazing thing in the World' that might have appeared in the *Philosophical Transactions* of the Royal Society; the phenomenon is captured. Peter's nature, however, although transparent to us, becomes increasingly magical to Youwarkee. His sense of inferiority at being unable to fly is matched by her initial suspicion that his graundee has been 'slit' (the only punishment among her people); but Peter's art soon appears superior to her nature, and the everyday picaresque story of a man called Wilkins she takes as enormously bizarre. When Peter finds a flageolet, which his family take to be a stick, the result is a literal Orphic 'enchantment':

> My Wife and Children . . . all stared as if they were wild, first on me, then on one another, whilst I played a Country Dance; but I had no sooner struck up an Hornpipe, than their Feet, Arms, and Heads had so many Twitchings and convulsive Motions, that not one quiet Limb was to be seen amongst them; till having exercised their Members as long as I saw fit, I almost laid them all to sleep with *Chevy Chase*, and so gave over. (pp.166–67; and see p.198)

A later (hostile) comment, that Peter 'sets up for a conjuror, and wants us all to dance to his pipe' (p.286), further alerts us to the possible misuse of such irresistible art.

This exchange between magic and art establishes Peter's domestic base. They live in a border zone, visited by Youwarkee's countrymen on rare occasions but largely unknown and now colonized by Peter. The next stage of his rise to dominion is the formal visit of Youwarkee's father (a regional governor) and his army. This gives Peter the opportunity for more displays of the magic of ordinary life, with increasing comedy: one Glumm attempts to eat his knife, it never having occurred to him to use a tool in eating. They have never seen fish or fowl, and assume that each grow on trees. Peter's control here serves to confirm him as a wondrous being; he is taken for 'something above the mortal Race' (p.216) and his 'secular' narrative is again reinvented as a tale of wonder for the troops. His adoption of full European costume adds to the effect and Youwarkee, now kitted out with the appropriate (though unnecessary) gown, is unrecognizably altered.

But once again it is the gun which most marks Peter as magical. It has already been established as an essential tool for signalling, protection and hunting; now it becomes a source of amazement and terror, even for the staunch and non-savage Glumms. Peter explains that it is 'but a common Instrument in my Country, which every Boy used to take Birds with' (p.196), and, 'being unwilling they should think me a Conjuror, agreed to make them Masters of Part of the Mystery of Powder and Ball'.[39] The painstaking lecture-demonstration that follows goes down to basics (they know nothing of iron), telling us nothing we do not know, but revealing the gun as 'very strange . . . the strangest thing they had ever seen' (pp.226–29). But the experience is quite opposite from Swift's destructive defamiliarization. The Glumms are initiated; the gun is still curious but not terrifying, and Peter instructs them in the use of other weapons, such as the cannon and cutlass; later, guns are offered as prizes in a race.

Though the gun becomes familiar, its value is respiritualized when the Glumms realize that Peter is the Messianic figure, mentioned in an ancient prophecy, who will 'with unknown Fire and Smoak . . . destroy the Traitor of the West', a figure then enjoying great success against their king (p.243). Peter is persuaded to leave his domain and travel to the court; to traverse this vast distance he constructs a flying machine, to be operated by the aerial power of the Glumms. We learn a great deal, from an enthusiastic account, about its specifications. After various experiments it is found workable and stands as the techological union between his constructive ability and their natural magic: Peter learns what it is to fly faster than an arrow, or (in a telling phrase) 'as quick as thought'.[40] On arrival at the court, the 'contrivance' becomes a curiosity; but its main function is to form the main plank of an airborne weapons system. The Glumms have only stone weapons; Peter brings swords, pistols and cannons to bear and is himself virtually covered with pistols and gunpowder, as we learn in his excited analysis of the battle-plan. We are offered the contrast between old and new fighting: Peter's general manages to defeat the opposing general in hand-to-hand combat of a traditional kind, upon which Harlokin, the traitor leader, comes on 'with Majesty and Terror mixt in his Looks; and seeming to disdain the Air he rode on' (p.297). His threatening words to Peter recall the defiant Satan, and his natural power seems awesome; but Peter kills him with a single shot, while his system of artillery effortlessly disperses the rest of the army. His general declares that 'we have had no Engagement at all; nor have we lost a single Man; *Peter* only sitting in his Chair, and commanding Victory'.[41] Swift's hellish vision of carnage is effaced; in an exact reversal of Milton's war in heaven, the gun becomes the weapon of the angels.[42]

Peter's flying arsenal marks the high point of the hybridization between magic and technology, but it is not the end of it. Peter's consciousness of the beauty of the Glumms and Gawrys is enhanced by the splendour of their natural magic on home territory: for once, Peter is the ignorant admirer. Their lamps do not run on oil: enlightenment is drawn from a naturally fluorescent creature.[43] They cook, to Peter's incredulity, in natural hot springs. Their city ('the most curious Piece of Work in the World') is extremely regular (like the cities in *Utopia* and *Blazing*

World), yet is not constructed but *dissolved* out of solid rock by naturally-occurring chemicals (pp.315–20). Their tools are of stone or wood, being like Eve's, 'guiltless of fire'.[44] Even their creation myth (in a pointed reversal of the Yahoo's degenerative saga) is natural, telling an evolutionary story of volcanic action, 'the dews of heaven' and the original unity of male and female bodies.[45] So much is impressively recounted, in a tone of wonder. And yet Peter himself is still fantastically empowered by his technological knowledge. His ship, though now distant, retains a cornucopian ability to replenish Peter's world of commodities; 'I think', the King tells him, 'a Man might find everything in your Country' (p.327). The King feels he has been in a dream ever since Peter's arrival.

Peter replaces their religious idol with God, here imagined as a sort of telekinetic thaumaturge in his own image.[46] The priests are taught to write and translate the Bible (a paper factory is also set up). But writing itself is a miracle to the Glumms. In an apt reversal of Gulliver's explanations to the Houyhnhnms, Peter has to explain what a horse is; he writes a message to one of his protégés (who can already read) instructing him to return a picture of a horse he had previously borrowed. No-one believes that a non-oral message can exist; the wonder that the written text can have such a distant effect is as great as the wonder at the horse as a strange beast. This episode also challenges the Houyhnhnms' own distrust of writing and preference for the immediacy and authenticity of verbal communication.[47] In another Gulliverian reversal, Peter's watch is taken as a live thing, an evil spirit which assists him in doing his 'wonders' (one remembers Gulliver's watch as his 'God'); yet as Peter explains how the mechanism works, he not only teaches them how to quantify time (they have no clocks), but also how to make such gadgets ('a hundred things as useful as this') to sell to one another: the watch becomes the chief teaching aid in a lesson about economic superfluity and desire (pp.325–26).

The final element of Peter's mystique is money, a subject with a surprising prominence in the fantastic voyage.[48] Crusoe famously hangs on to his money despite its uselessness on the island; when he escapes it becomes useful again, and in the twenty-eight years of his absence his plantations and other investments have increased bountifully. The bill of exchange becomes a telekinetic wonder, a paper writing which can transfer money and power the world over. The Houyhnhnms, by contrast, have to have money and trade explained to them by Gulliver, and as usual, the effect is to render them monstrous.[49] But to the equally innocent Glumms, Peter posits money as a magic producer, in a characteristic mode of mystification:

> You shall all be possessed of that, which will bring you Fruits from the Woods without a Lask [slave] to fetch it. Those who were before your Slaves, shall then take it as an Honour to be imployed by you; and at the same time, shall imploy others dependent on them; so as the great and small shall be under mutual Obligations to each other, and both to the truly industrious Artificer, and yet every one content only with what he merits. (p.325)

This mystic speech is taken for an impossible prophecy, yet the economic miracle is brought to pass in ten years. Peter abolishes slavery and installs a liberal capitalist monarchy (all with the consent of the people); but he also annexes by a new exploitation of his airborne weaponry the land of mineralogy on the other side of the volcano (which the Glumms take, from the noise and smoke, to be a sort of hell) as a source of wrought metal and economic material.[50] Peter, who as a child played at a nearby smithy, and who is used to the Cornish tin mines, replaces this mythology with economic dogma; the immense 'forge' allows metals to be traded, and money goes current. Colonies are instituted to trade with the outer world and to intercept smugglers, and a new technological town created to police the border, with building now accomplished by 'Shovels, Spades, Pickaxes, Hammers, and abundance of other Iron Implements' (p.355).

An entire economic system is fantastically replicated, with almost no misgivings.[51] We might simply see this as the last moment of wonder in a tale which has grafted a cleansed Gulliverian fantasy onto Crusoe's colonial ambition. Peter's whole tale is framed by the economics of narrative itself: he exchanges his story for passage back to England (the anonymous amanuensis then uses the manuscript to defray the expenses of Peter's funeral).[52] Yet Peter's death on arrival home, of which we learn before the story proper has begun, signals a questioning anti-climax to be borne in mind through the triumphal auxesis of the main text. Seduced by his own nostalgia for the now mythical realm of England, he takes a final voyage in his flying machine, which is taken as some sort of atmospheric disturbance by the worldly mariners, and is in effect shot down by the very sign of his own technological prowess, the signal gun. In the end, Prometheus has become Icarus—though the narrative format displaces any simple minatory reading. The fantasy of a union between a beautiful natural magic and a technology of renewed and re-imagined vitality is finally ambiguous, its genetic consequence in Peter's half-breed children curious but not useful, the scene of the interplay lost. No-one can go back (as Crusoe does to his island) to the land of flight with its aboriginal, easy power, its pre-technological completeness and contentment. It is easy enough to see why Coleridge and Southey, writing from the other side of an Industrial Revolution which *Peter Wilkins* ostensibly endorses, should concentrate on the mythic beauty of the Glumms and Gawrys, amphibiously at home in any element. In the end Paltock does not quite offer a fantastic *future* of science and magic in a powerful embrace so much as a serendipitous and unretrievable lightness of being, temporarily achieved by such an encounter.

This negative aspect is not, however, stressed in a project which glosses over many of the difficulties visible in Crusoe's colonialism and erases or sanitizes the critical moments of Gulliver's technological disillusionment. These are, on the other hand, issues which refuse to go away. Mary Shelley's *Frankenstein*, a novel which quite possibly borrows some of its formal features from *Peter Wilkins*, conspicuously questions the ethics of an unfettered Promethean technology, while Butler's *Erewhon* (1872) envisages a progression from technology to war. Both novels explore the limits of the eugenic science already becoming an issue in *Gulliver's Travels* and *Peter Wilkins*. The travel motif, through which the charting of intellectual and moral limits is presented in geographical terms, continues through the work of Poe and others, with the problem of colonialism already established in the three novels under discussion here becoming increasingly prominent. The future to which we look in this volume, that of a generically-stable science fiction, must include *Peter Wilkins* at least among its precursors for its juxtaposition of technological power and imaginative fantasy. For in its dramatic encounter between mechanics and superstition, its magical enhancement of ordinary technology, its linkage of gadgetry and economic expansion, and its all too credible mapping of a providential history onto imperial power, *Peter Wilkins* might be taken to look towards the cosmos of Asimov's *Foundation* saga.

NOTES

1. For the Pope quotation see *Rape of the Lock* (1714), IV.48. In these notes place of publication is London unless otherwise specified.

2. The classic survey is Marjorie Hope Nicolson, *Voyages to the Moon* (New York, 1948).

3. See for example *The Man in The Moon* (1820) and *The Man In The Moon. A Poem* (1839). For typical eighteenth-century examples see *The Tub and the Pulpit* (1710); *The Regular Physician* (1715); Thomas Killigrew, *Miscellanea Aurea* (1720), pp. 1–34; Thomas Gordon, *The Humourist* (1720); Captain Anstruther, *A Letter from the Man in the Moon* (1725).

4. See also *A Letter from the Man in the Moon; An Answer to the letter from the Man in the Moon*; and Joseph Browne, *The Mooncalf*; all published in 1705 in response to Defoe's satire.

5. See also 'Mr. Chamberlen', *News from Hell; or, a Match for the Directors* (1721).

6. *A Journey lately performed through the Air, in an Aerostatic Globe ... To the newly discovered Planet, Georgium Sidus* (1784). The author was also taking advantage of the balloon mania of that year, which of course began rather more serious exploration of human flight.

7. An exception might be made for David Russen, *Iter Lunare: or, a Voyage to the Moon* (1703).

8. *Kepler's Somnium: The Dream, Or Posthumous Work On Lunar Astronomy*, trans. Edward Rosen (Madison, Milwaukee and London, 1967), pp.63–64 (Note 56).

9. Wilkins, *The Discovery of a new World, ... With a Discourse Concerning the Possibility of a Passage Thither* (1640); Godwin's work, together with a bizarre prophecy of telecommunications called *Nuncius Inanimatus*, was edited by Grant McColley in *Smith College Studies in Modern Languages*, vol. xix, no. 1 (October 1937).

10. *Comical History*, in *The Man in the Moone: An Anthology of Antique Science Fiction and Fantasy*, ed. Faith K. Pizor and T. Allan Comp (1971), pp.64, 69, 73–74; *Trip to the Moon*, I, 21.

11. *Cacklogallinia*, in *The Man in the Moone*, ed. Pizor and Comp, pp. 108–11; *Trip to the Moon*, p.59.

12. See *Satires and Miscellaneous Poetry and Prose*, ed. René Lamar (Cambridge, 1928), pp.3–30.

13. The motif of hugeness is used, for example, by Lucian, Godwin and Kepler and 'Brunt'.

14. See also McDermot, *Trip to the Moon*, p.81.

15. *The Essential Thomas More*, ed. James J. Greene and John P. Dolan (New York and Toronto, 1967), pp.31, 65, 69, 75.

16. The edition used is that by Angus Ross (Harmondsworth, 1965) with page references in the text.

17. P.74; Crusoe's initial hoard is gathered over pp.66–82. A second shipwreck brings more goods, pp.196–97; and a ship's boat is ransacked, p.257.

18. Pp.69, 81; the contrast with the tool-less Spaniards, p.243, is pointed. Alexander Selkirk, the shipwrecked sailor whose narratives Defoe uses, had 'a Fire-lock, some Powder, Bullets, and Tobacco, a Hatchet, a Knife, a Kettle, a Bible, some practical pieces, and his Mathematical Instruments and Books'; he also made his own knives; *Crusoe*, pp.303, 305.

19. P.127; see also pp.77, 82, 83.

20. Apparently Selkirk had turnips on his island; *Crusoe*, p.305.

21. See *An Essay Upon Projects* (1697), ed. Henry Morley (London, 1887), p.31 for a comment upon the invention of gunpowder, as well as other contrivances; and *A Tour Through the Whole Island of Great Britain* (1724–26).

22. The edition used is the original one, in which the parts are separately paginated; references are placed in the text where possible.

23. Terry Eagleton, 'Écriture and Eighteenth-Century Fiction', in *Literature, Society and the Sociology of Literature*, ed. Francis Barker et al. (Colchester, 1980), pp.55–58, at p.58. Defoe's own allegorical reading of *Crusoe* is found in *Serious Reflections on Robinson Crusoe* (1720).

24. See for example, I.72, 126; II.13, 41–44; IV.10–12, 95, 171. The motif of the traveller as curiosity is from Cyrano's *Comical History*, but see also D'Urfey's *Wonders in the Sun*, p.14 and the moon voyages of Brunt and McDermot.

25. Defoe makes a playful reference to *Mechanical Operation of the Spirit* in *The Consolidator* (p.61).

26. III.25, 35–43. The confusion between magnetism and gravity is often found in early moon-voyages. For the standard accounts of Swift's 'science' here see M.H. Nicolson and Nora Mohler, 'The Scientific background of Swift's *Voyage to Laputa*', *Annals of Science II* (July 1937), pp.299–334; and Nicolson, 'Swift's "Flying Island" in the *Voyage to Laputa*', *Annals of Science II* (October 1937), pp.405–30.

27. III.160–62; see also II.128–29.

28. *Paradise Lost*, 2nd ed. (1674), I.670–730, VI.470–523, 568–655.

29. *Monthly Review*, IV (December 1750), p.157. The edition used here is that by Christopher Bentley (London, 1973), with page references in the text where possible.

30. See Robert Crossley, 'Ethereal Ascents: Eighteenth-Century Fantasies of Human Flight', *Eighteenth-Century Life*, VII.2 (January 1982), pp. 55–64.

31. *Gulliver's Travels*, I.112–14, II.84–87, 138–39, IV.122–23.

32. Compare the extensive propagation in *The Life and Adventures of John Daniel* (1751). Lucian's *True History* contains a bizarre account of asexual reproduction, and Cyrano is taken for a female in his voyage.

33. Cavendish's *New Blazing World* makes a fictional case of her own historical situation in a more conspicuous vein of personal fantasy.

34. See Georges Lamoine, 'Deux Utopies du dix-huitième siècle chez les hommes volants: quelques aspects', *Littératures*, V (Printemps 1982), pp.7–18.

35. See, however, Vita Fortunati, 'Utopia, satira e romance in *The Life and Adventures of Peter Wilkins* di Robert Paltock', *Il Lettore di Provincia*, XV (March 1984), pp.23–34.

36. Pp.45–55; for the appropriate reflection on cultural difference, see p.151.

37. Coleridge's admiring comment, 'I would try the marvellous line of Peter Wilkins ... rather than the *real* fiction of Robinson Crusoe' might relate also to the sense of ease so adeptly caught in the book; *Specimens of Table Talk* (London, 1835), II.337–39 (5 July 1834).

38. Pp.104–08, 115; one thinks also of Fevvers in Angela Carter's *Nights at the Circus* (1984).

39. P.226. Ordinary travellers are taken as conjurors in the voyages of Godwin, Cyrano and McDermot; on the other hand, Gulliver mistakes the supremely natural Houyhnhnms for metamorphosed magicians (*Gulliver's Travels*, IV.14). The question of sorcery is also utilized in Bacon's *New Atlantis*.

40. P.254; see also pp.262, 319. Top speed is apparently about 60 mph; p.350.

41. P.300; see plate VI (between pp. 296 and 297) for the scene.

42. This is explicitly a fantasy of world domination: 'had my Countrymen but the Graundee to convey their Cannon at so easy an Expense from place to place, the whole World would not stand before us' (p.293); the submarine war fantasy in *New Blazing World* has even more direct relevance to its historical situation. A celestial war is also imagined by Lucian (*True History*); for other treatments of gunpowder see D'Urfey, *Wonders in the Sun*, p.43, McDermot, *Trip to the Moon*, p.84, and Bacon, *New Atlantis*.

43. The 'light bulb' is anticipated in Cyrano's *Comical History*; in *Man in the Moone*, ed. Pizor and Comp, p.95.

44. *Paradise Lost*, IX.392.

45. Pp.321–24, and see *Gulliver's Travels*, IV.133–34, where possible material origins are mud, slime, ooze and froth.

46. For a more positive view, see Georges Lamoine, '*Peter Wilkins*: Bonheur et Religion au Pays des Hommes Volants', *Études Anglaises*, xxxv.2 (Avril–Juin 1982), pp.129–38.

47. *Peter Wilkins*, pp.308–11, 370–71; and see the praise of the English postal system, p.174. For the Houyhnhnms see *Gulliver's Travels*, IV.35, 138. Crusoe also tries to write to preserve sanity and identity (*Crusoe*, pp.81, 86), but runs out of ink.

48. Money is presented negatively in More's *Utopia* and Bacon's *New Atlantis*, comically in Bergerac's *Comical History* tragically in Cavendish's *Blazing World*, and satirically in Defoe's *Consolidator* and Brunt's *Cacklogallinia*.

49. *Crusoe*, pp.274–80, 296–99; *Gulliver's Travels*, IV.80–85.

50. Pp.255, 330–36. The thought is from Milton, *Paradise Lost*, Books I and II; again it is sanitized and converted.

51. His faintly troubled apology (p.215) is heard before the triumphal event itself. See also J. Cl. Dupas, 'Échange et circulation dans *The Life and Adventures of Peter Wilkins*', *Bulletin de la Société d'études anglo-américains des XVIIe et XVIIIe siècles*, XI (Novembre 1980), pp.77–94.

52. Pp.7–8, 376; and compare McDermot, *Trip to the Moon*, p.89. Paltock's own sale of the Wilkins manuscript was examined by Jas. Crossley in *Notes and Queries*, X (1854), pp.212–13.

Science Fiction by Gaslight: An Introduction to English-Language Science Fiction in the Nineteenth Century[1]

EDWARD JAMES

Nineteenth-century science fiction is mountainous territory which still remains to some extent impenetrable and uncharted. The obvious high points are well-known: it is easy enough to map a mountain range from the air by noting those peaks which emerge from the clouds. Brian Aldiss, for instance, in his standard survey, proceeds from Mary Shelley's *Frankenstein* (1818) and Edgar Allan Poe (d. 1849) through Edward Bulwer-Lytton's *The Coming Race* (1871), Samuel Butler's *Erewhon* (1872), Edward Bellamy's *Looking Backward* (1888), and William Morris's *News from Nowhere* (1890). He then crosses the Channel to discuss Jules Verne (d. 1905) and some French predecessors, and then returns to Britain to George Chesney, William Le Queux and Robert Louis Stevenson. After a quick side-step to Lewis Carroll and Edwin A. Abbott, and to W.H. Hudson's *A Crystal Age* (1887) and Richard Jefferies' *After London* (1885), he arrives at the safe, well-charted plateau of H.G. Wells.[2] The peaks, one notes, are generally British or French writers; one would not suspect from Aldiss that quantitatively there was more American science fiction in the nineteenth century than British, and one is left wondering what is being written in Russian, Italian, Portuguese, and other European or non-European languages. More significant, perhaps, is that the peaks are indeed there, and are familiar; but no historian of the genre has yet examined what sustains them, how they are linked, and whether the landscape between them is made up of deep, separating valleys, or a mass of connecting hills. The science fiction landscape of the nineteenth century is only gradually being revealed.

The revelations have come primarily from the bibliographers.[3] I.F. Clarke's *Voices Prophesying War* (1966) and Lyman Tower Sargent's *British and American Utopian Literature, 1516–1975* (1979) introduced scholars to some of the range of material within two sub-genres of science fiction, the future war story and the utopia. Darko Suvin's *Victorian Science Fiction in the UK* (1983) contained an annotated bibliography, as well as biographical studies of the writers; Thomas D. Clareson's *Science Fiction in America, 1870s–1930s* (1984) contained even fuller descriptions. Other more specialized bibliographies have filled some of the gaps, such as the list of primary sources in Kenneth M. Roemer's *The Obsolete Necessity: America in Utopian Writings, 1888–1900* (1976) or Carol Farley Kessler's 'Bibliography of Utopian Fiction by United States Women, 1836–1988' (1990). But the Everest of bibliographical study has come recently from Everett F. Bleiler, whose monumental work *Science-Fiction: The Early Years* (1990) has made the present discussion possible, and is going to be an essential source of information for any future scholars of the field. It is possible now to begin to make generalizations about the nature of nineteenth-century science fiction—although it is only the science fiction published in the English language. The French, German and other national traditions still await their Bleilers.

Bleiler, Clareson and Suvin did much of their work by exploring earlier bibliographies, library catalogues, and the shelves of specialized collections. But they each also grappled with a major problem: what is science fiction? For the period after 1930 the question is much easier to answer, particularly in America: the bulk of science fiction is what is published as science fiction, first in the specialized science fiction magazines (which appeared in growing numbers from 1926 onwards) and then in the science fiction paperback lines of British and American publishers. Even so, there are problems on the margins, and there are numerous books which science fiction critics would be happy to claim as science fiction which were not written or published as such, from George Orwell's *Nineteen Eighty-Four* (1948) to Margaret Atwood's *The Handmaid's Tale* (1985) and beyond. But before the 1930s the question of definition is even more problematic, because clear publishing categories had not emerged.

The phrase 'science fiction' does in fact first appear in 1851, in a treatise on the poetry of science by the English writer William Wilson:

Campbell [the Scottish poet Thomas Campbell] says that
'Fiction in Poetry is not the reverse of truth, but her soft and
enchanting resemblance'. Now this applies especially to
Science Fiction, in which the revealed truths of Science may
be given, interwoven with a pleasing story which may itself
be poetical and *true*—thus circulating a knowledge of the
Poetry of Science, clothed in a garb of the Poetry of Life.[4]

Wilson marvels at the poetry lying behind the wonders of creation—the fact that a tear-drop 'holds locked in its transparent cells
an amount of electric fire equal to that which is discharged during
a storm from a thunder-cloud', or that 'minute insects have built
whole islands of coral reefs up into light from the low deep bed
of the vast ocean'; his musings have a close relationship with the
'sense of wonder' which science fiction critics have discerned as
one of the major pleasures of the genre. Wilson also finds poetry in
current technological change, as no doubt did others in that year of
the Great Exhibition: 'The modern discoveries and applications of
Science throw deeply into the shade the old romances and fanciful
legends of our boyhood'. And stories and poetry about science,
replacing the old romances, will in future be a means of instruction
for children.

Except for an editorial response to a 1927 letter to *Amazing
Stories: The Magazine of Scientifiction*, no-one used that phrase 'science
fiction' again until 1929, when the New York publisher Hugo
Gernsback, who had just lost control of *Amazing Stories*, decided
to replace his own coinage 'scientifiction' by a less cumbersome
term for his new magazine *Science Wonder Stories*. The triumph of
the term 'science fiction' was rapid in the United States, at least
among readers and publishers of science fiction magazines. Before
1929, however, there was no generally accepted contemporary
terminology for stories of adventures in the future, of amazing
inventions, or of romances on other planets, and no terminology
which linked these tales with the much older and well recognized
genre of utopia. The stories of Jules Verne, published as *voyages
extraordinaires* in France, were published as 'scientific romances'
in Britain, and Wells was using that term informally to describe
his 'science fiction' as early as 1897: he sometimes referred
to his less plausible stories as 'scientific fantasies'. In Britain
'science fiction' books were often subtitled 'A Romance' or 'A
Romance of the Future'. There was more variety in the United
States. 'Romance' was used, and, as early as 1876, 'scientific

fiction'. The prolific American publisher of dime-novels, Frank Tousey, used the phrase 'invention stories' in the 1880s. Frank Munsey, publisher of the magazine *Argosy*, used phrases like 'off-trail stories' and 'impossible stories'. The most frequent label was simply 'different stories': that continued until the 1920s, when it was replaced by 'pseudo-scientific stories'. Gernsback's *Science and Invention* magazine published some fiction, and after 1922 these used to be referred to as 'scientific fiction'; *Argosy* itself started using that term in the late 1920s.

No-one before 1929, therefore, was writing within a self-conscious genre, or had begun to formulate any kind of definition of the type of fiction which they were writing. It is clear that if we apply the term 'science fiction' to a type of literature produced in the nineteenth and early twentieth centuries, we are applying our own late twentieth-century preconceptions and trying to impose the idea of a genre onto what would in the nineteenth century have been perceived as a disparate and almost random grouping of several different types of story: the future war story, the utopia, the lost race story, the invention story and so on. When writers of Victorian 'science fiction' decided to break out of the mimetic mould, they were doing so not because there was a ready-made market for a new kind of fiction but, normally, for one of two reasons. First, because they wished to express some kind of statement about the future: warning of the possibility of a French invasion, or of the chaos that would result from Irish Home Rule or from allowing women to vote, or, alternatively, advocating the desirability of living in a socialist future, or a society in which technological advances had made life easier and happier for the majority of citizens. Or, secondly, because they knew, as commercially-minded authors, that there was a growing audience for romance and adventure, for tales of the marvellous and the exotic, whether those tales were set on the uncharted frontiers of the British Empire, or the mysterious jungles of Central America, or the red plains of Mars. In general, said the Victorian science fiction writer W.H. Hudson, in words probably just as applicable to science fiction today, 'Romances of the future, however fantastic they may be . . . are born of a very common feeling—a sense of dissatisfaction with the existing order of things, combined with a vague faith or hope of a better one to come'.[5]

Bibliographers like Clareson, Suvin and Bleiler clearly have had to devote a great deal of attention to the question of what to include and what to exclude, of where the boundaries of this nascent Victorian genre of science fiction are actually to be placed. Suvin has tackled the problem more rigorously, though not necessarily more satisfactorily, than his colleagues. His definition of science fiction is that it is 'distinguished by the narrative dominance of a fictional novelty (novum, innovation) validated both by being contiguous with a body of already existing cognitions and by being a 'mental experiment' based on cognitive logic'.[6] Science fiction, he argues, has to be written in a realistic mode: he would exclude whimsy, moral allegory, or the tall tale (what Germans have called the *Munchhauseniade*). The novum ought to dominate: also excluded by him, therefore, are those stories in which there is one, minor and peripheral, science-fictional element, such as the automatic electric camera in Grant Allen's *Recalled to Life* (1891), which plays no major role in the narrative. The necessity for science fiction to be based on 'cognitive logic' (which seems to be a near-equivalent to 'scientific logic') excludes supernatural fantasy. There are different interpretations of 'scientific logic', of course, and few would follow Suvin in excluding Robert Louis Stevenson's *The Strange Case of Dr Jekyll and Mr Hyde* (1886) from the category of science fiction. Suvin's reasoning is that the transformation of Jekyll to Hyde takes place initially as a result of a chemical concoction but that thereafter Hyde begins 'returning' by force of desire and habit, without the chemical stimulus: it is fantasy and moral allegory which dominate, not scientific rigour. On those grounds, of course, much modern science fiction would have to be reclassified as supernatural fantasy. The fact that a scientific justification is only a token has really been regarded as a reason for exclusion.

A rather better test case than *Dr Jekyll* would be Marie Corelli's *The Romance of Two Worlds* (1886). Suvin is certain where this stands:

> I hope it is clear that her type of narration is not only fraudulent (e.g., in reconciling a totally superordinated world with all the Victorian sexual, religious, political, and ethical taboos), is not only a proto-Fascist revulsion against modern civilization, materialist rationalism, etc., is not only a narration based on ideology unchecked by any cognitive logic, but is also [. . .] cobbled together from orts and scraps of esoteric metaphysics, so that the narrative logic is simply ideology plus Freudian erotic patterns. If SF exists at all this is not it. (p.94).

But Suvin's own description demonstrates that it is largely his own profound disagreement with the fundamentals of Marie Corelli's beliefs that conditions his attitude. Certainly her novel is highly individual: it involves the description of a psychic voyage around the solar system, in the company of an angel, visiting the advanced societies on Saturn, Venus and Jupiter, and learning about the scientific basis for a somewhat deviant kind of Christianity. Corelli herself was highly indignant at the fun which her reviewers poked at her Electrical Christianity, and in later editions she incorporated testimonials from readers who had profited from her ideas. The ideas in the novel, hidden among 'hundreds of pages of gush' (Bleiler, p.160), certainly witness to an eccentric view of the universe, but do have many points of contact with those found in more conventional works of science fiction, and she does do what science fiction writers most typically do: use their fiction as a forum for speculations upon the nature of reality. It would be dangerous to start excluding works because they did not correspond to the accepted wisdom of late twentieth-century readers; and Corelli is only one of several late Victorian writers to use the medium of science fiction in an attempt to reconcile the worlds of science and religion, or to 'people' her solar system with angels and spirits.

The lost race tale is another marginal area.[7] These stories, of which Rider Haggard's *She* (1887) is the most famous example, involve the discovery, in one of the relatively unexplored parts of the globe, of a fictional community which had developed in isolation from the author's known world. Lost races are abundant in late nineteenth-century fiction—127 examples are listed by Bleiler, of which forty are British and eighty-four American—and they are usually to be found in Africa or Latin America. Latin American versions generally involve the discovery of a civilization of Mayas, Aztecs or Incas, preserving their pre-Columbian way of life intact; in Africa and elsewhere we find the Lost Tribes of Israel, and the long-lost descendants of Romans, Carthaginians, English explorers and so on; in the warm seas which many Victorian writers imagined to exist beyond the north polar ice-packs live (in five novels) the descendants of the Vikings. As R.D. Mullen has pointed out (in Suvin, p.95), most science fiction stories contain a 'what if?', and there is a latent 'what if?' in the lost race story: 'what would happen to a civilized society isolated for centuries from the Ekumene?' But very few lost race stories actually explore this question, says Suvin, and very few offer any

kind of novum. Most lost races have primitive barbaric slave-
owning societies; the plot usually revolves around the relationship
between a wicked high priest, a beautiful princess and a virtuous
white explorer. Suvin admits that this 'nostalgia of primitivism'
has been prominent in science fiction (the Mars stories of Edgar
Rice Burroughs, from 1912 onwards, are a prime example), but
does not feel that the great majority of them qualify. He is, on
the other hand, prepared to admit to the category another type
of story that most would exclude: the prehistoric tale. A story set
in the prehistoric past is indeed often, like a science fiction story,
a 'parable on the possibilities of novel relationships of psychozoa
(intelligent beings) to each other and the universe' (Suvin, p.4); it
is an application of the most recent speculations of scientists (in
this case archaeologists and anthropologists) to the understanding
of human development.

I would agree with Bleiler that the prehistoric story bears a far
more distant relationship to the primary concerns of science fiction
than the lost race story. For Bleiler prehistoric fiction is too remote
for it to be classified as science fiction at all: 'the story of prehistoric life (unless it has other elements) is simply a form of historical
fiction' (p.xii). The lost race story, on the other hand, is part, and
a significant part, of the category which he is studying:

> As a rule there is little or no quasi-scientific material
> present, beyond the survival of an occasional dinosaur or
> mammoth. Sometimes there is a certain amount of trivial
> supernaturalism, like prophecies that are fulfilled or rein-
> carnation, but this does not affect the basic rationality of
> the story type.
> A few critics, for doctrinary reasons [i.e. Suvin], do
> not accept the lost-race story as science-fiction, but the con-
> sensus has traditionally accepted it commercially, and I see
> no reason that it should be rejected. (p.xi)

There are rather better reasons for including the 'lost race' story
than Bleiler implies. The 'lost race' as a category merges imperceptibly with much less problematical categories, so that drawing
clear boundaries is impossible. A 'lost race' properly defined is a
group of people who once had contact with our own historical
past, but have since moved geographically and developed isolated
from western Europe until their rediscovery in the nineteenth century: specific examples might be *The Day of Resis* (USA, 1897) by
Lillian Francis Mentor, in which Europeans come across a lost

kingdom in Africa ruled by descendants of the Egyptians who escaped the plagues of Moses, or *The Fortress of Yadasara* (UK, 1899), by Christian Lys (pseudonym of Percy James Brebner) in which the lost race are descendants of Crusaders living in a secluded valley in the Caucasus. But this category merges imperceptibly into those stories of imaginary races who have no contact at all with the history that we have known, such as the peoples whom numerous Victorian stories depict as living within the interior of a hollow Earth, or, indeed, those peoples who inhabit Mars or Venus. Fascination with the Other is one of the basic sources of the science fiction imagination, and the traditional 'lost race' story may satisfy that fascination as well as stories of interplanetary travel.

For drawing up the two Tables, commentary upon which forms the central part of this chapter, I have taken the term 'science fiction' to include as wide a range as possible. The figures are derived from a data-base which I established from the various bibliographies mentioned above: primarily that by Bleiler, but with additions from Clareson, Kessler, Roemer and Suvin. The category of 'science fiction' has been drawn more widely than Bleiler does since I have included a number of stories (types of utopian fiction, for instance), which he rejects. I include, as Bleiler did, boys' stories, and also the eighty-three dime-novels which Bleiler lists, even though their science-fictional element—Suvin's 'novum'—is often only a single peripheral item, such as an airship or an electric submarine, or the appearance of a lost race.

The total number of science fiction stories (following the broadest possible definition of science fiction) published in the English language between 1801 and 1900 is 1024. That total includes all kinds of fiction, ranging from short stories a few pages long to the relatively few traditional three-decker British novels. There are 306 short stories in the total: 177 by American writers, 112 by British writers and seventeen by 'Other'. Some explanation is needed of the categories 'British', 'American' and 'Other' for an understanding of the Tables, or of what follows. By 'British' I mean that the writer is known to be British, or, very occasionally, can be assumed to be British by the place of publication. The work may occasionally be written, or even published, in a part of the British Empire, or even in the United States. For the sake of simplicity, and recognizing the political realities which existed under the Union between 1801 and 1922, the term 'British' is taken to include 'Irish'. (Though this is not a relevant comment here, it is

Table 1: English-Language SF Publications, 1801 – 1900

Year	British	American	Other	Total
1800 – 10	0	0	0	0
1811 – 20	5	2	1	8
1821 – 30	5	1	0	6
1831 – 40	3	15	0	18
1841 – 50	3	23	1	27
1851 – 60	6	6	0	12
1861 – 70	11	7	2	20
1871 – 80	39	49	13	101
1881 – 90	115	126	15	256
1891 – 1900	258	288	30	576
TOTAL	445	517	62	1024

perhaps worth noting that the bulk of the Irish writers hidden in the figures are Ulster Protestants.) The term 'American' means that the work is written by a citizen of the United States of America (even though the work may be published in the United Kingdom). The term 'Other' includes a multitude: these may be works translated from German or French (most notably the works of Jules Verne), or works written by Canadians (four in number), Australians (five) or New Zealanders (one), or works written by authors who are probably either American or British but whose actual origins are unknown.[8] In the Tables, the date of publication as far as possible is that of the original magazine publication, where applicable, rather than its subsequent publication in book form.

Table 1 shows very clearly the pattern of publication of science fiction novels and stories during the nineteenth century. There is a gradual growth in the numbers until the 1880s, when there is a sudden increase, both in Britain and in the United States. The anomaly of an increase in the number of stories published in the United States during the 1830s and 1840s is entirely due to the publishing careers of Edgar Allan Poe and Nathaniel Hawthorne: Poe wrote thirteen and Hawthorne twelve of those thirty-eight stories. Likewise, the increase of stories under the 'Other' heading during the 1870s is largely due to the publications of Jules Verne, who produced six out of the thirteen stories in that part of the Table. But from the 1880s an increasing number of authors contribute to the nascent genre, and perhaps these writers are different from earlier ones. Suvin's biographical study of British authors of science fiction (in *Victorian Science Fiction in the UK*, pp.127–251) suggests that before the mid-1880s, writers of science fiction were drawn from the same high professional class as most writers of 'high literature'; after the mid-1880s, the dramatic increase in the amount of fiction published 'brings an influx of lower-class or Grub Street writers, and changes the overall social status of S-F writers' (p.242).

Table 2 is a detailed breakdown of the figures from 1871 onwards; 1871 is certainly a crucial year. As I.F. Clarke wrote, the history of British science fiction virtually began on May Day in that year: Edward Bulwer Lytton's *The Coming Race* 'appeared on May 1st, 1871, the day when Blackwood's of Edinburgh also published Chesney's *Battle of Dorking* in their magazine, and by an even more extraordinary coincidence the day when Samuel Butler brought the manuscript of *Erewhon* to Chapman and Hall'.[9] Of the thirteen stories published in Britain in 1871, which included Chesney and Lytton, seven were direct answers to Chesney, while one or two others were probably also inspired by it. Apart from 1871, the single largest leap in production occurred in 1886. As in 1871, that might well have been caused largely by external events. The publication of *The Battle of Dorking* in 1871, which warned of British unpreparedness for war, and which inspired seven responses in that year, was a direct reaction to the catastrophic defeat of the French forces by the Germans in the Franco-Prussian War, and the sudden realization of the potential swiftness of modern warfare. Seven out of the twenty British items published in 1886, on the other hand, were directly inspired by internal politics: the Irish Home Rule Bill. These stories were mostly written by Ulster Protestants, warning of the dangers of a Papist state in Ireland.[10] The table also shows that with the exception of two groups of three years each—1885–1887 and 1896–1898—American writers were producing more science fiction than British authors, even though the difference is marginal and perhaps not significant statistically.

Getting beyond the bald figures in the Tables, it is possible to notice some differences between the British and American markets. As we have already seen, the lost race story was much more popular in America, with eighty-four examples to Britain's forty: this is largely due, however, to the popularity of the motif in

Table 2: English-Language SF Publications, 1871 – 1900

Year	British	American	Other	Total
1871	13	3	1	17
1872	1	3	2	6
1873	4	2	4	10
1874	4	4	2	10
1875	3	1	0	4
1876	2	9	0	11
1877	3	4	1	8
1878	2	5	1	8
1879	4	10	0	14
1880	3	8	2	13
1881	4	11	1	16
1882	6	9	0	15
1883	7	6	1	14
1884	7	6	2	15
1885	10	9	0	19
1886	20	10	1	31
1887	19	11	1	31
1888	19	8	3	30
1889	12	23	3	38
1890	11	33	3	47
1891	19	32	3	54
1892	22	29	4	55
1893	24	26	4	54
1894	25	32	4	61
1895	26	29	2	57
1896	34	24	4	62
1897	24	23	2	49
1898	41	32	4	77
1899	21	27	2	50
1900	22	34	1	57
TOTAL	412	463	58	933

American dime-novels, which account for thirty of the American total. Boy explorers like Frank Reade Jr., in their electric submarines or bat-winged air-ships, are continually finding lost races of Aztecs or Vikings: in one dime-novel the Toltecs have even managed to lose themselves in Australia.[11] The utopian story, too, was much more of an American genre than a British one. Counting only those utopian stories with science-fictional elements (and thus excluding, in particular, those stories dealing with life on a utopian commune in contemporary or near-future America), there are 105 American examples to thirty-eight British ones, out of a total of 154. Even before the publication of Edward Bellamy's *Looking Backward* in 1888, utopia was a theme which came much more readily to Americans—unsurprisingly, in a country which itself had utopian ideals and in which numerous experimental utopian communities were founded in the nineteenth century—and after Bellamy there was a great flurry of production. Novels were written which were sequels to Bellamy, following the adventure of Julian West Jr., the son of Bellamy's protaonist, or of Juliana West, or even purporting to be one of the novels produced by Berrian in Bellamy's utopian future.[12] The future war, however, was much more of a British phenomenon, with fifty-five examples from British authors and only seventeen from Americans (out of a total of seventy-seven). Chesney played the same inspirational role for the British future war story that Bellamy played for the American utopia.

One reason for this great increase in the production of science fiction, above all in the last fifteen years of the century, is clearly the influence of specific books, like Bulwer-Lytton's *The Coming Race*, Chesney's *The Battle of Dorking*, Bellamy's *Looking Backward* and the popular translations of Verne's early novels. These not only inspired direct response, but also accustomed people to the idea of writing within these particular categories, for instruction or entertainment, and helped to train a readership to be used to thinking in these terms. But there must also have been wider cultural changes which allowed for the rapid growth of these new categories of literature, most of which had something to do with the idea of historical change. No doubt the increased speed of technological change in the later nineteenth century, together with the *fin de siècle* feeling that one age was over and another about to begin, led people to speculate more about the future. There was much anticipation of the coming twentieth century not only in fiction, but also in non-fictional essays and popular journalism.

Familiarity with the idea of a fictional future, thanks to Verne, Bellamy and others, clearly encouraged people to express their hopes and fears in those terms: the phrase 'literature of ideas' was current in the 1890s, and much of British science fiction in the 1890s was part of that. When the Fabian socialist Beatrice Webb was working on her history of trade unionism in 1895, for instance, it seemed to her perfectly natural to think of writing a novel called *Sixty Years Hence*. This would not be a utopia, she hastened to tell her diary (i.e. not another *News from Nowhere*), but a tale of life in the future 'if we go on "evoluting" in our humdrum way': a collectivist future, and one in which 'the fully-fledged woman engaged in a great career should be pictured just as we should now picture a man'.[13] She never wrote it, but others did.

General trends in fiction may also have helped prepare the ground for the scientific romance, in Britain at least. Elaine Showalter has recently argued that in the Britain of the 1880s there was a conscious move away from the realistic novel as epitomized by women writers like George Eliot, concerned with domestic matters, love, marriage, and relationships between people, towards new forms of romance. Romance dealt with adventure, with Empire, with the deeds of men among men. Rider Haggard dedicated *King Solomon's Mines* (1885) 'to all the big and little boys who read'. Women were largely excluded from this world, as protagonists, as writers and as potential readers. 'If the critic is a woman', Walter Besant wrote to Haggard after the publication of *She* (1886), 'she will put down this book with the remark that it is impossible—almost all women have this feeling towards the marvellous.'[14] R.L. Stevenson, G.A. Henty, Haggard and Kipling all wrote stories in which male friendships are much more important than female relationships, and in which the imperial quest is also a flight from domesticity and marriage. The almost exclusively male writers of British 'scientific romance' in the period up to the Great War fit neatly into this trend.

People at the end of the nineteenth century, seeing their world changed out of all recognition from earlier times by the steam engine, by the mechanized factory, by gas and increasingly by electricity, were fascinated by machines and gadgets, and fully conscious that the lives of their children, even more than their own, were going to be transformed by them. A set of fifty cigarette cards produced by Armand Gervais of Lyons in 1899 shows the range of expected wonders: personal flying apparatus, helicopters, children being taught via electric head-sets and news coming through a superphonograph, mechanized house-cleaning and farming, and so on.[15] The fascination with invention, and an interest in writing what may be categorized as 'invention stories', in which a new invention supplies the main narrative theme, is perhaps more American than British. Of those 1024 science fiction stories we are examining, 178 may be categorized as 'invention stories', of which 111 are American, and only fifty-four British. The interest in 'invention stories' is part of what Neil Harris has called the 'operational aesthetic'; he has suggested that it is a particular manifestation of American culture in the nineteenth century. Ordinary Americans were disturbed by beauty, significance, spiritual values, but were fascinated by the absorption of knowledge: museums were much more popular than art galleries. 'This was an aesthetic of the operational, a delight in observing process and examining for literal truth.'[16] It is a significant element in the growth of science fiction. Readers then (as, frequently, younger readers today) had insatiable appetites for learning about the universe around them, and the lengthy disquisitions about science which were to be found in early science fiction stories were not then seen, by most of their readers, as literary flaws, but as an essential part of their reading pleasure.

The differences between science fiction in the United States and Britain are concerned not just with the different political and cultural histories of the two countries, but also with the different history of book publishing, and the different ways in which both publishers and authors treated science fiction.

In Britain, as is well known, the three-volume novel, the 'three-decker', dominated the respectable novel-writing scene in the nineteenth century, and there was an enormous unfilled gap in both price and quality between these and the penny dreadful market. Because three-deckers were so expensive, circulating libraries were established which in turn dominated the field, fixing prices and causing writers to self-censor themselves in order to achieve publication. Science fiction was outside this system. In Suvin's list of 360 items of Victorian science fiction, only eleven are three-deckers.[17] Even if the circulating libraries had been interested in such material on a large scale, the three-decker form simply did not lend itself to science fiction: the kind of detailed description and analysis required to fill hundreds of pages was very difficult to apply to scientific romance. At the other end of the scale, the penny dreadful (the English equivalent of the dime-novel) did not adopt science fiction themes either: for different reasons, it too preferred the familiar. Science fiction as it existed in Victorian Britain therefore mostly survived outside the generally accepted forms: as novelettes published in magazines like *Blackwood's*, as pamphlets, or as single-volume publications intended for boys (like the translations of Verne). But the situation changed radically in the 1890s, not only because the circulating libraries turned against the three-decker in favour of single-volume novels, but also because of the great expansion of middle-brow periodicals. *The Strand*, home of Sherlock Holmes from 1891 and of various science fiction short stories (including some by Doyle himself), is well known, but there were many others. These weeklies and monthlies published much of the science fiction of the 1890s and 1900s. *Pearson's Weekly* serialized George Griffith's *The Angel of the Revolution* from January 1893, the most imaginative yet in the 'future war' mould. (Griffith established himself as the best-known writer of science fiction in Britain in the early 1890s, and Wells, wanting to be taken seriously, always fumed at the obvious comparisons made between him and the popular Griffith.) Wells himself had his short stories published by *The Pall Mall Gazette* and others, while his novels were serialized in the magazines before book publication: *Pearson's Weekly* took his *The Invisible Man* (1897), for instance, and *Pearson's Magazine* published *The War of the Worlds* (1897; book publication 1898).

The proliferation of markets for imaginative romances was not just a British phenomenon. Magazines like *The Strand* and *Pearson's Magazine* both had American editions, which helped introduce some of these British science fiction writers to a much larger readership, while American magazines of similar type were created. There were all-fiction magazines too, like *The Argosy* (monthly from 1896) and *All-Story Magazine* (1905): there was also a smaller-circulation fiction magazine, published in Boston between 1895 and 1919, called *The Black Cat*, which specialized in fantasy fiction. These magazines allowed a large number of writers to establish themselves and to reach a very large number of readers: at its peak in 1907 *The Argosy* was offering some 135 000 words of fiction on coarse pulp paper, at a cost of 10 cents, to around half a million readers each month.

In the United States the increasing number of popular magazines had not had the profound effect upon the kind of fiction produced that it had in Britain. The three-decker had never been important, and the huge gap between 'literature' and the penny dreadful which existed in Britain until the 1890s had in the US been filled by a wide variety of 'popular' literature. In the US, romance had never been so marginalized by the realistic novel as it had been, earlier in the century, in Britain. Throughout the century, most of the respected (male) writers of fiction in the US had dabbled in what we could call science fiction: Edgar Allan Poe is the most obvious example, but there are also Charles Brockden Brown, Washington Irving, Nathaniel Hawthorne, James Fenimore Cooper, Fitz James O'Brien, Oliver Wendell Holmes, as well as, somewhat later, Mark Twain, Herman Melville, Henry James and Ambrose Bierce.

The American public was introduced to Wells and other English writers through these new periodicals, which also allowed the republication of older material and the appearance of some newer American writers, such as George Allan England and Garrett P. Serviss; on the whole, in this period British writers had more of an impact on the American market than Americans on the British, but there was considerable cross-fertilization, even if there were differences in taste. The themes of utopias and lost races were more popular in the US, the future war story in the UK, and that fiction aimed at a semi-literate readership was more common in the US (in the form of dime-novels). But the two markets also had a lot in common, and by the early part of the twentieth century it looked very much as if British and American markets and readerships had converged, and were destined to follow a similar evolution.

By 1910, however, much had changed. In Britain, many of the periodicals disappeared with the rise of the popular daily press, and those that were left, like *The Strand* and *Pall Mall Gazette*, were yearning for respectability and became reluctant to publish anything like the quantity of speculative fiction which they had done before. The fad for scientific romance declined. Interplanetary tales virtually disappeared from the scene until Olaf Stapledon in the 1930s; when such stories were written they tended to be published as 'boys' books'. Before the Great War, and particularly just after it, when scientific romance was written in Britain it was published not in magazines, but in book form. It rarely appeared in a cheap hardback series, like Collins' Shilling Fiction Library, or Newnes' Sevenpenny Series, just as, immediately before and after World War II in Britain, it very rarely appeared in paperback format: scientific romance was regarded as unlikely to achieve mass-market interest. Moreover, British scientific romance tended to be published in full-length novel form, not in the short story form which dominated American science fiction until the 1950s. Brian Stableford (whose excellent and indispensable *Scientific Romance in Britain, 1890 – 1950* is the otherwise unacknowledged source for much of this section) sees a highpoint in the production of scientific romance in Britain in 1898, with a steady decline thereafter to the trough of 1918, and only a slow recovery to a new phase of popularity, and a new generation of writers, at the beginning of the 1930s.

Publishing in the US took a totally different direction. Books had been cheap even before the 1890s, and widespread pirating of foreign books helped to keep prices down. The boom in periodicals, which the US shared with Britain, continued long after the decline in Britain, and publishers deliberately aimed their publications at a wider public than in Britain. There had been considerable indignation at the low literary level of such dime-novels as the *Frank Reade Library*, but the result was the replacement of the dime-novel by almost equally low-grade fiction magazines aimed at almost the same public—'the pulps'. The average pulp was a magazine measuring 10 inches by 7, printed on thick coarse paper; it was the development of the technique of producing cheap paper from wood-pulp, in the 1880s, that created the possibility of mass production of cheap magazines as well as the name by which they became known. The pulps often had ragged untrimmed pages and, later in their history, covers printed with cheap, lurid coal-tar dyes. Now, yellowing and fragile, they are expensive collectors' items; when published they were the kind of thing respectable readers shunned, or kept hidden. The publishers of the more upmarket middle-class magazines (printed on better quality, shinier paper, and hence known as 'the slicks') came to see the fast-paced adventure stories to be found in the pulps (which included science fiction) as tainted by their low-grade associations, and they stopped printing them. While early twentieth-century science fiction in Britain, when it was published, came out regularly in hardback, in America it was largely restricted to the pulps.

It was the later specialization of the pulps which gave birth to science fiction as a genre in America: this is part of the history of twentieth-century science fiction. Publishers of dime-novels had realized that there were readers who liked only one kind of fiction—westerns, perhaps, or detective novels—and eventually the pulps began to specialize as well. *Thrill Book* (which began and ended in 1919) was the first pulp to specialize in fantastic fiction; *Amazing Stories* (1926 to the present, in different guises) was the first 'scientifiction' pulp. In the 1920s specialisation reached spectacular heights: 'there were magazines specialising in railroad stories, sea stories, yellow peril stories, the exploits of crime-fighting superheroes, and even a short-lived pulp called *Zeppelin Adventures'*.[18] The success of *Amazing Stories* inspired not only *Astounding*, but numerous other science fiction pulps: modern science fiction was born.

The modern science fiction that was born in the twentieth century in the United States and, eventually, in Britain and other European and non-European countries, had very obvious roots in the science fiction of the nineteenth century. Verne and Wells (particularly Wells's stories and novels from the 1890s) remained strong influences for a long time, and not only in their countries of origin. From its first issue in 1926, and for years thereafter, *Amazing Stories* had a drawing of Jules Verne's tomb at Amiens on its title-page, the immortal Verne in the act of raising the lid of his tombstone to peer into his own future. In England the tradition of scientific romance was dominated by the memory of Wells well into the 1950s—science fiction was not infrequently called 'that Wells stuff'—and his influence was strong too in the United States, where, for instance, the first specialist science fiction magazine, *Amazing*, published twenty-six of his novels and stories in its first five years, between 1926 and 1930. But the nineteenth century had not only seen the emergence of the 'respectable' science fiction of Verne and Wells, but, rather more importantly for the future of science fiction, had also seen the writing of works which fore-shadowed other significant aspects of twentieth-century science fiction. Two British works may be singled out. Percy Greg's *Across the Zodiac. The Story of a Wrecked Record* (1880) offers not only a very precise account of space travel, but also invents an alien society on Mars, complete with philosophy, religion, language and proverbs. Robert W. Cole, *The Struggle for Empire. A Story of the Year 2236* (1900) introduces the concepts of galactic empires, giant interstellar space-ships travelling at ten million miles per hour, and space fleets of thousands of battleships fighting it out for mastery of the galaxy. It may be only a future war story writ large, with the British and German fleets being rewritten as the fleets of Earth and Sirius, but it had all that exuberance and extravagance that have been essential characteristics of twentieth-century science fiction but which were largely missing from the works of Verne and Wells. Studying the nineteenth-century predecessors of modern science fiction, indeed, in all their considerable variety and lack of conformity to any specific preconceptions of category or genre, we are reminded of something that twentieth-century terminology often forces us to forget: that the modern label 'science fiction' or 'sf' gives a spurious kind of unity to what is, in fact, a collection of disparate sub-genres, with differing literary histories and characteristics.

NOTES

1. The title is a homage to Sam Moskowitz, who has done so much pioneer work on early American science fiction, and in particular to his book *Science Fiction by Gaslight: A History and Anthology of Science Fiction in the Popular Magazines, 1891–1911* (Cleveland, Ohio, 1968). As he points out (pp.15–16), although the electric light was invented in 1879 (and although the science fiction of the 1880s and 1890s was obsessed with the infinite possibilities of electricity), gaslight does not reach its peak until the 1890s, and remained the dominant source of light until 1910 and beyond. Portions of this essay appear in Edward James, *Science Fiction in the Twentieth Century* (Oxford, 1994).

2. Brian Aldiss, with David Wingrove, *Trillion Year Spree: The History of Science Fiction* (London, 1986), chapters 1 to 4.

3. The full references to these works are as follows: I.F. Clarke, *Voices Prophesying War 1763–1984* (Oxford, 1966); Lyman Tower Sargent, *British and American Utopian Literature, 1516–1975: An Annotated Bibliography* (Boston, 1979; much expanded 1988); Darko Suvin, *Victorian Science Fiction in the UK: The Discourse of Knowledge and of Power* (Boston, 1983); Thomas D. Clareson's *Science Fiction in America, 1870s–1930s. An Annotated Bibliography of Primary Sources* (Westport, Conn. and London, 1984); Kenneth M. Roemer's *The Obsolete Necessity: America in Utopian Writings, 1888–1900* (Kent, Ohio, 1976); Carol Farley Kessler's 'Bibliography of Utopian Fiction by United States Women, 1836–1988' (*Utopian Studies*, 1 (i) (1990), pp.1–58); Everett F. Bleiler, *Science-Fiction: The Early Years. A Full Description of More than 3,000 Science-Fiction Stories from Earliest Times to the Appearance of the Genre Magazines in 1930* (Kent, Ohio and London, 1990).

4. Quoted by Brian M. Stableford, in 'William Wilson's Prospectus for Science Fiction: 1851', *Foundation: The Review of Science Fiction*, 10 (June 1976), pp.6–12, at pp.9–10.

5. W.H. Hudson, preface to his utopian science fiction novel *A Crystal Age* (London, 1887), p.2, quoted by Suvin, in *Victorian Science Fiction in the UK* (Boston, 1983), p.389.

6. This definition (*Victorian Science Fiction*, p.86) is a refined version of that which he discusses in his earlier *Metamorphoses of Science Fiction* (New Haven and London, 1979).

7. Recently, but unsatisfactorily, surveyed in Allienne R. Becker, *The Lost Worlds Romance: from Dawn to Dusk* (Wesport, Conn. and London, 1992). See also Nadia Khouri, 'Lost Worlds and the Revenge of Realism', *Science-Fiction Studies*, 30 (vol. 10, part 2) (July, 1983), pp.170–90.

8. The figures do not include the recently unearthed novella published in New Zealand in 1881: *The Great Romance*, by The Inhabitant (a common pseudonym for guide-books at the time). This is edited by Dominic Alessio, 'The Great Romance, by The Inhabitant', *Science Fiction Studies*, 61 (Vol.20, part 3) (November 1993), pp.305–40.

9. I.F. Clarke, *The Pattern of Expectation, 1644–2001* (London, 1979), p.144.

10. On which see Edward James, '1886: Past Views of Ireland's Future', *Foundation*, 36 (Summer 1986), pp.21–30 and 'The Anglo-Irish Disagreement: Past Irish Futures', *The Linen Hall Review*, 3 (4) (Winter 1986), pp.5–8.

11. Thomas P. Montfort, *Underground; Or, Adventures among the Toltecs* (1890): Bleiler no. 1533.

12. Mrs C.H. Stone, *One of 'Berrian''s Novels* (1890), mentioned by Kessler, op. cit., p.14.

13. Quoted in Elaine Showalter, *Sexual Anarchy: Gender and Culture at the Fin de Siècle* (London, 1992), p.63.

14. Quoted by Showalter, op. cit., p.88.

15. Edited by Isaac Asimov in *Future Days: A Nineteenth-Century Vision of the Year 2000* (New York, 1986).

16. Neil Harris, *Humbug: The Art of P.T. Barnum* (Chicago, 1973), p.79. I should like to thank my colleague Chris Clark for drawing my attention to this.

17. Darko Suvin, *Victorian Science Fiction in the UK* (Boston, 1983), p.125.

18. Stableford, op. cit., p.149.

Frankenstein and the Origins of Science Fiction

BRIAN STABLEFORD

Frankenstein is one of those literary characters whose names have entered common parlance; everyone recognizes the name and everyone uses it. The recognition and the usage are often slightly uncertain—most people know it from the film versions, which are significantly different from the book, and some people have to be reminded that the name is that of the scientist, not the monster that the scientist made—but this uncertainty is not entirely inappropriate to a work whose implication and significance are rather problematic.

The popularity of *Frankenstein* both as a literary classic and as a fuzzy set of ideas bears testimony to the remarkable vividness of Mary Shelley's vision, but it also reflects the protean quality of its central motifs, which can be interpreted in several different ways so as to carry several different messages. The most common modern view of the story—aided and perhaps sustained by Boris Karloff's remarkable performance in the 1941 film version and its sequels—is that it is an account of the way in which 'monstrousness' arises, involving diseased brains, inadequate control over one's actions and resentment against the unthinking horror with which most people react to ugliness. The most common view based on the book alone sees it as an allegory in which a scientist is rightly punished for daring to usurp the divine prerogative of creation. A closely-related interpretation regards Victor Frankenstein as an archetypal example of a man destroyed by his own creation; in this view the story becomes a central myth of the kind of technophobia which argues that modern man is indeed doomed to be destroyed by his own artefacts (and that such a fate, however tragic, is not undeserved).

There are, of course, more convoluted interpretations of the text to be found in the voluminous academic literature dealing with the story. Among the most widely-cited are accounts which see the story as a kind of proto-feminist parable about the male usurpation of the female prerogative of reproduction, and accounts which see it as an allegory of the evolving relationship between the *ancien régime* (Frankenstein is a hereditary peer) and the emergent industrial working class.

So far as can be ascertained, Mary Shelley does not appear to have had any of these theses in mind when she wrote the book, but champions of these various meanings are usually content to interpret them as the result of a coincidence of inspirational forces in which the author's role was that of semiconscious instrument. Support is lent to this view by the fact that Mary Shelley was only nineteen years old when she completed *Frankenstein* and by the fact that all her other books—with the partial exception of the majestically lachrymose jeremiad *The Last Man* (1826)—failed to excite the contemporary audience and are now rarely read or studied. However, the fact remains that *Frankenstein* is one of the most powerful stories produced in the course of the last two centuries and that it has better claims than any other to have become a 'modern myth' (whatever one understands by that phrase).

* * * * *

Frankenstein is often called a Gothic novel, on the grounds that the popular horror stories of its day mostly shared a set of characteristics which justified that label, but it ought not to be thus classified. Despite certain similarities of method and tone, its subject matter is very different from that of the classic Gothic novels. Horace Walpole's definitive *The Castle of Otranto* (1765), Anne Radcliffe's *The Mysteries of Udolpho* (1794), Matthew Gregory Lewis's *The Monk* (1796) and Charles Maturin's *Melmoth the Wanderer* (1820) all involve sinister ancient edifices, evil conspiracies, hideous apparitions (invariably interpreted as supernatural, though sometimes ultimately rationalized), the threat of sexual violation, and intimations of incest. The pretence that *Frankenstein*—which employs none of these motifs—belongs to the Gothic sub-genre serves mainly to obscure the remarkable originality of its own subject-matter, which is broader and more forward-looking.

Victor Frankenstein might be regarded as a distant literary cousin of the diabolically-inspired (or seemingly diabolical) villains of the Classic Gothic novels, but his personality and his ambitions are very different. Although he takes some early inspiration from occult writings of a kind which the inquisitorially-minded might regard as the devil's work, he undertakes a decisive change of direction when he decides that it is modern science, not ancient magic, that will open the portals of wisdom for scholars of his and future generations.

By virtue of this move, *Frankenstein* began the exploration of imaginative territory into which no previous author had penetrated (although that was not its initial purpose). For this reason the novel is more aptly discussed as a pioneering work of science fiction, albeit one that was written at least half a century before its time and one which does considerable disservice to the image of science as an instrument of human progress.

It is entirely appropriate that Brian Aldiss should have worked so hard to establish *Frankenstein* as the foundation-stone of the modern genre of science fiction; the underlying world-view of the novel entitles it to that position. Its only significant competitor in terms of content is Willem Bilderdijk's *A Short Account of a Remarkable Aerial Voyage and Discovery of a New Planet* (1813), which is far less plausible and was far less influential, remaining untranslated into English until 1989. (The third book of Jonathan Swift's *Travels into Several Remote Nations of the World by Lemuel Gulliver*, 1726, must be disqualified on the grounds that its vitriolic parody of the activity and ambitions of scientists alienates it completely from the kind of proto-scientific world-view which Mary Shelley is ready to embrace, albeit in desperately anxious fashion.) On the other hand, given the nature of the most common interpretations of the text, it is by no means surprising that Isaac Asimov should have felt that the technophilic optimism of his work—which was, of course, central to the historical development of genre science fiction—was framed in frank opposition to a 'Frankenstein syndrome'. The central myth of *Frankenstein* seemed to Asimov to be an ideative monster, which must be slain by heroic and sinless robots for the benefit of future generations.

Ambivalent attitudes to science are not particularly unusual in works of speculative fiction. A great deal of the fiction nowadays categorized as science fiction is horrific, and much of it is born of a fear or even a deep-seated hatred of the scientific world-view, whose acknowledged intellectual triumph over older concepts of natural order seems to many observers to be unedifying and undesirable. Given this, it would not necessarily be inappropriate to trace the origins of the genre back to a science-hating ancestor—but it is not at all clear that the author of *Frankenstein* set out with the intention of attacking or scathingly criticizing the endeavours of science, even though many modern readers think that the text carries a bitterly critical moral.

Mary Shelley's life story srongly suggests that she was not the kind of person who might be expected to produce an anti-scientific parable. Her actions and the opinions she held in the years which led up to the writing of *Frankenstein* were such that one suspects that she might have been rather distressed to discover that so many readers interpreted her work in that way, although it must be admitted that she did little to discourage such an interpretation. If, however, one assumes that she had no such intention, there remains the problem of explaining how and why the book turned out to have such a semblance at all.

The full title which Mary Shelley gave to *Frankenstein* is *Frankenstein: or, The Modern Prometheus*. In attempting to assess the significance of this choice it is necessary to bear in mind her beloved husband's fascination with the character of Prometheus. To a devout atheist like Percy Shelley, Prometheus was a great hero whose condemnation to be chained to a rock throughout eternity while eagles came daily to devour his perpetually-regenerated liver was firm proof of the horrid unreasonableness and downright wickedness of godly tyrants. Shelley knew quite well that the atheism he proclaimed so loudly and the free love which he and Mary preached and practised so brazenly were—in the eyes of his enemies—tantamount to Satanism but like Blake before him he was fully prepared to champion Satan himself, let alone the safely-obsolete Prometheus, as a revolutionary light-bearer unjustly slandered and condemned by a monstrous God. To Percy Shelley—and to Mary too, at least while Percy lived—no modern Prometheus could possibly be reckoned a villain, and any terrible fate a modern Prometheus might meet must be reckoned as a tragedy, not an exercise of any kind of justice, divine or otherwise.

Given all this, it is unlikely in the extreme that a book which Mary Shelley elected to call *The Modern Prometheus* was planned as an assault on the *hubris* of scientists, or a defence of divine pre-rogative. It is true that Mary Shelley added a new introduction to the revised edition of the book issued in 1831, in which she seemed not unsympathetic to the demonization of Frankenstein (and also to the notion that she had been a mere instrument of creative forces for whose product she was not to be held responsible), but this was nine years after Percy Shelley's death—which

circumstance had forced her to compromise and make her peace
with all the tyrannies of convention that he was able to despise
and defy quite openly. (In Victorian times, even the most determinedly heroic woman had far less leeway than a man.) Even
if the 1831 introduction can be reckoned sincere—and it almost
certainly cannot—it must be reckoned the work of a person who
bears much the same relation to the author of *Frankenstein* as the
humbled Napoleon who came back from Moscow bore to the all-
conquering hero who had set out.

The fact remains, however, that whether Frankenstein's fate
was intended to be an awful warning to scientists or not, it certainly looks that way. How could this have come about?

* * * * *

The text of *Frankenstein* begins with a series of letters written by
the explorer Robert Walton, who has been trying to navigate
his ship through the Arctic ice in the hope of finding a warm
continent beyond it, akin to the legendary Hyperborea. Modern
readers know full well that this was a fool's errand, but that was
not at all certain in 1818. Thus, although Walton's situation is clearly
symbolic—one of the Gothic conventions which *Frankenstein* does
adopt is that the weather is symbolic of human emotions, so his
entrapment in the ice signifies that Walton's noble ambitions have
unfortunately alienated him from the warmth of human compan-
ionship—it should not be taken for granted that Mary Shelley saw
him as a lunatic who should have known better. Nor should we
assume that Walton's encounter with Victor Frankenstein, who
is similarly lost in the ice-field and in whom Walton recognizes
a kindred spirit, was in her eyes a meeting of damned men.

Victor's story is essentially that of a man who once had 'everything' but lost what he had through desiring even more. The
'everything' which he had includes material goods, but its
most precious aspects are friendships and love, embodied in
his relationships with Henry Clerval and his cousin Elizabeth.
His ambitions become inflated when he leaves home for university, where he becomes enamoured of the grandiose dreams
of Renaissance magicians like Paracelsus and Cornelius Agrippa.
One of his teachers dismisses this fascination with frank contempt,
but another points out that modern scientists are beginning to
achieve results even more marvellous than those which the
optimists and charlatans of earlier eras had claimed. Victor
then makes his crucial intellectual move, turning his attention

to science—specifically to the science of electricity, the 'vital fluid' whose implications in the mechanics of muscular movement had recently been demonstrated—as a possible means to achieving an unprecedented victory over the greatest of all tyrants: death.

(It is worth noting here that Mary Shelley, even at the tender age of nineteen, had good cause to be preoccupied with the oppressions of this particular tyrant. Her mother's glittering intellectual career had been cut short when she died shortly after bearing Mary, and Mary's first child by Shelley had already died before the fateful night at the Villa Diodati which set in train the sequence of events ultimately leading to the writing of *Frankenstein*. The death of Shelley's first wife Harriet—who drowned, probably by suicidal design, while Mary was engaged in the writing of the book—freed Shelley so that he and Mary could marry. This last episode presumably added an uncomfortably guilty ambivalence to her preoccupation with mortality.)

While Victor is completing his experiments in resurrection he becomes withdrawn and intellectually isolated, no longer able to find any joy in social intercourse. This process reaches a frightful climax when the work is finally complete; the patchwork man which he has made has only to open a cold eye for Victor to be suddenly overcome by repulsion at what he has done. When the monster departs in confusion, Victor gladly reverts to type, renewing his relationships with his friend and his family—who gratefully nurse him back to health when he falls terribly ill.

One of the more ingenious academic interpretations of the plot suggests that from this point onwards much, if not all, of what happens is a hallucination of Victor's and that the monster which subsequently appears to him is a projection of his own personality, his own *doppelgänger*. Although this is superficially the most bizarre of the academic reinterpretations, its adherents rightly point out that it does make rather more sense than the literal interpretation of the puzzling events which follow.

When Victor's young brother is murdered Victor becomes afraid—and later becomes quite certain—that the monster is the murderer, and yet he does not say a word to prevent the wrongful conviction of an entirely innocent servant. The immorality of this inaction is so striking as to have convinced some readers that Victor himself must be the true murderer, and that his subsequent account of the monster's activities, like his failure to speak up for the servant, is a pathological denial of his own guilt. Although this interpretation is certainly over-ingenious as an account of the author's intentions, and does not sit well with the conclusion of the story, it must be admitted that the monster's story is hardly more credible and that the monster's explanation of his own motivation is, in its way, every bit as peculiar.

The monster tells Victor that he too has craved the fellowship and love which provided a safe refuge for the sick scientist, but that it was denied him absolutely. He was rejected by his creator at the moment of his first awakening, and was subsequently reviled by everyone who caught sight of him; even his desperate attempt to make a home with a blind man had inevitably come to nothing. It was, he claims, the madness born of this rejection which led him to kidnap a child, and the revelation that the child was the brother of his creator that drove him to murderous frenzy. In consequence of all this the monster demands that a companion be made for him, given that he is too repulsive to be accepted into the community of men.

Victor initially agrees to this request, and sets out to accomplish it on a remote islet in the Orkneys, but he is no longer insulated by obsession, and becomes terrified of the thought that he is giving birth to an entire race of monsters whose co-existence with mankind will be—to say the least—problematic. This prospect causes him to abandon the work, and no immediate repercussions ensue. In time, though, the monster sets out to exact his revenge, not upon Victor himself, but upon his friends and loved ones. First, Clerval is murdered—Victor is charged with the crime but eventually acquitted—and then, on her and Victor's wedding-night, Elizabeth.

Isolated once again by these deprivations, Victor has little difficulty recovering the motive force of obsession, but this time his obsession is to rid the world of his creation, and the consequent pursuit has led him into the Arctic wastes. He looks to Walton for aid, but when he learns that his host has already turned back from his own quest and is now heading out of the ice-field he realizes that he cannot carry through his purpose. He gives up and dies.

The final confrontation with the monster—the only corroborative evidence of his actual existence—is left to Walton. He finds Victor's adversary every bit as fearful as Victor led him to expect, but also confused, agonized and contrite. One of the few books the monster has had the opportunity to read, since he learned the uses of language by secretly observing a family at work and play, is Goethe's Romantic classic *The Sorrows of Young Werther*, which waxes lyrical about the appropriateness of suicide as a solution for those bereft of any meaningful connection with their fellows, and it is hardly surprising that the monster chooses to continue into the wilderness of the Arctic ice.

'I am content to suffer alone while my sufferings shall endure', the monster says, regretfully; when 'I die, I am well satisfied that abhorrence and opprobrium should load my memory.' He could not possibly have guessed how prophetic these words would prove to be.

* * * * *

We are nowadays familiar with the circumstances of *Frankenstein*'s genesis, on the stormy night on which Lord Byron, Percy and Mary Shelley, Claire Clairmont and Dr Polidori amused themselves at the Villa Diodati by reading tales from a volume entitled *Fantasmagoriana*, which consisted of horror stories translated from German into French. They subsequently agreed that each of them would write a horrific tale of his or her own—although Polidori was the only one apart from Mary to produce anything substantial, and that was eventually published without his knowledge, under circumstances which caused considerable embarrassment to him (and, of course, to Byron, to whom the work was falsely attributed).

The significance of the story's first inspiration to an understanding of the construction of *Frankenstein* is that its author was charged from the very beginning with the task of writing *a horror story*. The particular horror story she settled on grew from a fragment of an actual nightmare she experienced soon afterwards. If Mary's later claim is to be believed—and there seems no reason to doubt it—this nightmare displayed to her a creator's first confrontation with his creation.

Thus, Mary did not begin the work of ideative elaboration with the premise of her story, but with its crucial image. The beginning and the end of the story are both extrapolations of that single instant, the one constructed in order to explain how it came about and the other to follow it to its implicit conclusion. Both are consistent, to a degree, with the visionary moment, but they are not really consistent with one another, in the way that they would have been had the author extrapolated an ending from the apparent premises contained in the beginning. Because the fact that the story was to be horrific was accepted as an axiom,

much of what was eventually presented as the logic of the story
—the 'explanation' of how the nightmare confrontation came
to take place—was formed by way of ideative apology, not as a
set of propositions to be examined on their own merits.

Given all this, it is not entirely surprising that the logical
patchwork which leads up to the true point of origination is
somewhat ill-fitting. Had the author actually started to make
up a story about a 'modern Prometheus' she would surely have
come up with something very different; that first awakening of
the resurrected man might have been a joyous and triumphant
affair had it not been already set in place as the horrific *raison
d'être* of the whole exercise. Alas for the modern Prometheus, his
endeavour was damned before he was even thought of, let alone
characterized.

The reason Mary made poor Victor Frankenstein a scientist,
therefore, had nothing to do with a desire to comment on science as
an endeavour. It was simply the result of wanting to do something
different from the Gothic novels of supernatural horror which had
already become tedious and *passé*. The preface to the first edition,
which was probably written by Percy Shelley on his wife's behalf,
treads a delicate argumentative line in speaking of such matters.
'I am by no means indifferent to the manner in which whatever
moral tendencies exist in the sentiments or characters it contains
shall affect the reader', 'Mary' says, 'yet my chief concern in
this respect has been limited to avoiding the enervating effects of
the novels of the present day and to the exhibition of the ami-
ableness of domestic affection, and the excellence of universal
virtue.' 'She' further insists that 'the opinions which naturally
spring from the character and situation of the hero are by no
means to be conceived as existing always in my own conviction;
nor is any inference justly to be drawn from the following pages
as prejudicing any philosophical doctrine of whatever kind'.

There is certainly some self-protective rationalization here—the
author of the preface is shrewdly anticipating and trying cleverly
to deflect the charge that the book promotes atheism—but 'she' is
not trying nearly so hard to do that as she was later to attempt in
the 1831 introduction, and it must be noted that 'any philosophical
doctrine whatsoever' includes science as well as religion.

If the build-up to the moment of confrontation between creator
and creation is a fairly haphazard rationalization, then so is the
subsequent unfolding of that horrific moment in the later pages of
Frankenstein. What happens in the remainder of the novel makes

little sense—rationally or morally—precisely because the horror of that moment can never be undermined or reduced, and thus can never undergo any kind of imaginative transformation, no matter how hard the unfortunate monster tries to find a solution. The machinery of the plot remains totally subordinate to that instant of revulsion, and revulsion remains the inescapable condition of the key characters, no matter how they may regret it. Victor and the monster are sealed within it and united by it, all possible avenues of escape being ruled out by the fact that this is, essentially and definitively, a horror story. It is only to be expected that the narrative expansion of the crucial moment should seem to some readers to be akin to a hallucination—especially to the kind of hallucination which allegedly packs a lifetime into the space of a single incident.

Thus, while the long prelude which precedes and sets up the visionary moment invents—more or less by accident—the modern genre of science fiction, the long coda which follows and expands upon it constitutes—again, more or less by accident—a giant leap for the not-so-modern genre of delusional fantasy which had recently been invented by E.T.A. Hoffman. This double triumph assured that the book would become a landmark in the evolution of modern imaginative fiction as well as a popular success. It *is* a landmark, because rather than in spite of its inherent internal contradictions; because of its struggle to be something other than it is. It is a great book precisely because its author could not and would not settle for writing an *ordinary* book, which would hang together by reproducing some familiar pattern of clichés.

* * * * *

It would, of course, be foolish to regret that *Frankenstein* is the kind of book it is, or to wish that Mary Shelley had written another book instead. Life being what it is, we have to be grateful for whatever we have, and *Frankenstein*-the-novel is a book well worth having even if *Frankenstein*-the-myth is a nest of viperish ideas we could well do without. Given, however, that *Frankenstein* is a pioneering work of science fiction it might be appropriate to wonder what Mary Shelley—doubtless with Percy's active encouragement and assistance—might have achieved had she decided, once the beginning of the story had been written, to cease taking it for granted that what she was writing was a horror story and had cast aside the nightmarish seed.

So let us, briefly, wonder...

What if the scientific miracle that Victor Frankenstein had wrought had been allowed to be a miracle indeed, and the resurrected man no monster at all? What if the monster, in spite of his ugliness, had been allowed to win the respect of others with his intelligence and moral sensibility? (Perhaps, like Remy de Gourmont after his face had been ruined by discoid lupus, he might have become a recluse illuminating the work with the wise produce of his pen!)

What if Victor, and Mary, had been allowed to proclaim that a Promethean man of science—a bringer of energetic fire and a creator of new life—would be the greatest benefactor imaginable by man, *and that the day of such fire-bringers and creators was indeed at hand?*

What if Victor, and Mary, had boldly proclaimed that there *are* no divine prerogatives except wilful ignorance and vile intolerance, and that the produce of scientific creativity ought not to be feared by religious men, nor by feminists, nor by political conservatives, and that such fear is merely the unreasoning electrical reflex of blinkered fools?

What if Mary had attached to her vivid romance the moral which Percy's preface would surely have delighted in celebrating: the moral that the only hope men have for any kind of salvation is that they might find the technological means to redeem themselves from every kind of earthly damnation?

What then?

The overwhelming probability, sad to say, is that such a book could never have been published in 1818. It would have been considered so horribly indecent and blasphemous that anyone who so much as read the manuscript would have screamed in horror. We may be reasonably confident of this conclusion because, sad to say, it is far, far easier even today to publish and find an appreciative audience for the ten thousandth rip-off of *Frankenstein* (*Jurassic Park*, to name but one example) than it is to publish and find an appreciative audience for the kind of novel which *Frankenstein* might have been. The modern Prometheus remains a prophet without honour in his own country.

This is, in its way, a tragedy: a tragedy which has caught up in its toils the entire genre of science fiction which descends from *Frankenstein*. The great bulk of modern science fiction still grows, by means of dubious patchworks of apologetic 'logic', from moments of nightmarish vision born of fear and dyspepsia; it fails to work the kind of imaginative alchemy that would be necessary to transform those moments of nightmare into something saner.

Let us be clear, though, about one thing: it was *not* our mad technological monsters that made the world the way it is and murdered so many of the things which we ought to hold dear; *it was us*. To think otherwise is a delusion which might easily possess us until we are irredeemably lost in the icy wilderness of our own moral cowardice.

Mary Shelley knew that. It is a pity that those who are heir to the perverse produce of her imagination mostly do not.

From Mary Shelley to
The War of the Worlds:
The Thames Valley Catastrophe

PATRICK PARRINDER

I

'"Fearful massacres in the Thames Valley!"' cries a news-vendor in H.G. Wells's scientific romance *The War of the Worlds* (1898).[1] To readers of popular fiction he must have seemed somewhat late with the news. The Thames Valley was already well-established as a favourite location both for catastrophe fictions and for romantic idylls ranging from Jerome's farcical *Three Men in a Boat* (1889) to Morris's visionary fable *News from Nowhere* (1890). Massacres take place in the Thames Valley in Sir George Chesney's *The Battle of Dorking* (1871)—where the Surrey hills form the last line of defence which fails to stop the invaders from reaching the London basin—and in William Le Queux's *The Great War in England in 1897* (1893). London and its region are overwhelmed by natural disasters in Richard Jefferies' *After London* (1885), in Robert Barr's 'The Doom of London' (1894) and in Grant Allen's 'The Thames Valley Catastrophe' (1897). Wells's *The Time Machine* (1895) portrays the end of civilization, and the imminent end of all life on Earth, in a Thames Valley setting radiating out from the site of the Time Traveller's former home at Richmond. (There are massacres in *The Time Machine*, too.) The tradition of Thames Valley catastrophes continues in the twentieth century with, for example, J. Leslie Mitchell ('Lewis Grassic Gibbon')'s *Gay Hunter* (1934), John Wyndham's *The Day of the Triffids* (1951) and Brian Aldiss's *Greybeard* (1964). The unsung precursor of all these novels is Mary Shelley's *The Last Man* (1826), which W. Warren Wagar has described as 'the first major example of secular eschatology in literature'.[2]

What is already very evident in *The Last Man* is the contrast between London, the 'overgrown metropolis' and 'great heart

of mighty Britain', and the 'greenwood shade' of its supposedly Arcadian hinterland.[3] London and its surroundings represent
the extremes of urban bustle and rural tranquillity, yet in the
catastrophe novel this is frequently reversed, with terrible forces
emerging from the countryside to engulf the unsuspecting city-
dwellers. The timeliness of the flood of Thames Valley catastrophe
stories at the end of the nineteenth century is a result not only
of London's pre-eminence as the imperial capital and hub of the
world's trading system, but of the threat that suburbanization
posed to the countryside, and, more specifically, the growth of the
modern transport network which turned the river above London
into a leisure resource for the capital.

The River Thames in the early nineteenth century was a
commercial thoroughfare linking the port of London to the
canals serving the Midlands and the West Country. The building
of the railways not only freed the Thames of commercial traffic
but opened it up to commuters, day-trippers and holiday-makers.
The huge demand for excursion trains to the seaside and into
the country was one of the first effects of the railway age, and
both modern business and modern holidays were shaped by the
railways.[4] William Morris was an early beneficiary; his acquisition
of Kelmscott Manor on the upper Thames as a holiday retreat was
one consequence of the extension of the railway to Faringdon and
Lechlade. Morris was in the habit of running down to Kelmscott
from London by train for a day's fishing. On one occasion, it is
true, he did row from Hammersmith to Kelmscott, as his characters do in *News from Nowhere*; but his busy personal life was in
sharp contrast to the leisurely pace of his utopia. Another rowing
enthusiast, Jerome K. Jerome, had once worked as a railway clerk.
In *Three Men in a Boat* he is careful to detail the train journeys that
take J. and Harris to Kingston to pick up their boat, and George
to Weybridge to join them. *News from Nowhere* likewise begins with
the narrator's journey in a 'stinking railway carriage' from London
to Hammersmith.[5]

Mary Shelley's *The Last Man*, written before the railway age,
ignores the river and stresses instead the immemorial tranquillity
of Windsor Forest. The later Thames Valley romancers, however,
are writers freed by the railway to contemplate a river which has
lost its function as a commercial artery. The peaceful river tends
to evoke a poetic symbolism of impermanence and flux. 'Who
looks upon a river in a meditative hour', Emerson once asked,
'and is not reminded of the flux of all things?'[6] Not only is the

river older than the city but in the late nineteenth century its contemplation leads inexorably to thoughts of evolution, of the vastness of prehistoric time, and of the open-ended future. To look long enough at the Thames is to envision the passing of London. The city reverts to a 'greenwood shade' in *News from Nowhere* and to a decadent Arcadia in *The Time Machine*. The majority of Thames Valley romances, however, portray London not as a development of the garden city but as a sinister wasteland. Marlow in Conrad's *Heart of Darkness* (1899) begins his long narrative by looking back to the Roman invasion and settlement of the River Thames: '"And this also . . . has been one of the dark places of the earth"', he reminds his listeners.[7] *Heart of Darkness* is a river romance in which the savagery of the (unnamed) River Congo supplants that of the Thames. Marlow later connects the Congo—and thus, by implication, the Thames—with the beginnings of the world. For the authors of Thames Valley catastrophe fictions the disappearance of London signifies or anticipates the end of the world. In Grant Allen's story, a cyclist on holiday near Cookham witnesses a volcanic eruption which sends a river of molten lava rolling down the valley to engulf the metropolis. London is abandoned, and Manchester takes over as the seat of British government—an outcome not everyone would regard as catastrophic. Nevertheless, London's destruction is 'the greatest calamity which had befallen a civilised land within the ken of history'.[8] Another fin-de-siècle story, 'London's Danger' by Cutcliffe Hyne, sums up the devastation of the capital in a second Great Fire with the claim that 'Civilisation has received no such shock since Atlantis sank beneath the ocean waves'.[9] The early H.G. Wells is still more confident of the global ramifications of London's eclipse. In *The War of the Worlds*, London and the Thames Valley are the sole targets of a Martian invasion apparently intended to subdue the whole Earth.

Significantly, the best-known twentieth-century versions of Wells's story have changed the location to North America. The Martians land in New Jersey in Orson Welles's 1938 radio adaptation, and in northern California in the later Hollywood film version. London's predominance as the site of global catastrophes was short-lived, since only to the late Victorians could it be convincingly presented as the universal city. In *The Last Man*, written earlier in the century, the hero resides in the Thames Valley, but (as we shall see) his last pilgrimage takes him to Rome for a symbolic purpose that London was not yet able to serve.

II

The Thames Valley catastrophe as I have outlined it above is a species of topographical romance sharing the general features of catastrophe fictions. *Catastrophe*, like *comedy* and *tragedy*, is a word of theatrical origin which has come to be applied to social and natural events. The Oxford Dictionary defines a catastrophe in this sense as a 'ruinous overthrow', an 'event producing a subversion of the order or system of things'. It has a strong suggestion of finality and closure—the narrator of Mary Shelley's *Frankenstein*, for example, introduces the concluding scene by remarking that 'the tale which I have recorded would be incomplete without this final and wonderful catastrophe'.[10] However, a catastrophe rarely is an end, and sometimes it seems more like a beginning. The panic-stricken sailors who abandoned the *Patna*, in Conrad's *Lord Jim*, inaugurated a series of events as a result of identifying a catastrophe prematurely. If, conversely, the whole universe were to be destroyed instantaneously and without warning in five minutes' time, a catastrophe would have happened but there would be nobody to identify it as such. A catastrophe is an occurrence of such magnitude that it can only be confirmed retrospectively. It needs an audience, or at least a sole surviving interpreter: hence the popularity of 'last man' tales. It is also, characteristically, an event that has been foretold. Many catastrophe fictions incorporate a prophetic voice or voices, and the fictions themselves may be read as prophecies or warnings. A catastrophe also has an outcome—the events after the end, as it were—which as readers or spectators we are anxious to learn about. The outcome determines whether or not a fresh start is to be hoped for.

A catastrophe may have either human or natural causes. The typical image of a catastrophe with human causes before the advent of nuclear weapons was a military defeat leading to conquest, enslavement or the overthrow of the social order. The typical images of natural catastrophe reflect humanity's age-old fears of plague and flood. In nineteenth-century fiction the imagery of social and natural catastrophe tends to overlap and sometimes to become interchangeable. Military defeat is attributed to the workings of so-called laws of nature, while plague and flood carry the Biblical suggestion of a 'judgment of God'. *The Last Man*, set in the late twenty-first century, shows the spreading of a plague which first becomes apparent in the siege of Constantinople. *The War of the Worlds* is a double 'last man' tale in which humanity is overcome

by military conquest, while the Martians are overcome by plague.
Wells to some extent reconciles the nineteenth century's opposing
belief-systems by invoking the rhetoric of evangelical Christianity
in support of his explicitly Darwinist outlook.

Many of the generic features of catastrophe fictions are present
in one of the central Victorian poetic texts, Tennyson's 'Morte
d'Arthur'. In *The Idylls of the King* (the full version of Tennyson's
Arthurian cycle) the military defeat of the Round Table is foretold by
Merlin and inscribed on the magical double-edged sword Excalibur.
Merlin does not appear in the first version of the 'Morte d'Arthur',
but Tennyson refers to the prophetic legend of Arthur's second
coming. Sir Bedivere is the indispensable witness to the passing
of Arthur. We follow his thoughts as the King sends him down
to the lake-shore after the Last Battle, with instructions to cast
the magnificent sword into its waters. Three times the dying King
sends Bedivere to the lake, and on the first two occasions Bedivere
disobeys orders. It seems that he has good reasons for doing so.
Why should so priceless a national treasure be cast away, rather
than being preserved for posterity to admire? (If Bedivere had had
his way, Excalibur might now be on show in the British Museum.)
On the third occasion, when the knight does what he is told, the
mysterious gloved hand of the Lady of the Lake emerges from the
waters to catch the sword and spirit it away.

Excalibur stands for the strength and authority of Arthur's
kingdom, and Bedivere, lacking his master's faith in prophecy,
must resign himself to seeing it sink into the lake like a stone.
Here the imagery of drowning serves to intensify the desolation
of military defeat. Some strangely vehement lines in the epilogue
'To the Queen', which immediately follows the 'Morte d'Arthur'
in the final version of the *Idylls*, invoke the idea of drowning and
flood as a figure for the contemporary fate of the nation. Tennyson
had been reading a leader in the *Times* advocating Canadian
independence, on the grounds that the colony was becoming too
expensive to maintain. Was this, the Poet Laureate thundered,

> The voice of Britain, or a sinking land,
> Some third-rate isle half-lost among her seas?

A decade later, Jefferies' *After London* could be seen as taking
Tennyson's metaphor literally. A comet passing too close to the
Earth's surface has caused the land of England to sink, leaving
much of the southern half of the country covered by two enormous
lakes, with only the weald and downland exposed. Later, in 'To the

Queen', Tennyson tries to reassure his sovereign in the face of other contemporary prophets of doom and last battles:

> for some are scared, who mark,
> Or wisely or unwisely, signs of storm,
> Waverings of every vane with every wind,
> And wordy trucklings to the transient hour, . . .
> . . . their fears
> Are morning shadows huger than the shapes
> That cast them, not those gloomier which forego
> The darkness of that battle in the West,
> Where all of high and holy dies away.

It is tempting to suppose that Chesney might be one of the false prophets Tennyson had in mind. His best-selling tale of catastrophic military defeat, caused by Britain's unpreparedness in the face of the Prussian threat, was written in response to the French defeat at Sedan and published the year before the *Times* leader which so exasperated Tennyson. *The Battle of Dorking* is a moral tale portraying invasion as a just punishment for a nation which has failed to maintain its defences. The defeat at Dorking leads to the bombardment of Central London with explosive shells and to a second bloody battle at Sevenoaks. With Chesney's vivid narrative the site of the Last Battle had decisively shifted from a mythical West to the suburban Home Counties.

I.F. Clarke has surveyed the large number of successors and imitators spawned by *The Battle of Dorking*. Very few of these were genuine catastrophe novels. Most are pseudo-catastrophes warning, not of the end of the world, but of the possible defeat of the political causes espoused by their authors. Darko Suvin's excellent annotated bibliography of *Victorian Science Fiction in the UK* offers many examples. Somebody's *Radical Nightmare*, by 'An Ex-M.P.' (1885), is possibly somebody else's radical utopia. There are novels in which England comes under female rule, or in which London is burnt by a socialist mob, or in which the Irish fight for and claim their independence. Then there is the novel in which Ireland, having gained its independence, makes such a mess of things that it has to beg for readmission to the British Empire.[11] And what of *'Down with England'* (1888), described by Suvin as a 'vindictive tale of total British defeat by France and loss of whole Empire'?[12] It turns out that this is a translation of a French work, *Plus d'Angleterre* (1887): not so much a catastrophe as a triumph. The major late Victorian catastrophe fictions involve non-human causes and administer a rebuke to humanity's, not merely England's, pretensions. Some of them reflect the ecological anxieties famously expressed in John Ruskin's lecture *The Storm Cloud of the Nineteenth Century* (1884). Ruskin's semi-metaphorical 'storm cloud' and 'plague-wind' are meteorological effects of industrial pollution which portend the 'moral gloom' of the British nation.[13] A plague-wind of poisonous gases emanates from the ruins of London in Jefferies' novel. In M.P. Shiel's *The Purple Cloud* (1901), a lone survivor enjoys the unlimited resources of a world depopulated by volcanic eruptions of cyanide gas. In *The War of the Worlds* one of the Martians' weapons, the noxious Black Smoke, both recalls Ruskin's storm cloud and anticipates the smoke-bombs and poison gas of the First World War.

Both *After London* and *The Purple Cloud* revel in the destruction of civilization and the opportunity it provides for a return to an idyllic, barbaric existence. 'How often it consoles me to think of barbarism once more flooding the world', William Morris wrote two weeks after reading *After London*.[14] Jefferies' hero Felix Aquila is a boat builder, a pioneer navigator who sails across Southern England to the former site of London, and later a tribal chieftain. Shiel's Adam Jeffson roams the deserted world until he discovers a fellow-survivor, a beautiful Turkish princess who has spent twenty years sheltered from the purple cloud in an airtight cellar, where she has kept alive on an ample supply of wine and dates. The plot resembles that of Fred T. Jane's *The Violet Flame: A Story of Armageddon and After* (1899), succinctly annotated by Suvin as follows: 'All annihilated save narrator and girlfriend as new Adam and Eve'.[15] Reading these fin-de-siècle catastrophes we should perhaps recall Dorian Gray's wish that 'it were *fin du globe*', since 'Life is a great disappointment'.[16] In the post-catastrophe worlds of Jefferies and Shiel, life for those lucky enough to survive is no longer disappointing.

III

In *The War of the Worlds* there is one character, the Artilleryman, who embraces the prospect of a newly barbaric age as eagerly as do Jeffson and Felix Aquila. He plans to lead a guerrilla band against the Martians, and exults over the demise of the middle classes whose softness and cowardice stand brutally revealed. Wells's narrator, however, regards him as a ridiculous braggart. In *The Time Machine*, likewise, what follows the collapse of civilization is an enfeebled, not an invigorated world. W. Warren Wagar estimates that about two-thirds of the (mainly twentieth-century) novels surveyed for his book *Terminal Visions* portray a 'new start' after the catastrophe, involving the setting-up of a different kind of society which is often described in tones of intense euphoria.[17] This is the literary equivalent of the psychological state that Martha Wolfenstein identifies as that of the 'post-disaster utopia'.[18] Its prototype is the Christian Kingdom of Heaven, coming after the apocalyptic Last Days. The narrator of *The War of the Worlds*, looking back on the Martian invasion, does concede that it 'has done much to promote the conception of the commonwealth of mankind'.[19] Apart from this his intimations of a post-disaster utopia are much more muted and suppressed than are those in Jefferies and Shiel, not to mention some of the later Wells.

Nor is there any sign of a new start in *The Last Man*. Even when the astronomer Merrival predicts the coming of a 'universal spring' as the pole of the Earth coincides with the pole of the ecliptic in six thousand years' time, he adds that this will be succeeded by an 'earthly hell or purgatory' (pp.159–60). Merrival seems oblivious of the fact that, for Mary Shelley's other characters, life in the Thames Valley is a paradisal state already drawing to a close. As the plague advances, Lionel Verney briefly considers his home at Windsor Castle as a place of safety and a 'haven and retreat for the wrecked bark of human society' (p.189). But his hopes are delusive, and soon he joins a motley band of English survivors wandering across a depopulated Europe in search of 'some natural Paradise' (p.226). This ghastly parody of the Grand Tour takes them to Paris, Versailles, Geneva and Milan. For a brief moment the remaining fugitives believe they have found an Eden beside Lake Como. There have been other paradisal landscapes in Verney's well-travelled past, notably in Greece, where he joins the Byronic Lord Raymond in the struggle against the Turks, and in the Lake District where he grew up as a solitary shepherd. But every paradise in this novel becomes a lost paradise, and every garden contains a serpent. Verney's ultimate status as the Last Man makes him comparable to Adam and Eve only in the sense that 'Like to our first parents, the whole earth is before him, a wide desert' (p.234).

We cannot speak with certainty of *The Last Man*'s influence on Wells or any other late nineteenth-century writer, though it is tempting to suppose that Wells did read it. Shelley's novel remained virtually forgotten (in sharp contrast to the fate of *Frankenstein*) from shortly after its publication in 1826 until 1965 when it was first reprinted in the United States. As fiction it is ill-served by its cumbersome three-volume format and vapid, endlessly effusive style. The powerfully mythic plot is frequently obscured by the flood-tides of emotional melodrama, yet there are also sufficient passages of documentary realism and topographical accuracy to remind us that one of Mary Shelley's avowed models is Defoe's *A Journal of the Plague Year*. In its own time, *The Last Man* was one of a whole series of texts exploiting the motif of the lone survivor. The only one to remain very long in the popular memory was Thomas Hood's burlesque ditty in which the last man left alive is the hangman. The ancestor of these works was *Le Dernier homme* (1805) by Jean-Baptiste François Cousin de Grainville, which appeared anonymously in English translation in the following year.[20] Grainville, unlike Shelley, follows the pattern of the Biblical Apocalypse and gives no dates for the events that he recounts.[21] The events of Shelley's novel take place between the formation of the English Republic in AD 2073 and the year 2100, 'last year of the world', which the narrator commemorates with an inscription on the topmost stone of St. Peter's in Rome (p.340).

The Last Man opens with an oracular Introduction in which the author tells in abundant circumstantial detail of her visit to the cave of the Cumaean Sibyl at Baiae in 1818. On the floor of the cave were strewn leaves and bark covered with writing in various languages, including English. Mary Shelley and her companion hastily removed the scraps written in English, and these 'slight Sibylline pages' turned out to contain Lionel Verney's narrative (p.3). Among Mary's predecessors in the Sibyl's cave was Virgil's Aeneas, who heard the prophetess foretell future wars and the Tiber foaming with streams of blood. She then told Aeneas how he might go down to Hades and return alive. In English catastrophe novels the Tiber becomes the Thames (which in *The War of the Worlds* is turned red by the proliferation of the Martians' Red Weed), and England itself is the hell on earth, in which the solitary last man survives long enough to leave a record of his experiences for the dubious benefit of anteriority.

Mary Shelley will have known Pope's *Windsor-Forest*, in which 'Thames's glory' is said to have surpassed that of the Tiber. Just as Pope's Windsor is the Arcadian hinterland of the modern Rome, so *The Last Man* is framed by constant journeys between London, the scene of political turbulence and the worst ravages of the plague, and the tranquillity of Windsor and its 'antique wood' (p.28). Verney is a regional administrator residing at Windsor Castle, while his brother-in-law Adrian stays in London once he has been elected Lord Protector of England. The doom of humanity has already been foretold by prophetic voices within the narrative—those of the dying Lord Raymond and his rejected ex-lover Evadne. After many delays Verney abandons his beloved Windsor Forest and sets out on what will become his solitary pilgrimage to Rome, the city of monuments in which his last act, he tells us, will be to leave a monument to himself (presumably the one that we are reading). He too has had the role of a prophet forced upon him, since he is fated to solve the riddle of the Sphinx and 'reveal the meaning of the enigma, whose explanation closed the history of the human race' (p.311). One of his successors was to be Wells's Time Traveller, another Last Man who arrives in the year AD 802 701 only to find himself immediately confronting the riddle of the Sphinx.[22] The front cover of the first edition of *The Time Machine* is illustrated with the device of the winged sphinx.

IV

Not only is Wells's White Sphinx an obvious symbol of prophecy, but many of his futuristic narratives (though not *The War of the Worlds*) are 'dream books' with elaborate Sibylline frameworks. *The Shape of Things to Come* (1933), for example, is introduced as the 'Dream Book of Dr. Philip Raven'. What Raven dreams is a 'Short History of the Future. It is a modern Sibylline book'.[23] (The Sibylline books—collections of oracular utterances attributed to the Cumaean Sibyl—were preserved in ancient Rome and consulted by the Senate in times of emergency.) Wells's writings throughout his long career are the expressions of a composite prophetic stance combining the classical images of the prophet as Delphic priestess, Sphinx and Sibyl with the Hebrew notion of the preacher and sage, and with an attempt to define a new, scientific basis for prophecy.[24] Prophecy is always on the point of becoming futurology in Wells, though it never quite does so.

The narrator of *The War of the Worlds* is an amateur futurologist who, at the time of the Martian invasion, was 'busy upon a series of papers discussing the probable developments of moral ideas as civilisation progressed'.[25] His failure as a futurologist is signified by his unfinished sentence, '"In about two hundred years, we may expect—"' (p.190), written on the afternoon when the Martians emerged from the cylinder which had crash-landed on Woking Common. The Martians, it turns out, resemble the 'After-Man', or 'Man of the Year Million', foreseen by another Wellsian avatar, 'a certain speculative writer of quasi-scientific repute', in the *Pall Mall Budget* in 1893 (p.151). By a carefully-assembled chain of reasoning drawing on the nebular hypothesis, the law of entropy, and natural selection, *The War of the Worlds* argues that future evolution on Earth must follow the same course as the evolution of the Martians, thus confirming Wells's earlier journalistic prophecy—for 'The Man of the Year Million' was one of his own articles. Meanwhile, the narrator's perilously close observations of the Martians change him from a tentative and faltering futurologist to a historian with immense authority and narrative drive. We see this as early as the ending of his opening paragraph: 'And early in the twentieth century came the great disillusionment' (p.51).

The War of the Worlds reflects the lively contemporary interest in whether or not there could be life on Mars. The novel refers to the report in the summer of 1894 of a 'strange light' on Mars, and this astronomical observation aroused widespread comment, with the leading scientific journal *Nature* suggesting that it could have been caused by a forest fire (p.50). Wells had put some of the arguments for the existence of life on Mars in a college debate in 1888. In 1896, however, he wrote that any inhabitants on Mars would be 'inscrutable to us', their nature 'impossible to imagine'.[26] In *The War of the Worlds*, as any writer on alien intelligences must do to some extent, he portrayed them as creatures with some anthropomorphic traits which his narrator found it possible to struggle to comprehend. At the same time he endowed them with superhuman technology and a capacity for terrible violence. They are the appointed scourge of our species and—despite the setbacks they experience—the most dangerous antagonists of humanity in the future: 'To them, and not to us, perhaps, is the future ordained' (p.193).

The Martians are at once superior men and non-anthropoid monsters: the ancestors of the hideous aliens of twentieth-century science fiction and horror movies. They are also new and terrible gods. With intellects 'vast and cool and unsympathetic' (p.51), they have been watching the Earth for a long time. The narrator in turn manages to scrutinize them, first through an astronomical telescope, then through a convenient crack in the wall of the ruined house overlooking their encampment at Sheen, and finally at the South Kensington Museum where a specimen is preserved in spirits in a glass tank. If the Martians scrutinize human beings as closely (but also as uncomprehendingly) as biologists scrutinize micro-organisms, we for our part find that 'the attraction of peeping [is] . . . irresistible' (p.154). There is one moment in the book at which man and Martian appear to exchange an equal glance. As the first Martian emerges from the cylinder, 'Two large dark-coloured eyes were regarding me steadfastly' (p.63). However, the Martians, as a would-be master-race of colonists, cannot tolerate this reciprocal watching; far from acknowledging human beings as fellow intelligences, they turn on the Heat-Ray. The unfortunate bystanders find themselves in the position of the natives of Tasmania who were exterminated by European settlers, or that of the lower animals condemned by humanity as vermin.

Zoologically, the extraterrestrial creatures which accomplish the 'dethronement' (p.165) of humanity are themselves grotesque lower animals, combining the most repellent features of reptiles, molluscs, crustaceans, insects and even fungi (p.63). It is their machines that give them the stature of giants and gods, like Briareus (p.160) or the Titans (p.90). If their spacecraft are stars falling from heaven, their first appearance is like locusts emerging from the bottomless pit—both images from the Book of Revelation, which the Curate (an unsound individual, but a good theologian) quotes just before his death (p.159; cf. Rev. 8.13). The 'pitiless sword' (p.71) of the Martians' Heat-Ray is at once an instrument of divine wrath and a startling forecast of late twentieth-century warfare. Their armoured Fighting Machines anticipate the tank, an invention in which Wells was to take a continuing interest. Nor is Wells's foresight in *The War of the Worlds* limited to the field of weaponry. 'Never before in the history of warfare had destruction been so indiscriminate and so universal' writes the narrator, whose vivid realism and topographical detail suggest the reports of a first-rate war correspondent (p.91). His grasp of the totality of military strategy—communications, intelligence, supply-lines, firepower, morale, and the problems of evacuating the civilian population—is far superior to that of most future-war writers.

Journalism and the spreading of rumours, reports and announcements fascinate Wells just as they had done that earlier journalist-novelist, Daniel Defoe. *A Journal of the Plague Year* begins by recounting the first signs of the impending catastrophe, while reminding the reader that 'We had no such thing as printed newspapers in those days to spread rumours and reports of things, and to improve them by the invention of men, as I have lived to see practised since'.[27] *The War of the Worlds* takes account of newer forms of communication such as heliographic signalling and the telegraph. Wells's narrator always has an eye for the newspapers, beginning with *Nature*, the *Daily Telegraph* and *Daily Chronicle*, taking in 'a pre-Martian periodical called *Punch*' (p.151), and ending with the 'placard of the first newspaper to resume publication—the *Daily Mail*' (p.188). Like Defoe, Wells constantly asserts the authenticity of his account by the technique of correcting previous reports. His narrative is strictly ordered in the interests of lucid description and factual plausibility. Though we see a long procession of anguished, panic-stricken and tortured fugitives, expressions of personal emotion are kept to a minimum. All this is in great contrast to *The Last Man*, where the high-born protagonists face the onslaught of the plague with courage, dignity and large reserves of sentimental rhetoric. The same contrast is present in Wells's and Shelley's depictions of landscape. In *The War of the Worlds* there are unforgettable descriptions of the Martians at night, lit up by the green fire of smelting aluminium or by flashes of lightning in the midst of a storm. The portrayal of the Home Counties landscape by day is strictly functional, though no less effective for that. The best editions of Wells's novel nowadays contain a map or a gazetteer as aids to the reader. Any such map will show the extent to which Wells's story (with the exception of the two chapters following the narrator's brother's escape across Hertfordshire and Essex) is dominated by the topography of the Thames Valley.

Mary Shelley had lived in Marlow and on the edge of Windsor Great Park. Wells likewise chose the setting for *The War of the Worlds* as a result of his move to Woking (where his house was considerably less grand than the one the narrator occupies) in 1895. The first three Martian cylinders land in the area of Woking and Horsell Commons, between the River Thames and the River Wey. The remaining four cylinders all land quite close to the Thames, at Hampton Court, Sheen, Wimbledon, and Primrose Hill respectively. Three chapters of Book I and virtually the whole of Book II tell of the narrator's journey on foot from Woking to London. He witnesses a pitched battle between the Martians and the artillery at the confluence of the Thames and the Wey, submerging himself in the river to escape from the Heat-Ray. Subsequently he and the Curate follow the Thames towpath. After sheltering in the ruined house, he meets the Artilleryman on Putney Hill and proceeds towards Central London by crossing Putney Bridge. Once in the dead and deserted city, he becomes persuaded that, like Lionel Verney, he is the 'last man left alive' (p.167), or, at least, the last man in full possession of his faculties. But his sense of solitude is delusive. He does not know that help is on its way and that, hours before he makes his reckless and potentially suicidal approach to the Martian camp on Primrose Hill—'An insane resolve possessed me. I would die and end it' (p.183)—other wanderers have discovered the invaders' overthrow and have telegraphed the news to Europe. But Wells, in a stunning reversal, transfers the pathos attaching to the Last Man to the last Martian. The narrator becomes a farcical figure, deliriously wandering the streets singing 'some inane doggerel about "The Last Man Left Alive! Hurrah!"' (p.187). We have earlier heard the Martian on Primrose Hill wailing in its solitary death-agony, '"Ulla, ulla"'—a sound, at first unearthly, which is actually the classical ululation or lamentation over the dead (p.181). The double catastrophe of Martians and human beings is an effect that has been prepared for throughout the story.

What becomes evident in the 'Dead London' chapter is that the crucial war of the worlds was not fought on a human scale but between rival squads of bacteria. The Martians bring their bioorganisms with them, so that the River Thames becomes choked by the growth of the Red Weed. But they are also recklessly vampirish creatures feeding off injections of human blood, with the result that they rapidly succumb to a plague since they have no immunity against terrestrial bacteria. This is certainly bad science, for it is quite implausible for the highly civilized Martians to have lost all the knowledge of bacteria and immune-systems that they must once have possessed, and it is undignified to make their defeat depend solely upon a military blunder. Wells certainly intends more than this, and his euphoric narrator draws a grandiose moral:

> By the toll of a billion deaths man has bought his birthright of the earth, and it is his against all comers; it would still be his were the Martians ten times as mighty as they are. For neither do men live nor die in vain. (p.184)

Thus Wells's narrator, like Defoe's but unlike Shelley's, is able to reside in a belief in Providence—though it is fair to add that he is also left tortured by nightmares and by an 'abiding sense of doubt and insecurity' (p.193).

We know from Wells's correspondence that the magazine publisher Pearson was unwilling to buy the serial rights of *The War of the Worlds* until he saw how it ended.[28] When it appeared, however, it was hailed by W.T. Stead as 'The Latest Apocalypse of the End of the World'. The final paradox of Wells's story is that, without the sympathy we are made to feel at the last for the defeated Martians, who are being forced by the cooling of the solar system to evacuate their planet and move sunwards, *The War of the Worlds* might have seemed something less than a world-ending narrative.

LIST OF WORKS AND EDITIONS CITED

Aldiss, Brian W. *Greybeard* (St. Alban's: Panther, 1968).

Alkon, Paul K. *Origins of Futuristic Fiction* (Athens, Ga. and London: Georgia U.P., 1988).

Allen, Grant. 'The Thames Valley Catastrophe', in *Beyond the Gaslight: Science in Popular Fiction 1895–1905*, eds. Hilary and Dik Evans (London: Frederick Muller, 1976), pp.37–45.

Barr, Robert. 'The Doom of London', in *The Face and the Mask* (London: Hutchinson, 1894), pp.78–94.

Chesney, G.T. *The Battle of Dorking*, in *Before Armageddon*, ed. Michael Moorcock (London: Wyndham, 1976), I, pp.19–71.

Clarke, I.F. *Voices Prophesying War 1763–1984* (London: Panther, 1970).

Conrad, Joseph. *Heart of Darkness*, ed. Paul O'Prey (London: Penguin, 1983).

Defoe, Daniel. *A Journal of the Plague Year* (Harmondsworth: Penguin, 1966).

Emerson, Ralph Waldo. *Essays and Other Writings* (London: Cassell, 1907).

Hyne, Cutcliffe. 'London's Danger', in *Beyond the Gaslight: Science in Popular Fiction 1895–1905*, eds. Hilary and Dik Evans (London: Frederick Muller, 1976), pp.64–69.

Jefferies, Richard. *After London and Amaryllis at the Fair* (London: Dent, 1939).

Jerome, Jerome K. *Three Men in a Boat (To Say Nothing of the Dog)* (Bristol: Arrowsmith, 1889).

Mitchell, J. Leslie. *Gay Hunter* (London: Heinemann, 1934).

Morris, William. *Letters of William Morris to his Family and Friends*, ed. Philip Henderson (London: Longmans, 1950).

—*News from Nowhere*, ed. James Redmond (London: Routledge, 1970).

—*Nature*, 50 (1894).

Palacio, Jean de. 'Mary Shelley and the "Last Man": A Minor Romantic Theme', *Revue de littérature comparée*, 42 (1968), pp.37–49.

Parrinder, Patrick. 'Experiments in Prophecy', in *H.G. Wells: Reality and Beyond*, ed. Michael Mullin (Champaign, Ill: Champaign Public Library, 1986), pp.7–21.

Perkin, Harold. *The Age of the Railway* (Newton Abbot: David and Charles, 1971).

Pope, Alexander. *Poetical Works* (London: Warne, n.d.).

Ruskin, John. *The Storm Cloud of the Nineteenth Century* (Orpington: George Allen, 1884).

Sambrook, A.J. 'A Romantic Theme: The Last Man', *Forum for Modern Language Studies*, 2 (1966), pp.25–33.

Shelley, Mary. *Frankenstein, or The Modern Prometheus*, ed. M.K. Joseph (London: Oxford U.P., 1971).

—*The Last Man* (London: Hogarth Press, 1985).

Shiel, M.P. *The Purple Cloud* (London: Allison and Busby, 1986).

Stead, W.T. 'The Latest Apocalypse of the End of the World', *Review of Reviews*, 17 (1898), pp.389–96.

Suvin, Darko. *Victorian Science Fiction in the UK: The Discourses of Knowledge and of Power* (Boston: G.K. Hall, 1983).

Tennyson, Alfred Lord. *Poetical Works* (London: Macmillan, 1911).

Wagar, W. Warren. *Terminal Visions: The Literature of Last Things* (Bloomington: Indiana U.P., 1982).

Wells, H.G. *Early Writings in Science and Science Fiction*, eds. Robert M. Philmus and David Y. Hughes (Berkeley, Los Angeles and London: California U.P., 1975).

—*Experiment in Autobiography: Discoveries and Conclusions of a Very Ordinary Brain (Since 1866)* (London: Gollancz, 1966).

—'The Man of the Year Million', *Pall Mall Gazette*, 57 (6 November, 1893), p.3.

—*The Time Machine* (London: Heinemann, 1895).

—*The War of the Worlds: A Critical Edition of H.G. Wells's Scientific Romance*, eds. David Y. Hughes and Harry M. Geduld (Bloomington and Indianapolis: Indiana U.P., 1993).

Wilde, Oscar. *The Picture of Dorian Gray*, ed. Isobel Murray (Oxford: Oxford U.P., 1981).

Wolfenstein, Martha. *Disaster: A Psychological Essay* (Glencoe, Ill., 1957).

Wyndham, John. *The Day of the Triffids* (Harmondsworth: Penguin, 1954).

NOTES

1. David Y. Hughes and Harry M. Geduld (eds.), *The War of the Worlds: A Critical Edition of H.G. Wells's Scientific Romance* (Bloomington, 1993), p.113.

2. W. Warren Wagar, *Terminal Visions: The Literature of Last Things* (Bloomington, 1982), p.13.

3. Mary Shelley, *The Last Man* (London, 1985), pp.188, 264. Subsequent page references to this work are incorporated in the text.

4. Harold Perkin, *The Age of the Railway* (Newton Abbot, 1971), p.201.

5. William Morris, *News from Nowhere*, ed. James Redmond (London, 1970), p.8.

6. Ralph Waldo Emerson, *Essays and Other Writings* (London, 1907), p.380.

7. Joseph Conrad, *Heart of Darkness*, ed. Paul O'Prey (Harmondsworth, 1983), p.29.

8. Grant Allen, 'The Thames Valley Catastrophe', in *Beyond the Gaslight: Science in Popular Fiction 1895–1905*, eds. Hilary and Dik Evans (London, 1976), p.41.

9. C.J. Cutcliffe Hyne, 'London's Danger', *Beyond the Gaslight*, eds. Hilary and Dik Evans, p.69.

10. Mary Shelley, *Frankenstein, or The Modern Prometheus*, ed. M.K. Joseph (London, 1971), p.218.

11. The novels referred to are: [Walter Besant], *The Revolt of Man* (1882); Donald McKay, *The Dynamite Ship* (1888); 'An Ex-Revolutionist', *England's Downfall* (1893); and C.A. Bland, *Independence* (1891). For these and similar, see Darko Suvin, *Victorian Science Fiction in the U.K.: The Discourses of Knowledge and of Power* (Boston, 1983), pp.11–85.

12. Suvin, p.35.

13. John Ruskin, *The Storm Cloud of the Nineteenth Century* (Orpington, 1884), p.62.

14. Philip Henderson (ed.), *Letters of William Morris to his Family and Friends* (London, 1950), p.236.

15. Suvin, p.77.

16. Oscar Wilde, *The Picture of Dorian Gray*, ed. Isobel Murray (Oxford, 1981), p.179.

17. Wagar, p.195.

18. Martha Wolfenstein, *Disaster: A Psychological Essay* (Glencoe, Ill., 1957), pp.189–98.

19. *The War of the Worlds*, p.192.

20. See Jean de Palacio, 'Mary Shelley and the "Last Man": A Minor Romantic Theme', *Revue de littérature comparée*, 42 (1968), pp.37–49 and A.J. Sambrook, 'A Romantic Theme: The Last Man', *Forum for Modern Language Studies*, 2 (1966), pp.25–33.

21. Paul K. Alkon, *Origins of Futuristic Fiction* (Athens, Ga., 1988), p.171.

22. H.G. Wells, *The Time Machine* (London, 1895), pp.33–34.

23. H.G. Wells, *The Shape of Things to Come. The Ultimate Revolution* (London, 1933), p.14.

24. See Patrick Parrinder, 'Experiments in Prophecy', in *H.G. Wells: Reality and Beyond*, ed. Michael Mullin (Champaign, 1986), pp.7–21.

25. *The War of the Worlds*, p.55. Subsequent page references to this work are incorporated in the text.

26. H.G. Wells, *Early Writings in Science and Science Fiction*, ed. Robert M. Philmus and David Y. Hughes (Berkeley, 1975), pp.177, 178.

27. Daniel Defoe, *A Journal of the Plague Year* (Harmondsworth, 1966), p.23.

28. H.G. Wells, *Experiment in Autobiography: Discoveries and Conclusions of a Very Ordinary Brain (Since 1866)* (London, 1966), Vol.II, p.555.

Breaking the Bounds: The Rhetoric of Limits in the Works of Edgar Allan Poe, his Contemporaries and Adaptors

DAVID SEED

In the course of defining the science fiction genre, Darko Suvin argues for the centrality of the voyage towards a distant island. He continues: '. . . it is not only the basic human and humanizing curiosity that gives birth to SF. Beside an undirected inquisitiveness . . ., this genre has always been wedded to a hope of finding in the unknown the ideal environment, tribe, state, intelligence or other aspect of the Supreme Good'. The journey can articulate the desire for this possibility, and the genre of the 'adventurous voyage as an inner quest', which Suvin proposes as a key American literary tradition, clearly relates to the history of that nation's mercantile expansion.[1] Similarly, in his history of the same genre Brian Aldiss proposes that Poe's central theme is the notion of elsewhere: '. . . he knows Another World. He cannot tell us where it is: perhaps it is beyond the tomb, perhaps in a lost continent, perhaps through a mirror, perhaps in another stage of mind, another time, another dimension.'[2] This disparity between conviction and utterance, 'knowing and being unable to say', would make Poe's poem 'Eldorado' the very paradigm of his oeuvre in describing a quester after an elusive land which can only be figured in relational terms as lying beyond the present.

Poe's critics have differed as to whether he was the 'father' of science fiction or simply a 'pioneer' of the genre; Clarke Olney, for instance, sees his use of the device of extrapolation as crucial for the subsequent development of science fiction.[3] There is, however, an emerging consensus that Poe was a formative figure and one important sign of his influence lies in his handling of place. He waxed positively eloquent on the achievement of American merchant adventurers. In 1836 he pleaded for an unrestrained expansion into the Pacific and right across the North American continent:

> Our pride as a vigorous commercial empire, should stimulate us to become our own pioneers in that vast island-studded ocean, destined, it may be, to become, not only the chief theatre of our traffic, but the arena of our future naval conflicts. Who can say, viewing the present rapid growth of our population, that the Rocky Mountains shall forever constitute the western boundary of our republic, or that it shall not stretch its dominion from sea to sea.[4]

Yet Poe's conviction of technological progress and his unembarrassed support of American naval rule in the South Seas are not matched by his travel-narratives which repeatedly problematize the act of travelling, the processes of perception and the identity of goals. Although he incorporates acknowledgements of commercial purpose, Poe's journeys are characteristically ambiguous in their significance and as often as not take their protagonists into unknown areas where the stability of the self is brought into question. In his survey of nineteenth-century American science fiction, H. Bruce Franklin rightly plays down the scientific element in Poe, stressing instead the speculative nature of his fiction.[5]

Poe's travel fictions obviously capitalize on the fact that there were untravelled regions within America and in the Antarctic region, but John Cleves Symmes added a bizarre further dimension to possible exploration by positing the theory that the earth consisted of concentric spheres. In his 1818 manifesto he made the following claim: 'I declare the earth is hollow and habitable within . . . that it is open at the poles'.[6] This theory became known familiarly as 'Symmes's Hole' and in 1822 Symmes petitioned Congress to equip a polar expedition to test it out. One nineteenth-century commentator described Symmes as a visionary who 'believed that there were beneath our feet miles and miles of wondrous unclaimed domain; . . . splendid visions of untold wonders, misty dreams of splendors unnameable, floated through his nightly and daily thoughts, and greater than all burned within him the ceaseless desire to become the discoverer of this unknown land'.[7] The symbolic barrier to such discovery was the supposed ring of ice around the poles which Poe's Hans Pfaall traverses by balloon. He reads this 'huge rim' as the 'limit of human discovery in these regions' and from his vantage point confirms Symmes's theory by recording a concave depression at the North Pole. In the meantime *Symzonia; A Voyage of Discovery* by one Adam Seaborn was published in 1820 purporting to give first-hand confirmation of the theory. This work is now accepted to have been written by Symmes himself and exerted a powerful influence on Poe's related fiction.[8]

Symzonia combines two genres: the imaginary voyage and the utopia. The narrator identifies his purpose as a combination of economic and intellectual expansion: 'I flattered myself that I should open the way to new fields for the enterprise of my fellow-citizens, supply new sources of wealth, fresh food for curiosity, and additional means of enjoyment'.[9] For all his apparent confidence, Seaborn has to conceal his exploratory ambitions from his crew by disguising his voyage as one after seals. His caution turns out to be eminently justified because as the *Explorer* nears the 'icy hoop' off Antarctica the crew mutinies. Seaborn patiently expounds Symmes's theories to the leading mutineer who then retorts that the crew signed up, as they thought, for a bonafide commercial voyage and not to indulge their captain's 'mad passion for discovery'. Seaborn at this point becomes caught between rival impulses, like Walton in the frame narrative to *Frankenstein*. In the latter novel Walton's imagination has been fed by his reading of earlier voyages and he dreams of breaking through the ice barrier to a place of ideal beauty: 'we may be wafted to a land surpassing in wonders and in beauty every region hitherto discovered on the habitable globe'.[10] As the ice closes in on his ship the sailors plead to return but Walton remains haunted by his dream of future glory right to the end of the novel when his decision to return makes his dream recede ('it is past'). In *Symzonia* the moral crux is diverted by circumstances; the mutiny peters out when the ship sights land. But the fact that a mutiny has taken place at all identifies an ambiguity in the central project which later developments confirm.

Symmes writes himself into the narrative as a precursor along with Captain Ross, and establishes his credentials by detailing the outfitting of the *Explorer* and by giving precise particulars of the islands he visits. *Symzonia* thus alternates between narrative (the voyage sections) and expositions of flora and fauna common to the genre. As the ship approaches the pole the crew become disoriented: 'They were perfectly bewildered; they knew not which way was north, south, east or west'. Seaborn is the only one to retain a sense of direction but keeps it to himself as dangerous knowledge. At last they reach the edge of Symmes's concave sphere which marks the key point of geographical transit: 'We had a regular recurrence of day and night, though the latter was very short, which I knew was occasioned by the rays of the sun being obstructed by the rim of the earth . . . ' From this point on the men experience the strange new world of Symzonia which is first apprehended as an idealized picturesque landscape: 'gently rolling hills within an easy sloping shore, covered with verdure, chequered with groves of trees and shrubbery, studded with numerous white buildings, and animated with groups of men and cattle'. All in all the effect is, once Seaborn has penetrated the interior, of 'one beautiful and highly cultivated garden'.[11] The garden becomes an emblem of the Symzonians' harmonization of industry and beauty, a reflection of their civic order which is confirmed by lengthy expository chapters on their institutions.

So far the process of assimilating Symzonia might sound to be uniformly pleasant but a Swiftian recoil from the self takes place. Confronted by the ideally fair inhabitants of this country (the women's complexion resembles 'alabaster slightly tinged with rose'), Seaborn begins to loath his 'dark and hideous appearance'. The Symzonians are not referred to as 'natives', never placed along a civilized/savage axis, but rather designated 'instructors' or 'conductors'. From the very first Seaborn places them in a superior relation to himself and the fact that they are called 'internals' and the visitors 'externals' suggests that the former are inverted mirror-images of the latter. A connected reversal takes place between the Best Man's (i.e. the premier's) exposition of Symzonia to the captain followed by his own description of America to the Best Man. As with Gulliver's conversations with the King of Brobdingnag, the result is horror and condemnation, especially when the question of weaponry comes up: 'Instead of exciting his admiration, I found it difficult to convince him that my account was true, for he could not conceive it possible that beings in outward form so much like himself, could be so entirely under the influence of base and diabolical passions, as to make a science of worrying and destroying each other, like the most detestable reptiles'.[12] Here utopia is used directly to criticize the values of contemporary America, and to destroy Seaborn's self-image in the process. There is even an anti-Symmes in this society, a philosopher who proposes the theory of an external world and for his pains is dismissed as a 'maniac' and 'enthusiast'. Not surprisingly, Seaborn's departure from Symzonia becomes tantamount to an expulsion from paradise although even here his gaze wavers between worlds. On the one hand he registers humiliation ('I felt like a culprit exiled to Botany Bay for his crimes'), on the other he dreams of being feted as a celebrity once he returns to the United States. And even in the latter case he is forced to conceal the true nature of his discoveries from fear of ridicule. The polarization of his attitudes suggests a central ambivalence on Seaborn's part towards national enterprises, which gets stronger in the second part of the narrative. So his proud ritual of appropriation performed on a new island in the name of America actually paves the way for greater and greater humiliation.

Read superficially *Symzonia* could appear to be a 'voyage of discovery' undertaken with the confidence that God has underwritten commercial expansion by providing empty lands for the disposal of American merchant adventurers. But the new land is peopled by citizens whose rational meritocracy highlights the failings of America and the final part of the book appropriately narrates the remorseless diminution of Seaborn from explorer-hero to bankrupt. A storm at sea means that he loses his Symzonian specimens; he has to pay a high government levy on profits; his ship is wrecked at sea and he finally incurs financial ruin by trusting his affairs to a prosperous merchant named 'Mr. Slippery'. Even the status of the book itself slides from an instructive narrative to the means of raising a few badly needed dollars. The narrative's play on inner and outer space thus could be read as a means of transforming the voyage into one of self-exploration which results in a total alienation of Seaborn from his own culture.

In the same year as the publication of *Arthur Gordon Pym* there appeared a narrative which follows the same trajectory as *Symzonia* and which was thought by A.H. Quinn to be the work of Poe himself.[13] Peter Prospero's 'The Atlantis' (1838–39) describes a similar voyage to the south resulting in the discovery of Atlantis, which Prospero takes to be Swift's Terra Australis Incognita. Like Seaborn he dreams of becoming the 'projector and executor of a great undertaking' which will even rival the voyage of Columbus, and like Mary Shelley's Walton he becomes impatient with the limits to knowledge: 'I endeavoured to penetrate to its lowest foundations, fathom all its depths and compass its most extended boundaries'. These tropes of measuring and mapping the domain of knowledge are easily transposed on to the voyage south, and at the transition from the known to the unknown Prospero, unlike Adam Seaborn, falls victim to disorientation along with his crew. In *Symzonia* transition was marked by the confusion of the means

of measuring direction. Now the effect is more extreme and correspondingly more threatening:

> From a region of intense and intolerable cold and
> tempestuous weather, we were transported to a thick
> and murky atmosphere, in the gloomy and darkened
> state of which, we found respiration difficult, all our
> senses seemed disordered, and through the gloom every
> frightful and fantastic form floated that could be conceived
> as crude and monstrous. During our passage through this
> tract of ocean, all our usual prescriptions were suspended,
> and we sank into what appeared an incurable slumber, or
> deliquium.[14]

Traversing this barrier area inner and outer space blur together into
a state of perceptual disorder comparable to that experienced by
the Ancient Mariner embarking on his journey. Since this narrative
concerns the realization of the legend of Atlantis, it is also important
to note the mythical allusions to Cimmerian darkness which suggest
the bounds of the known world.

The transition into a utopian land of perfect order then is
marked by a confusion of the senses and next by a sharpening
of the voyagers' perceptions which is synchronized with a shift
in the weather towards the temperate. Symzonia similarly
was a place of ideally ordered industry, but its very order
renders the appropriation-by-naming absurd because Seaborn is
finally expelled. The newly discovered Atlantis, in contrast, is
immediately related by the narrator to American sights and his
guide around the capital city Saturnia proves to be none other
than Benjamin Franklin. The utopia therefore combines a number
of functions. As an egalitarian meritocracy it embodies a socio-
political ideal; its technological efficiency suggests the possible
progress of America; and its Philosophical Society draws together
the greatest minds of the past. In other words, place is used to
juxtapose the best elements of past and future which at no point
are brought to bear confrontationally on the narrator as happens
repeatedly in *Symzonia* and its precursor text *Gulliver's Travels*.

In contrast with 'The Atlantis', *The Narrative of Arthur Gordon
Pym* has much greater ambiguity of purpose and method. When it
was published in 1838 the reviewers almost with one voice compared it to *Robinson Crusoe* and not surprisingly found it wanting in
probability. 'A more impudent attempt at humbugging the public
has never been exercised', huffed William Burton.[15] Although Poe

expressed great respect for Defoe's engagement with the 'idea of a man in a state of perfect isolation', what the reviewers failed to recognize was that *The Narrative* had moved away from the limits of a single genre and accordingly combined elements of the Gothic, the fictitious journal, and the adventure narrative.[16] G.R. Thompson has shown convincingly that the novel thrives on indeterminacy and digressions, so much so that the central notion of the voyage becomes ambiguous: 'more than just a journey to the South Pole, Pym's adventures symbolically suggest a journey within the self and back in time, a quest for origins and ends'. Having established the paradoxical conflation of direction (backwards/forwards) and aims, Thompson even qualifies the destination of the journey: the quest is 'less for any ultimate "truth" and more for the "astounding" as a kind of permanent penultimate apocalypse'.[17] In the preamble to 'Eleonora' Poe states as much when attributing value to daydream: 'In their grey visions they obtain glimpses of eternity, and thrill, in awaking, to find that they have been upon the verge of the great secret'. Since this 'secret' can scarcely be conceptualized, Poe can only figure the progression as an entry into boundless space where the self loses any means of control or measurement: 'They penetrate, however rudderless or compassless, into the vast ocean of the "light ineffable"'.[18] In *The Narrative*, then, the different domains of experience are rendered as spaces with their own modalities.

Boundaries function in Poe's writings as both spatial limits to be crossed and as perceptual frames. In 'Eureka', for instance, the attempt to conceive of the infinite becomes virtually impossible because it involves losing such a frame: '. . . no fog of the mind can well be greater than that which, extending to the very boundaries of the mental domain, shuts out even these boundaries themselves from comprehension'. The result is a shifting mental expanse, a 'shadowy and fluctuating domain, now shrinking, now swelling, with the vacillating energies of the imagination'.[19] The perception of space in *The Narrative* similarly fluctuates according to the circumstances and particularly the physical state of Pym. When he is first shown his hiding place on the *Grampus* it is praised as an 'apartment' and 'palace'. However, after sleeping for three days this luxurious accommodation contracts to a tomb while Pym's dreams project his fears of impending death into arid wastelands: 'deserts, limitless, and of the most forlorn and awe-inspiring character, spread themselves out before me . . . The scene changed; and I stood, naked and alone, amid the burning sand-plains of

Zahara.'[20] These descriptions grow immediately out of Pym's consuming thirst, but they also suggest a loss of bearings which is repeated several times in the novel, particularly as Pym drifts across the ocean after the cannibalism episode or when he is almost buried in the landslide (the latter a 'living inhumation').

Defoe presents Robinson Crusoe's sufferings as a result of disobedience, because he has defied his earthly and spiritual fathers. Although the religious dimension has attenuated down to perfunctory prayers immediately before or after deliverance, Poe also dramatizes his action as a transgression. Like Defoe he introduces his narrative with a preliminary shipwreck which demonstrates the sinfulness of his protagonist in going to sea. And again like Defoe, Pym denies his family (this time his grandfather) in the process. But the main transgression in *The Narrative* is the act of cannibalism which breaks the limits of Pym's species assumptions. As he drifts with other survivors of the mutiny they encounter a deathship which derives directly from 'The Ancient Mariner'. The eery vessel is introduced within a context of hallucination and it veers symbolically to and fro between extremes of life and death, hope and despair. As Pym gazes in horror at a seagull gorging itself on a corpse there occurs a comment which is censored even before it is expressed: 'May God forgive me, but now, for the first time, there flashed through my mind a thought, a thought which I will not mention . . .'[21] For all Pym's pious finessing it very quickly becomes evident what that thought concerns. The killing and eating of Parker is an episode suppressed by Pym as challenging the power of language itself. This whole section of the novel presents images of human beings reduced to matter and Pym's horror at the human merging into the non-human, a metaphorical loss of moral bearings, is only relieved when the castaways are picked up by the *Jane Guy*. At this point they re-enter the map (through specific bearings) and the familiar social world.

It is of course a truism that *The Narrative* alternates episodes of confusion and of relative clarity. Pym's internal account of being shut up in the hold of the *Grampus* is followed by Augustus Barnard's external narrative of the mutiny. The castaway section is in turn followed by a quasi-historical summary of South Sea voyages. One result of this method is to disperse the act of narrating and to raise constant questions about Pym's own reliability. The latter issue is foregrounded at the beginning of the last episode by Pym's admission that he is now basing his account on possibly faulty memories. To a certain extent this admission counters the reader's expectations of revelation, which have earlier been set up by references to the ice barrier and hypotheses of a southern continent and temperate zone. This time the boundaries are physical and limits to prior exploration. Thus the 84th parallel which is highlighted on the novel's title page refers to the southern-most point reached by James Weddell.[22] However, when Pym and his companions land on newly discovered islands the flora, fauna and even the rocks themselves are described as so alien that they cannot be related to the familiar. When Pym escapes into a 'region of novelty wonder' this effect increases. Now natural phenomena become surreal and paradoxical. Though the season is winter the temperature rises; the men fall into a 'dreaminess of sensation'; and all things become a monochrome white. Dimension also shifts bewilderingly:

> The range of vapor to the southward had arisen pro-digiously in the horizon, and began to assume more distinctness of form. I can liken it to nothing but a limitless cataract, rolling silently into the sea from some immense and far-distant rampart in the heaven. The gigantic curtain ranged along the whole extent of the southern horizon. It emitted no sound.[23]

Vapour assumes density and then immobility in these two analogies, which suggest an indefinite regression of boundaries since the horizon is no longer an ultimate limit but a barrier ('rampart', 'curtain') to fresh discoveries and further barriers. The reader is drawn into Pym's projected opposition between upper and lower space mediated by the vapour which establishes a sublime and awe-inspiring sense of scale. However, before Pym can approach and particularize this apparition his journal breaks off.

The voyage-narrative which most clearly takes its protagonist out of life is Poe's 'MS. Found in a Bottle'. The narrator identifies himself from the beginning as exiled from country and family, and suffering from a 'nervous restlessness'. Setting out from Indonesia, his voyage passes through climatic extremes (heat, stillness and storm) to a state where all light is blanked out: 'we were enshrouded in pitchy darkness'. The narrator and his sole surviving companion experience a kind of pre-death, a descent into a 'watery hell' where the normal dimensions of nature are radically altered. Instead of having extent, twilight discloses an abyss within which an enormous black ship towers over the narrator's. As it crashes on to the latter the narrator is flung on to its rigging and apparently transported to an earlier period where the ghostly crew never registers his presence. This shift is figured as another death, this time of the first vessel. So far the descent is comparable to 'A Descent into the Maelstrom' where the issue of plausibility is written into the tale as a dialogue between primary and secondary narrators. Now, however, the progression into the depths is only followed by the implicit rise of the narrative itself suggested by the tale's title.

As events become more and more extreme the lacunae in the manuscript reveal a conspicuous absence of explanatory connectives which for G.R. Thompson reflect directly on the narrator's credibility: '. . . the incredible events are the delusions of a man driven mad. Seen as a voyage of "discovery", the ludicrous "supernatural" events act as a grotesquerie of the discovery of what lies beyond the normal world or beyond death, for the tale abruptly ends at the very verge of revelation in apparent final destruction and silence.'[24] Thompson's eagerness to demonstrate the narrator's unreliability leads him to understate the metaphorical consistency of the narrative, which moves further and further away from life. The sequence is clear. First the narrator moves beyond the limits of known navigation. Then he experiences a figurative death, a descent into a world of shades followed by a loss of language ('a feeling, for which I have no name . . . a sensation which will admit of no analysis'); until finally the Southward current sweeps him towards a climactic insight: 'To conceive the horror of my sensation is, I presume, utterly impossible; yet a curiosity to penetrate the mysteries of these awful regions, predominates even over my despair, and will reconcile me to the most hideous aspect of death. It is evident that we are hurrying onwards to some exciting knowledge—some never-to-be-imparted secret, whose attainment is destruction'.[25] The tale must halt abruptly at a point of imminence because access to the innermost secrets of Nature is predicted as a moment where the self merges with Nature in death. Unlike the Maelstrom there will be no ascent from the polar vortex in this most literal demonstration of the 'desire for undifferentiation' which Rosemary Jackson argues lies at the heart of fantasy literature.[26]

The narrator of the above tale is typical of Poe's protagonists in being displaced from a notional point of origin. He suffers from the existential 'homelessness' described by Schlegel, one of Poe's literary mentors. In his *Lectures on Dramatic Art and Literature* Schlegel describes mankind's tragic predicament through metaphors which are pointedly relevant to this discussion:

> When ... we contemplate the relations of our existence to the extreme limits of possibilities:... when we consider how weak and helpless, and doomed to struggle against the enormous powers of nature, and conflicting appetites, we are cast on the shores of an unknown world, as it were, shipwrecked at our very birth; ... every heart which is not dead to feeling must be overpowered by an inexpressible melancholy, for which there is no other counterpoise than the consciousness of a vocation transcending the limits of this earthly life.[27]

By this account man is caught between a longing for infinity offset by a recognition of humanity's limited capacities, and displaced from an inaccessible point of origin. Schlegel's figure of shipwreck stresses the individual's vulnerability to uncontrollable forces, which is also one reason why Poe's sea narratives are usually far more powerful than his descriptions of journeys by land. Cut off from origins and tantalized by unrealizable goals, man is doomed to endless searching like the knight in Poe's poem 'Eldorado' who pursues his quest towards the limits of his own mortality. In a similar way the protagonist of Poe's unfinished narrative of land exploration, *The Journal of Julius Rodman* (1840), is totally detached from any family origins and driven forward by a 'romantic fervour'.

In 1837 Poe testified to his fascination with this subject of exploration by publishing one of the longest reviews of his career, a detailed discussion of Washington Irving's *Astoria*. Most of the review was summary, but Poe did declare that Irving's account of a land expedition across the Rockies was unsurpassed: 'no details more intensely exciting are to be found in any work of travels within our knowledge'.[28] *Astoria* was designed to realize Irving's youthful admiration for what he called 'these Sindbads of the wilderness' and also to put on record his fascination with the expansion westward of the American fur trade. John Jacob Astor is therefore presented as a culture hero whose eyes are set on something higher than personal gain: 'he now aspired to that honourable fame which is awarded to men of similar scope of mind, who by their great commercial enterprises have enriched nations, peopled wildernesses, and extended the bounds of empire'. Irving describes the merchant adventurers' land expedition as a triumph of physical endurance in traversing the natural barrier of the Rockies and as a future filling of the blank space on the North American map since 'these treeless wastes between the Rocky Mountains and the Pacific, are even more desolate and barren than the naked upper prairies on the Atlantic side; they present vast desert tracts that must ever defy cultivation, and interpose dreary and thirsty wilds between the habitations of man . . .'[29] Irving's emphasis on open featureless space obviously points up the heroism of his travellers, and also reinforces the symbolic importance of the West as the area of American national expansion. It should also be noted, however, that the period 1821–1842 was one characterized by border disputes between the USA and Canada so that fixing boundaries was a charged political issue, as both Poe and Irving recognized.[30]

Poe's imagination was so fired by *Astoria* that he tried his own hand at a similar work, but the result was quite different from Irving's. *The Journal*, for instance, contains two narrative voices, that of Rodman and the second voice of an editor who is constantly selecting passages and commenting on them. Furthermore Rodman is described as one who travels for pleasure and as the first man to cross the Rockies. Despite the ostensible date of his expedition in 1791–92, Poe actually borrows liberally from Irving's work.[31] However, in contrast with Irving's protagonist, Rodman gradually erases the commercial usefulness of the landscape about him and registers a mounting urgency to see the 'wonders and majestic beauties of the wilderness'. Not for him Irving's horror of empty space. On the contrary, Rodman is driven by a compulsion to leave even the traces of human habitation far behind.

> As yet, however, I felt as if in too close proximity to the settlements for the full enjoyment of my burning love of nature and of *the unknown*. I could not help being aware that *some* civilized footsteps, although few, had preceded me in my journey; that *some* eyes before my own had been enraptured with the scenes around me . . . I was anxious to *go on*; to get, if possible, beyond the extreme bounds of civilization; to gaze, if I could, upon those gigantic mountains of which the existence had been made known to us only by the vague accounts of the Indians.

This fantasy of the first gaze on 'absolutely virgin' territory appears to be realized in 'A Tale of the Ragged Mountains' when Augustus Bedloe penetrates the Virginian hinterland but he falls prey to disorienting fantasies of an oriental landscape worthy of the Arabian Nights, rendered all the more ambiguous by his adventures paralleling the Indian Mutiny. The narrative thus takes him out of familiar space and time, and even out of his body as he contemplates his own corpse. Where Poe sheds every possible doubt on Bedloe's narrative credentials he follows the opposite tactic in *The Journal*, since the editor pays explicit tribute to Rodman's style: 'with all his evident enthusiasm, our traveller is never prone to the exaggeration of facts'.[32]

The delivery of *The Journal* follows a procedure common in many of Poe's works whereby the primary narrator acts as editor of a framed secondary narrative. Here the editor contextualizes Rodman's journal within the history of exploration, claims the privilege of knowing unpublished letters and memoirs by Rodman and others, and takes the liberty of selecting at will from the journal. The narrative thus moves between the third and first persons, alternating between Rodman as object and Rodman as subject. Furthermore the editor anticipates our reactions even before the narrative has begun: 'He stalked through that immense and often terrible wilderness with an evident rapture at his heart which we envy him as we read'.[33] The chronology of the editorial comments occurs not only after Rodman's travels have finished but also after all other available travel narratives; in that respect it is quite distinct temporally from the day-by-day episodic sequence of the journal, which revolves around local presents. The narrative of *The Journal*, as so often happens in Poe's works, is mediated by an editor who is familiar with the accounts of Irving, Lewis and Clark, and others; and who selects passages from the journal proper. Although Rodman is pursuing the chimera of the primal gaze he can never realize this since he has always been preceded by others, if only Indians; and so he attempts to flee from the conditions of his very journal which 'shadows' *Astoria* at many points. The editor unconsciously draws our attention to this janus-quality in the text every time he interrupts the flow of the journal because he resorts to authenticating strategies by comparing Rodman's account to later exploration narratives. Although the latter postdate Rodman's journal, their authenticating force grows out of their status as models, i.e. as texts *preceding* Poe's. *The Journal* is thus constructed on the basis of a radical ambiguity between before and after which was never resolved as the work was left unfinished. One reason for its abandonment might have been once again a shift in Poe's conception of the work since, as one commentator has pointed out, Rodman 'practically disappears as a distinct character' and 'becomes merely a recorder of the progress and rather mild adventures of the whole party'.[34] In contrast with *The Narrative* Poe never exploits the dramatic potential of his protagonist.

Along with many subsequent writers and critics, Jules Verne claimed that *The Narrative of Arthur Gordon Pym* like *The Journal* had been left unfinished, but in so doing confused Pym's record with Poe's novel, and in 1897 Verne published his sequel *The Sphinx of the Ice-Fields* (*Le Sphinx des Glaces*). The action takes place in 1839 and concerns an American geologist named Jeorling who is planning to return home from the Kerguelen Islands. With difficulty he persuades a Captain Guy to take him on board the *Halbrane* and is startled to hear the latter discussing Pym as if he were a real person. Jeorling is finally swayed by a second person's corroboration that he knew Pym and the decision is taken to alter course south to retrace Pym's course in the hope that they will find survivors. It is clear from a very early stage in the narrative that Verne is concerned to close the gap between romance and history and between the editorial frame and Pym's narrative, thus losing any means of questioning the reliability of the latter; Jeorling and the characters from *The Narrative* are all situated on the same level of illusion. This is achieved partly by 'believers' engaging with Jeorling's scepticism and partly by introducing a character called Hunt who turns out to be none other than Dirk Peters. He is convinced that Pym is alive somewhere in the south, hence his functionalist name.

To establish the reality of Pym is only the preliminary stage of *The Sphinx*. That done, the narrative works almost like a palimpsest on Poe's work. Indeed Captain Guy possesses a copy of *Arthur Gordon Pym* whose margins he has covered with annotations. Although Verne told his publisher that a prior knowledge of Poe's work was not essential, its absence would make it less easy for the reader to follow a sequence of recognitions and repetitions: the discoveries of the wreck of the *Jane*, Tiger's collar, the body of a seaman in an iceberg, and so on. Verne declared: 'I have used everything that Poe left in suspense and have developed the mystery surrounding certain characters'.[35] It is precisely the element of mystery which *The Sphinx* works against. Thus Verne is not concerned with spatial limits. When the crew mutiny at one point (an echo of *Symzonia*?) there is no moral crux raised, simply a retarding of the narrative's steady progression towards understanding. Similarly, when Tsalal Island is described as a wasteland following an earthquake, the significance is that possible landmarks have been erased so that the sailors must look for different traces. *The Sphinx* offers an unusually explicit example of a general process Pierre Macherey has located in Verne's works: 'The journey, in all its progressive stages, is disclosed as having ineluctably happened before . . . To explore is to follow, that is to say, to cover once again, under new conditions, a road already actually travelled.' *The Sphinx* is exactly a narrative of pursuit which attempts to write away the aporias in Poe's work and the uncertainties in the landscape. It is no coincidence that the climax should contain the simultaneous discoveries of Pym's corpse and of the central natural object in Antarctica.

Macherey describes this rationalizing operation in Verne's works as an attempt to 'draw a straight line over the world' and certainly *The Sphinx* devotes a considerable amount of space to specifying nautical bearings and discussing the likely fates of Poe's characters, in other words to establishing a common level of factual accuracy.[36] This process is written into the novel as a temporary loss of the real experienced by Jeorling as he strains to penetrate the Antarctic mists:

> Then it was that I felt myself falling into an hallucination—one of those hallucinations which must have troubled the mind of Arthur Pym. I seemed to be losing myself in his extraordinary personality; I was beholding all he had seen! Was not that impenetrable mist the curtain of vapour which he had seen in his delirium? I peered into it, seeking for those luminous rays which had streaked the sky. I sought in its depths for that limitless cataract, rolling in silence from the height of some immense rampart lost in the vastness of the zenith! I sought for the dreadful white giant which guarded the South Pole.
>
> At length reason resumed her sway, and I descended to our camp.[37]

Just for a moment Pym opens up an imaginary vortex to the observer. Perceptual confusion licenses a temporary identification with another, dangerously unlimited way of seeing which Verne cuts off abruptly to return the reader to the safer level of rational clarity. Verne's choice of title was strategic because it raises a question of identity so strongly that when it is answered the result inevitably is anti-climax: 'The Antarctic Sphinx was simply a colossal magnet', a magnetic rock which has drawn Pym's boat to its destruction. For all its resemblance to the Sinbad story and to a key episode in *Peter Wilkins*, the explanation effectively closes off the reader's curiosity and therefore the narrative.[38] The general impulse towards 'exact scientific detail' in Verne which *The Sphinx* demonstrates is used by Verne's biographer Peter Costello as evidence that he is the true inventor of science fiction, but Costello then hedges his bets and admits: 'Yet the love of the unsolved and the unknown are essential qualities for a scientist'.[39] Poe, therefore, does not fare so badly after all.

Verne's desire to explain away the ambiguities of Poe's *Narrative* also informs Charles Romyn Dake's *A Strange Discovery* (1899). This work was written in answer to a question which contains a fundamental flaw: why did Poe not complete his novel? Having confused, as many readers would after him, Poe's novel with Pym's narrative, Dake comes to the following conclusion: 'My explanation is that the story has a foundation in fact, and that Poe himself never learned more than a foundation for the portion which he wrote'.[40] The English narrator is staying in the town of Bellevue, Illinois and meets a doctor who is a fervent admirer of Poe. His conviction that Dirk Peters is still alive is confirmed by a colleague, whereupon Dr. Bainbridge visits the old man and obtains the narrative which fills the final two thirds of the volume. Bainbridge has already discovered a fictitious precursor text which purports to be the record of one of Drake's sailors on his voyage of 1594. After coming through the Strait of Magellan their ship was driven south to a harbour on the shore of a huge city. This work establishes an analogy before the fact with Peters' own narrative since both fill gaps in existing accounts, and the former predisposes the reader to accept the possibility of an unknown Antarctic civilization. Peters' narrative disposes quickly of Pym's great white curtain; this turns out to be merely a curtain of fog which they traverse. Similarly, the ominous white figure is demystified as the 'large statue of spotless marble' standing at the entrance to the bay of a city and island named Hili-li. The transition from the known to the unknown, so crucial to earlier writers, is hardly given a mention by Dake. Far more important is his account of the islanders who prove to be the descendants of European refugees of the fourth century. The perfect beauty of the city and its female inhabitants particularly convince the newcomers that they have found a 'paradise on earth', but all is not quite as perfect as it seems. This new world contains dissidents, a small criminal class, and even madness. The royal maiden Lilama is abducted and then rescued by Pym and Peters. She shows her gratitude to the former by marrying him but falls victim to one of the waves of intense cold which sweeps the area, and dies. In deference to the grieving Pym the islanders make an exception to their general rule and allow the two men to leave, which they do, proceeding together to Montevideo.

Dake sets up a long cumbersome frame to Peters' narrative in the first part of the novel, which excludes the marvellous and forewarns the reader not to expect another Lilliput or flying people. Despite the novel's title the term 'discovery' refers to the meetings with Peters, not to any gradual process of exploration in Peters' narrative. The Antarctic is shown all at once in a map depicting concentric mountain ranges, at the centre of which lies an active volcano. The only travel carried out by Pym and his companions is a 'pleasure excursion' round the islands of the region. Nothing is at stake; there is no suspense from the unknown; and Dake's emphasis falls rather on the precarious isolation of Hili-li. As one islander predicts, 'whilst the ring-like continent of ice-covered volcanoes will long protect us, the warm strait will be discovered and mapped, and then design will carry to us many, over the same course by which chance has conveyed a few'.[41] The new world, in other words, might appear to be an earthly paradise, a Shangri-la of the southern hemisphere, but its inhabitants possess a historical awareness of their ancient connections with Europe, and a sense of imminent change. By prefacing Peters' narrative with a map, Dake's desire for authenticity leads him to realize the islanders' fears since the map promises accessibility and therefore the demise of Hili-li as a distinct and separate place. On the other hand, the fact that Pym's marriage does not last long suggests an ideological commitment on Dake's part to keeping Hili-li quite separate from the known world.

The ambition to continue or extend *The Narrative of Arthur Gordon Pym* must have reached its culmination in a recent novel by the American mathematician Rudy Rucker. *The Hollow Earth* (1990) is the narrative of a young Virginian named Mason Reynolds who is tricked when trying to sell his father's homebrew, becomes a fugitive and falls in with Poe's scheme to sail over the Antarctic mountains in a balloon. After a voyage south the two men and their companions make a successful flight only to crash near the South Pole. Here they fall through an opening in the polar ice and descend into a phantasmagoric inner world which becomes stranger and stranger as they approach the centre of the Earth. Discovering an abandoned bathysphere they pass through the centre and resurface

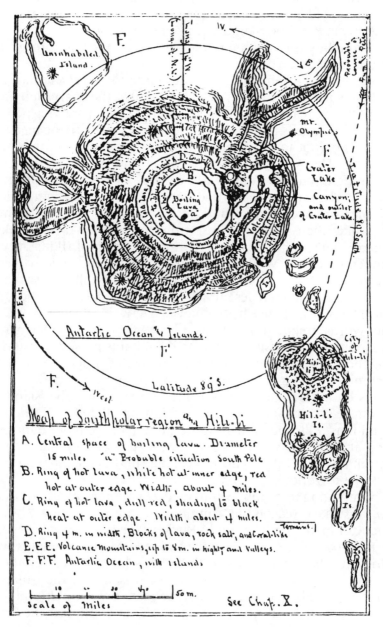

The SOUTH POLAR REGION *and* HILILILAND.

Charles Romyn Dake: *A Strange Discovery* (1899)

in Chesapeake Bay. Returning to Baltimore they discover that years have passed in their absence. It should be clear already that Rucker has produced a clever pastiche of a number of American and science fiction narratives. The flight of Reynolds with a negro servant in the opening section clearly echoes *Huckleberry Finn*; the return out of time looks back to 'Rip Van Winkle'; and the descent into the earth conflates *Alice in Wonderland* and Jules Verne. Above all the novel is a positive compendium of quotations from and allusions to Poe's works, with their implications now made clear. Poe the trickster is demonstrated in a scheme to forge bank bills ('diddling'); the suppressed sexual fear in his stories is written into an episode where Poe allows the young Reynolds to have sex with his wife Virginia; and the racial theme of *The Narrative* is signalled by Poe embarking on the *Wasp* and by a transformation of pigment which takes place within the Earth so that all the white characters return to Baltimore as negroes.

Rucker shadows Poe's *Narrative* in his description of the voyage south and outdoes *Symzonia* by taking his characters into a world of virtual reality where, as we shall see, dimensions shift unnervingly. Commenting on the new mode of science fiction where he places Rudy Rucker's works, Brian McHale has stated: 'Most cyberpunk motifs have precedents in earlier SF; some, indeed . . . , are among the hoariest of SF clichés'.[42] *The Hollow Earth* explicitly recycles such motifs, usually with a reductive humour; Dirk Peters appears as 'an empty-headed drifter who lived only for the moment' and Pym's dog now becomes Arf. Not even the figure of Poe himself is exempt from this process since he is revealed as a stowaway on the *Wasp* embracing the putrefying corpse of Virginia in a box! Rucker constantly reminds the reader of the novel's status as a pastiche by introducing blatant contradictions within the form. Thus the dust-cover to *The Hollow Earth* announces a 'Science Fiction Novel' by Rucker whereas the title page identifies it as 'The Narrative of Mason Algiers Reynolds of Virginia', *edited* by Rucker.[43] Similarly, the narrative dates events from 1836 but throughout uses an idiom packed with twentieth-century locutions. The overall result of these strategies is to refuse any consistent level of illusion and to prepare the reader for the radical shifts in the real which take place within the Earth's interior.

The first half of the novel repeats the limits familiar from *The Narrative* and *Symzonia*, namely the great ice barrier which the characters traverse without difficulty. Once they begin to fall, however, direction reverses ambiguously (up or down?) until they come to rest on a 'gravitational shelf'. In other words, they simply pause before their fall continues. But as they approach the centre of the Earth light and time warps, and gravity stops, as does the narrative while Rucker attempts theoretical explanations:

> Suppose that at the Hollow Earth's center there were a large shiny ball. Outside this mirrorball would be the Umpteen Seas, the Inner Sky, then Htrae, the thick planetary Rind, and, beyond the Rind, the Earth I came from and its outer sky with Sun, Moon, and Stars. Suppose that all of this were reflected in the central mirrorball, so that staring into the mirror one could see Umpteen MirrorSeas, an Inner MirrorSky, a MirrorHtrae, a MirrorRind and, beyond the MirrorRind (were the MirrorRind transparent), a MirrorEarth beneath an outer MirrorSky with MirrorSun, MirrorMoon, and MirrorStars. Imagine all this and then imagine that the central ball is no mirror at all but simply a window between two worlds—an open airy window. This is what is true.[44]

Rucker's equivalent to the fictitious naturalistic descriptions we have already noted is to posit such hypotheses about reality which totally destabilize our sense of boundaries. This passage, for instance, refers to an *inner* sky *outside* the mirrorball. The real becomes reversed and then reflected so that the mirror ceases to be a barrier and becomes instead a point of access to another world. The very notion of limits must be abandoned here in favour of a shifting space-time continuum where space might take on many possible dimensions.[45] Rucker follows through the logic of this hypothesis by describing confrontations between duplicate figures after his characters return to America. 'Eddie' Poe comes face to face with Mirror Poe, an older, more successful and oppositely figmented version of himself. In a paroxysm of rage the latter kills the former, repeating the climax of 'William Wilson' so that even the text itself becomes duplicitous in its play on different diegetic levels. Rucker throws out a strategic hint of this instability when Reynolds plans to write an account of his 'unparalleled journey'. The adjective clearly alludes to Poe's own balloon-narrative, 'The Unparalleled Adventure of one Hans Pfaall,' and extends even farther the levels of duplicity. Perhaps the 'hollow' in Rucker's title ultimately comes to refer to absence of a stable centre in his own text.

NOTES

1. Darko Suvin, *Metamorphoses of Science Fiction: On the Poetics and History of a Literary Genre* (New Haven, 1979), pp.5, 139.

2. Brian W. Aldiss with David Wingrove, *Trillion Year Spree: The History of Science Fiction* (London, 1986), p.60.

3. Clarke Olney, 'Edgar Allan Poe—Science-Fiction Pioneer', *Georgia Review*, 12 (1958), pp.416–21; David Ketterer lists critical comment on this aspect of Poe in his 'The SF Element in the Work of Poe: A Chronological Survey', *Science-Fiction Studies*, 1 (1974), pp.197–213.

4. Edgar Allan Poe, *Essays and Reviews*, ed. G.R. Thompson (New York and Cambridge, 1988), p.1231.

5. H. Bruce Franklin, *Future Perfect: American Science Fiction of the Nineteenth Century* (New York, 1966), p.95 ('Rarely in Poe's science fiction does one find science itself as a subject and nowhere does one find any kind of true scientist as a consequential figure'), p.102.

6. Quoted in *The Science Fiction of Edgar Allan Poe*, ed. Harold Beaver (Harmondsworth, 1977), p.10. Symmes's Hole was taken seriously as late as the 1870s: v.P. Clark, 'The Symmes Theory of the Earth', *Atlantic Monthly*, 31 (1873), pp.471–80.

7. E.F. Madden, 'Symmes and his Theory', *Harper's New Monthly Magazine*, 65 (1882), p.743.

8. The attribution of authorship is made in the *British Library Catalogue*. There are allusions to *Symzonia* in 'MS. Found in a Bottle' and 'The Unparalleled Adventure of One Hans Pfaall': v. Beaver, pp.334, 335, 346, 349. In the course of a biographical essay on J.N. Reynolds, Robert F. Almy similarly concludes that 'imaginary pictures of the polar regions in Poe's early tales strongly resemble the image publicized by Symmes and Reynolds' ('J.N. Reynolds: A Brief Biography with Particular Reference to Poe and Symmes', *Colophon*, n.s.2 (1937), p.238).

9. 'Adam Seaborn', *Symzonia; A Voyage of Discovery* (New York, 1820), p.13.

10. Mary Shelley, *Frankenstein, or The Modern Prometheus*, ed. M.K. Joseph, (London, 1969), pp.15–16.

11. *Symzoniar*, pp. 82, 99, 118.

12. *Symzoniar*, p.153. Also alluding to *Gulliver's Travels*, Arthur Gordon Pym by contrast concludes that the South Sea islanders he encounters 'were among the most barbarous, subtle, and bloodthirsty wretches that ever contaminated the face of the globe' (Poe, *Poetry and Tales*, ed. Patrick F. Quin (New York and Cambridge, 1984), p.1150).

13. A.H. Quinn, *Edgar Allan Poe: A Critical Biography* (New York, 1920), pp.757–61.

14. Peter Prospero, 'The Atlantis', *The American Museum of Science, Literature, and the Arts*, 1.i (September 1838), p.46. This unfinished work was serialized in the numbers for September–December 1838, and

January, May and June 1839. The first four chapters are reprinted in Sam Moskowitz's *A Man Called Poe* (1970).

15. I.M. Walker (ed.), *Edgar Allan Poe: The Critical Heritage* (London and New York, 1986), p.96.

16. Poe, *Essays and Reviews*, p.202. J.V. Ridgely and Iola S. Haverstick take the shifts in narrative mode to indicate that during composition Poe changed his conception of the work several times away from his original idea of a 'serial story of adventures aboard ship and in the South Seas': 'Chartless Voyage: The Many Narratives of Arthur Gordon Pym', *Texas Studies in Literature and Language*, 8 (1966), pp.63–80.

17. G.R. Thompson, 'Romantic Arabesque, Contemporary Theory and Postmodernism: The Example of Poe's *Narrative*', *ESQ: A Journal of the American Renaissance*, 35.iii–iv (1989), p.194.

18. Poe, *Poetry and Tales*, p.468.

19. Poe, *Poetry and Tales*, p.1275.

20. Poe, *Poetry and Tales*, p.1026. These descriptions probably derive from the dreams section of De Quincey's *Confessions of an English Opium Eater* ('The Pains of Opium').

21. Poe, *Poetry and Tales*, pp.1086–87. The travesty hospitality of the death-ship's crew, who would receive the castaways into their 'goodly company', makes a half-quotation from 'The Ancient Mariner', VII.20.

22. This bearing is stressed as a limit by Poe in his discussion of South Sea voyages (*Essays and Reviews*, p.1249).

23. Poe, *Poetry and Tales*, p.1179.

24. G.R. Thompson, *Poe's Fiction: Romantic Irony in the Gothic Tales* (Madison, 1973), p.168.

25. Poe, *Poetry and Tales*, pp.195, 198.

26. Rosemary Jackson, *Fantasy: The Literature of Subversion* (London and New York, 1991), p.72.

27. Augustus William Schlegel, *A Course of Lectures on Dramatic Art and Literature*, trans. James Black. Revised ed. (London, 1846), p.45. G.R. Thompson presents the evidence for Schlegel's influence on Poe in his *Poe's Fiction*, pp.29–34.

28. Poe, *Essays and Reviews*, p.629.

29. Washington Irving, *Astoria; or, Anecdotes of an Enterprise beyond the Rocky Mountains*. Revised ed. (London, 1857), pp.18, 187.

30. There were disputes over the borders of Maine and over the 45th parallel, but particularly over the ownership of the territory which was to become Washington State, a key area of reference in *Astoria* and, by implication, in Poe's *Journal*.

31. Both narratives contain a leading character called Pierre; both recount a meeting with a solitary Ponca tribesman. Irving describes the view from near Papillion Creek as follows: 'From the summit of a range of bluffs on the opposite side of the river ... they had one of those vast and magnificent prospects which sometimes unfold themselves in

these boundless regions' (*Astoria*, p.99). Rodman summarizes the view from Council Bluffs more tersely: 'From the cliffs just above us we had one of the most beautiful prospects in the world' (Poe, *Poetry and Tales*, p.1210).

32. Poe, *Poetry and Tales*, pp.1237, 1206. In 'A Tale of the Ragged Mountains' Bedloe too has the fantasy of being the 'first adventurer'. The primary narrator as usual in Poe's tales stresses Bedloe's 'profound melancholy' and thereby hints at his susceptibility to illusion.

33. Poe, *Poetry and Tales*, p.1190.

34. John Frank Ligon, Jr., 'On Desperate Seas: A Study of Poe's Imaginary Journeys' (Ph.D. thesis, University of Washington, 1961), p.223. Ligon sees the only value of *The Journal* as lying in its cameo romantic landscape descriptions.

35. Quoted in Peter Costello, *Jules Verne: Inventor of Science Fiction* (London, 1978), p.194.

36. Pierre Macherey, *A Theory of Literary Production*, trans. Geoffrey Wall (London, 1978), pp.189, 177.

37. *The Mystery of Arthur Gordon Pym* by Edgar Allan Poe and Jules Verne, ed. Basil Ashmore (London, 1960), p.164.

38. The Sinbad story is mentioned near the beginning of *Symzonia*. The relevant episode from *Peter Wilkins* occurs in Chapter 8, where his ship crashes violently into a magnetic rock immediately before Wilkins' entry into the 'new world' of the flying Indians. Poe knew this novel well and refers to it when reviewing a spurious pamphlet on the Moon (*Essays and Reviews*, p.1218).

39. Costello, pp.18, 79.

40. Charles Romyn Dake, *A Strange Discovery* (New York, 1899), p.38.

41. Dake, p.246.

42. Brian McHale, *Constructing Postmodernism* (New York and London, 1992), p.246.

43. The Editor's note, where Rucker purports to speak *in propria persona*, insists that the narrative is an 'authentic nineteenth-century manuscript'.

44. Rudy Rucker, *The Hollow Earth* (New York, 1990), p.208.

45. Rucker has explained this effect as a 'bridge between possible worlds, whereby world 2 is seen as in a spherical mirror at the end of a tunnel, but once the sphere is entered the visual perspective reverses so that world 1 appears to be the reflection' ('Magic Doors to other Worlds' in Rucker's *The Fourth Dimension: Toward a Geometry of Higher Reality* (Boston, 1984), p.118).

Verne's Amazing Journeys

M. HAMMERTON

Jules Verne (1828–1905) has been variously estimated as a writer of poetic force, the father of science fiction and 'a typical little bourgeois'.[1] It is still the case that his purely literary reputation stands higher in France than in English-speaking countries; but the reasons for this are not his fault, and not far to seek. Verne has been wickedly served by his translators.

His books were first translated, usually within a few years of their first appearance, by various hacks who seem to have known little English, less French, and no Science. Some of their renderings would make a schoolboy blush. I think my favourite howler is in *Vingt Mille Lieues*, where an irate captain calls for *someone more skilled* and is made to demand *another, more to the right* (ch.6: '"A un autre plus adroit!" cria le commandant . . .'). There are comparable gems, however, in almost every chapter of every book, besides blunders in elementary arithmetic. Subsequent hacks copied from the earlier ones, unless by some miracle they happened to make exactly the same arithmetical blunders;[2] and his most recent editors, though properly respectful, have tended to cut out the very passages which, though they may give pause to the unenlightened, delight the connoisseur (such as the minute account in *L'Île Mystérieuse*, of how to make nitroglycerine from the rawest of raw materials).

By this time, the reader may have surmized that I am something of an admirer of Verne. I do not deny it; and will attempt to offer some defence of this position. Certainly he had failings, some of which are regarded more sternly now than in his own time: for example, his racial prejudices read offensively today.[3] But many Victorians could believe in the natural inferiority of some races whilst regarding their oppression with genuine horror. There is no logical fallacy here—far less is there hypocrisy. Oppression is a moral act, which can be condemned irrespectively of any conclusions about abilities, which are an empirical matter. His xenophobia, usually mild, could be unpleasant at times. This, however, did not prevent him creating heroes and heroines—some of whom are surprisingly 'modern' and 'liberated'—who were English, Dutch, American, Russian, Indian or Chinese. And his humour was a saving grace.

A quality almost wholly lost by his translators is the ironic wit which pervades his work, especially the earliest books. Nevertheless, though his manner is light, his intentions were pervaded by a deep seriousness. His publishers produced his books in a series—collectively called *Les Voyages Extraordinaires*—explicitly dedicated to education as well as to entertainment; and Verne had no doubt that he intended to instruct as well as to amuse.

He was typically Victorian in this at least: he wished his instruction to be moral as well as factual; and his heroes are sometimes rather tryingly virtuous. They are brave, honest, determined, generous, kindly, and cheerful in the face of danger; and whilst twentieth-century readers smile cynically at the string of adjectives, can they deny that they are indeed desirable qualities? Cynicism might equally be aroused by the prodigious learning of some of his heroes; but some astonishingly well-schooled persons do exist, and why not have one as the hero of an adventure tale?

The term 'adventure tale' was used advisedly. Although Verne is mainly remembered for his science fiction—and it is with this that we are naturally most concerned—such works constituted less than a third of his enormous output. Out of over seventy volumes altogether only a score or so are properly 'science fiction'. The remainder are adventures, packing a great deal of geographical and other information, and favouring a 'with-one-bound-Jacques-sprang-free' method of escaping from tight corners.

It was, perhaps, his high Victorian morality which led Verne to take the care he did over his future technology. It was not acceptable for him to deceive the aspiring young with vague phrases and graceful evasions. If he wanted to go to the moon, he checked the Earth's velocity of escape (though, as we shall see, he made some mistakes in that area). If he wanted a balloon to remain airborne for weeks, he at least devised a theoretically workable method of doing it. If he wanted a submarine, he calculated its dimensions faithfully.

In various novels, Verne sent his heroes under the oceans, to the moon, in aircraft, navigable balloons and in a flying-submarine-car. Another, though a villain rather than a hero, unintentionally launched an unmanned satellite, and yet other villainous wretches were armed with guided weapons, and a variety of assault vertical take-off and landing machines. This makes a rather impressive list, the more so as many of these devices are described in enough detail to invite serious criticism.

Verne's first novel, and one which set the pattern for many to come, was *Cinque Semaines en Ballon* (1862). In this, three Britons cross then unknown Africa in a balloon, on the way establishing the source of the White Nile, discovering a gold mine, rescuing a missionary, eating an elephant, having an air-battle with some vultures, dispensing large dollops of geographical information for youthful readers, speculating on the future of the world, saving one another's lives and generally behaving as true Verne heroes always would.

The problem with balloons, grasped within a very short time of their invention in 1783, was that they would only go where the wind happened to blow them. By Verne's day, it was known that winds often blow in different directions at different altitudes; so, in principle, the problem could be solved by probing at various altitudes until the right wind was found. However, in order to rise, ballast must be shed; and to sink gas must be valved away; and a very few vertical sweeps soon exhaust the reserves of both. Verne's way round this impasse was at once ingenious, odd, and terrifying.

Suppose a balloon, in shape a prolate ellipsoid, is completely closed, and contains exactly enough gas to be, with its payload, precisely in equilibrium with the surrounding air at ground level. Now warm the gas: it will expand, and the balloon will rise; let it cool again, and the balloon will sink. In order to achieve this happy result, Verne suggested what was, in effect, an electric central-heating system. A pipe was to lead from the lower part of the balloon to the heating system, another from there to the upper segment. Thus, as heat was supplied, a circulation would be set up, and the whole body of gas eventually warmed. Thus far his ingenuity; the oddity lay in the heating system itself. A battery was used to separate the constituent hydrogen and oxygen in a tank of water; the gases were to recombine in an oxy-hydrogen flame heating the inside of a metal cone, the other side of which convected heat to the gas itself. Now why the complexity? You must, according to basic thermodynamics, recover *less* energy from the combustion of the gases than you put into the water to separate them. Therefore, it would be better and simpler to use the electricity directly in an element built into the inside of the cone.

It is, alas, decidedly possible—as we shall have cause to see again—that Verne quite simply never understood the ineluctable limitations of the laws of thermodynamics. More than one of his ideas depends on forbidden cheating of this kind; including precisely the above mistake again, in an aside in *L'Ile Mystérieuse*. To justify the adjective terrifying, I will merely observe that the reader is welcome to play with a flame near a balloon full of hydrogen—even a supposedly hermetically sealed one—but that I want to be a long way away when he does it.

A little arithmetic casts some further interesting light on Verne's ideas. He carefully tabulates the mass of balloon and payload; and we readily compute (in close agreement with him, by the way) that the mass of the gas in the balloon was just under 130 kg. To attain an altitude of 300 m—no great height—would roughly (necessarily roughly: the exact value would depend on the local temperature lapse-rate and other unknowns) require a 10°C increase in temperature. Since hydrogen has the rather high specific heat at constant pressure of 3.4 cal/gm/°C, this operation would require roughly 4 kw hr from the battery, making no allowance at all for inefficiency or loss. Making reasonable assumptions, the batteries would have needed to supply at least 500 kw hr during the journey. In 1862 that would have been a very remarkable battery indeed, and not a negligible one today. But Verne had a weakness for super-batteries.

It is worth noting this curious point. For Verne always seems to have shown the same two failings: he rarely solved the energy equations; and he never allowed for development—for the ironing out of bugs which is so invariable a part of making a new machine work. The power requirements of *Cinq Semaines* are typical, as is the assumption that the very first flight of the balloon is also its voyage: there is no test programme, no need for modification in the light of trials. The second of these failings we might ascribe to an excess of Victorian confidence; but the first must be due to mere lack of knowledge. Let us not complain too much; at least four of his most enjoyable tales would never have been written if he had been too tender about power sources, and he always produced an ingenious and theoretically sound means of using the power he so blithely assumed.

Usually, the power he assumed was electric. Indeed, Verne may, with some justice, be called the Erasmus Darwin of Electricity, for the following lines can surely be compared with the famous ode to 'Unconquer'd Steam':

'Listen', said Captain Nemo . . . 'A powerful, controllable,
and flexible form of energy is used for every purpose, and
really runs my ship. It is used for everything: lighting,
heating and power for the motors. I refer to electricity.'
(my translation)[4]

The narrator expresses astonishment, reflecting how little anyone
had achieved, at that time, in electrical engineering. And indeed,
it was so. No electric motor was commercially available in 1870
with the power output of a good Watt beam engine, far less one
which could compare with the best high pressure steam engines
of the time.

The principle of the electric motor had been demonstrated by
Faraday as early as 1821; but it remained a principle only. Gramme
did not demonstrate his D.C. motor until 1873, nor Siemens his little
(2 h.p.) traction engine until 1879. Also the problem of supplying
current was only being satisfactorily solved when Verne wrote.
Gramme was building his generator whilst Verne was working on
Vingt Mille Lieues; though some rather less satisfactory machines had
been produced a few years before. Otherwise, if you wanted electricity, you had to use chemical means: in other words, batteries. A
lot of effort was devoted, during the nineteenth century and since,
to finding better and more powerful kinds of batteries; but with
only modest success. The re-chargeable battery (accumulator) was
being developed by 1870; but the best of these today cannot supply
the kind of energies for the kind of weight that Verne demanded
and confidently, if wrongly, expected.

He was not in the least inhibited by the 'state of the art'. His submarine—the splendid *Nautilus*—incorporated many features that
had already been tried by brave, if not very successful, pioneers
(e.g., in *La Plongeuse* of 1864), or which were obvious enough. Any
thoughtful engineer of the time would have agreed that such a
craft would need ballast tanks to submerge it, horizontal rudders
to control it in a vertical plane, a pressure hull, and, above all, a
form of motor which was not air-breathing. Verne realized that an
electric motor would satisfy that requirement, and contributed to
the whole a stupendous zest and confidence.

Nautilus is described as a 1500 ton boat, 70 m (230 ft) long and
8 m (26 ft) in maximum diameter. It would therefore be comparable to a modern nuclear attack submarine, though rather smaller
and slimmer. No nuclear submarine, however—indeed, no million-

aire's yacht—boasts the luxurious splendours with which Verne endowed his creation: a library of 12 000 volumes (no less), a saloon 10 m by 6 m, 'truly a museum . . . [containing] all the treasures of Nature and of Art', and an organ, whereon the enigmatic Captain Nemo was wont to extemporize melodies in the Scottish style. To descend from Verne's exuberance to numbers, it would require roughly 400 h.p. to drive such a craft at 10 kt;[5] and to drive it at its full speed of 50(!) kt would require about 10 000 hp. During a journey of 80 000 km the batteries were only charged once; so assuming the lower speed for cruising, and only a small margin for high-speed bursts and contingencies, the batteries would have needed to hold a charge of the order of a million kilowatt hours. Today, the motor would be no problem; but even if the hull were so full of batteries as to reduce the accommodation to a very spartan level, it would be impossible to run for more than, at most, a few days without re-charging. (Consider the performance of the best type of 'conventional' submarines.)

Evidently, then, Verne was both reasonably confident and right about electric motors; but was his confidence in a new generation of super-batteries defensible, even though wrong as it turned out? Unfortunately, the answer is no, given that he could not have foreseen nuclear energy. Fuels offering the most energetic chemical reactions known, even if that energy were converted into electrical energy with 100% efficiency, would have required more mass than the *Nautilus* could have carried, even without engines and crew, to provide the charge he needed. Nevertheless, *Vingt Mille Lieues* is a great piece of technical prediction. Even though designers would have to content themselves with shorter voyages between re-charging, it summarized all the hints and suggestions of the pioneers, boldly provided them with a suitable motor (which was a bull's-eye) and transmuted the whole, with a soaring Victorian confidence, into a tale of assured wonder and great fun.

The element of Great Fun was present, if sometimes with a faintly gruesome tinge, when Verne temporarily deserted the sea for interplanetary space (*De la Terre à la Lune* and *Autour de la Lune*). The instigators of Verne's Moon-trip are a peace-weary (truly!) group of firearms fanatics, who have formed themselves into the Gun Club of Baltimore—a body comprising 1833 full members and more than 30 000 corresponding members, despite the criterion of entry being to have made some contribution to the design or development of weapons. As a result of practical experience on the battlefields of the American Civil War and sundry disasters in testing, they are a somewhat battered lot, having 'not quite one arm between four persons, and exactly two legs between six'.[6]

To keep these bloodthirsty cripples out of mischief, and for the sheer glorious fun of the thing, their (intact) president suggests firing a projectile at the Moon. Later, a splendid and eccentric Frenchman, Michel Ardan (actually an affectionate portrait of Verne's old friend Felix Tournachon, who was, among other things, the first man to take an aerial photograph from a balloon) insists on travelling in the projectile, taking with him the club president, and a rival engineer. To achieve these noble ends, Verne's heroes fire an aluminium shell 9 ft in calibre (he gives all the dimensions in English measure) out of a gun 900 ft long, which has been cast *in situ*, in a specially prepared excavation on top of a hill in Florida: the muzzle is at ground level. A charge of 400 000 lbs of gun-cotton expels the projectile which, for fine control in space, is equipped with steering rockets.

It is easy enough to laugh at this scheme. It was evident at the time that Verne made no allowance for air resistance: indeed, the shell would be vaporized before it even left the gun muzzle. Evidently also, the acceleration would have spread the heroic voyagers over the base of the inside at the initial shock. Nevertheless, it seems to me, the whole idea is worthy of the greatest praise.

Verne was not the first to write of travel to the Moon; but he was the first to talk about it as a great engineering problem, to be discussed in terms of quantity and material: he brought it from the merest fantasy to calculation. That he gave the escape velocity correctly is not, by itself, remarkable; the value had been estimated by Newton, and derived closely after Cavendish's work at the end of the previous century. Verne was the first to make any sort of serious suggestion of how such a velocity could be attained, and (for once!) his energetics were in the right bracket. A body travelling at escape velocity has an energy of rather less than 16 000 calories per gramme of its mass; gun-cotton yields around 1 500 cal/gm; and, of course, not all the energy of the charge is conveyed to the projectile. In allowing 20 kg of propellant for each kg of projectile he was very reasonable (Apollo did rather better a century later). He realized that rockets would work in vacuum, and made the brilliant suggestion of using them for what is now called vernier control. Why, one wonders, did he not take the next step of using rockets for the whole job? Above all, it is worth repeating, he treated the project as a vast engineering enterprise, which indeed it was to be. Not for him the solitary genius and his one assistant fabricating a space-ship in a back yard—an improbable supposition which recurred again and again over the following decades. Reaching the Moon was a goal, he rightly saw, which would require the labour of thousands and the expenditure of millions.

Certainly, he made a lot of minor errors, some of them surprisingly silly ones. For example, his heroes encounter a tiny, hitherto-unknown close satellite of the earth; and the values Verne gives for its orbit and period do not match, although the computation is very easy. But these are trivial failings in the light of the major mental saltation he achieved: he made space-flight something to be rationally talked about.

Also, let this be noted: for him space-flight was a glorious and soul-stirring enterprise. He would have scorned our mean-minded contemporaries who merely sneered and carped about the expense. Nothing, indeed, could be further from such baseness than the fictional welcome he planned for his astronauts, who, owing to unforeseen perturbations, had orbited the Moon, and returned to splash down in the Pacific. They toured the U.S.A. in a special train, whilst, at each station upon the way, local inhabitants dined on the platform, everything being so timed that they could toast the heroes as they came through; the dauntless three were thus enabled to drink with almost the entire population of the States. What a pity that N.A.S.A. did not take up this superlative idea!

Even today, space-flight remains worthy of remark; but flying has become such a commonplace that it needs some effort to remind ourselves that, within the life-time of persons still living, an aircraft was a sign and a wonder. Verne's story *Robur le Conquérant*—always known in English-speaking areas by the title *The Clipper of the Clouds*—when published in 1886 was considered almost as daring as his earlier Moon journeys.

It is, I hope, no denigration of a number of distinguished pioneers to say that the decades from the death of Cayley in 1853 to the work of Lilienthal in the 1890s were unhappy ones in the story of powered flight. Cayley's own work might never have been done, for all the notice that was taken of it; and failure followed failure as one designer after another tried to start from scratch. One of the greatest physicists of the century, Lord Kelvin, went on record as believing that heavier-than-air flight was impossible; and such minor successes as there were came in the realms of lighter-than-air flight, i.e. with airships. Giffard, the Tissandiers and others, mostly in France, could justly claim that they had at least got off the deck; and if their craft were somewhat flattered in being called 'dirigibles', at least they had some finite capacity for movement and control. In these circumstances, disputes between confident airship men and hopeful aircraft designers could become somewhat heated—though not, I imagine, quite as heated as Verne makes the row between his Philadelphia balloon enthusiasts and his hero Robur.

Verne came down firmly in favour of machines which were heavier than air. As he clearly stated, to be stronger than the air, it is necessary to be heavier; and he quoted with approval the indisputable observation of another pioneer that, after all, birds fly.

The Clipper of the Clouds is thin as a story. Two balloonists, arguing fiercely amongst themselves about the design of an airship they are planning, and more fiercely with a mysterious engineer named Robur, who interrupts one of the meetings of their club to tell them (rudely) that they are wasting their time, are kidnapped by their mysterious opponent, who takes them on board his helicopter, and demonstrates its paces in a world cruise. Subsequently, they escape and obstinately finish building their airship, which bursts when challenged to a climbing-match by Robur in his machine, who concludes by reading everyone a lecture and flying off into the unknown.

Somehow the magic, which remains in *Vingt Mille Lieues* despite our familiarity with submarines, has disappeared. Perhaps also the character of Robur does not help; he is less credible than Nemo and much more offensive. However, *Albatros*, the helicopter (the word coined by Verne is 'Aeronef', which never won acceptance: it was in fact a helicopter), is described in considerable detail. The fuselage of the *Albatros* is exactly the shape of the hull of a small clipper ship complete with three deck-houses: it is 30 m (98 ft) long by 4 m (13 ft) in beam. Whereas modern helicopters generally have one large rotor, the *Albatros* boasts no less than thirty-seven contra-rotating pairs of small ones, in three parallel rows: fifteen on each side and seven rather larger ones on the centre-line. These rotors are purely for lift; they are not tilted to provide translational movement. Instead, a four-bladed tractor propellor in the prow, and a similar pusher in the stern, suffice for a maximum speed of 200 km/hr (124 mph). The machine is built of a compressed, chemically bonded paper—apparently rather like Tufnol. The engines, one need hardly say, are electric; and power is drawn from batteries and accumulators. There is a crew of eight and the craft is armed with a 60 mm gun, which comes in handy for rescuing sacrificial victims from anthropophagous celebrations in Dahomey. *Albatros* makes a complete circuit of the earth without re-charging.

Once again, the batteries are simply absurd. Electric motors would be worth considering for aircraft—their power-to-weight ratio can be quite reasonable—were it not for the problem of power sources. In effect, Verne was compelled to imagine it solved because no type of motor was then known which yielded enough power for sufficiently low weight. The internal combustion engine was in its infancy, hot air engines were manifestly too feeble, and steam required massive boilers, condensers and fuel supplies.

For the rest, multiple small rotors would be less efficient than one very large one; though no one knew that at the time. Contra-rotation was a splendid idea, as it would obviate the need for the counter-torque rotor which is a feature of the modern helicopter, although it is not evident that Verne realized this; probably it should be put down to a fine stroke of intuition. The 60 mm gun is quite acceptable. During the Second World War some marks of Mosquito aircraft carried a 57 mm piece, and 75 mm ones were mounted in some Mitchells.

Verne's main contribution, once again, is the utter confidence he manages to convey. The thing can be done, he says, given only a lighter prime mover than we have at the moment. And of course, he was right and the sceptics were confounded.

The predictions of his later years tend to be less explicit, and, it must be admitted, less consistent and less carefully thought out. Probably the ageing writer, maintaining a tremendous output, found it increasingly difficult to keep abreast of technical developments, and to work out the details of contrivances as he devised them. For example, I am unable to make sense of the description of the aircraft (called 'planeurs', though they are not gliders) in the posthumously published *L'Etonnante Aventure du Mission Barsac*. It is, of course, the case that some parts of this book were only partially completed, and that it suffered from the editing of lesser hands. In any case, it contains the world's first radio-guided missile. The missile, apparently in the form of a model aircraft, is controlled, admittedly over short distances only, by means of Herz's electromagnetic waves, it being explained that an Italian named Marconi has recently discovered how to send them efficiently.

So evidently Verne had managed to keep track of one growing aspect of technology. However, the description of the flying-submarine-car with which the disagreeable Robur, now gone quite crackers, returns to attempt the conquest of the world in *Maître du Monde* includes some decided oddities.

The machine was spindle shaped, sharper for'ard than aft, the fuselage being aluminium, though I could not decide what material was used for the wings. It rested on four wheels . . . the spokes being broadened into paddles, which helped the *Epouvante* along when on or under the water. But . . . the principal drive comprised two Parsons turbines, one on either side of the keel. Driven with extreme rapidity by the machine, they acted as propellors in the water; and I wondered whether they were not also used in flying. (my translation)[7]

It really seems that Verne did not realize that Parsons turbines were *steam engines*; particularly as the narrator (predictably) goes on to say 'The force which drove all these mechanisms could only be electricity'.[8]

I, at least, am baffled here. Had he read of Parsons turbines driving generators—a set often being called a 'turbo-alternator'—and, when he read of their use in ships (*Turbinia* made her famous demonstration in 1897), assumed that the alternator was being used as a motor? It seems scarcely credible, yet I cannot think of another explanation.

Confusion likewise appears in *Les 500 millions de la Bégum* though, in this case, the book as a whole is, perhaps, too lighthearted to warrant too nice a critical study. A Frenchman and a German each inherit half of a vast fortune left by an Indian Begum; and each decides to use his new wealth to found an 'ideal city' in parts of the newly opened lands of the American West. Verne, no doubt getting something of his own back for the Franco-Prussian War, has his French hero found a Home of Culture and the Arts; whilst the German (surprise!) sets up an enormous armament works. Finding the close proximity of this model of French civilization offensive, the German (Herr Prof. Schultze) decides to eliminate it by firing a single enormous poison-gas shell from a monster cannon of his own design. What the Federal authorities were doing about this is nowhere made clear; but, although the gun is built, loaded and fired, all is well. The muzzle velocity is even greater than intended, and the deadly shell passes into orbit as an unintended artificial satellite!

Of course, this is nonsense—though such cheerful nonsense that one suspects that Verne knew it. It is not possible to fire a projectile straight into closed orbit from the surface of a planet: it would necessarily return to the surface. (Rocket-launched satellites receive their final urge whilst in flight, and roughly parallel to the surface.) Even forgetting this ineluctable conclusion of orbit mechanics, however, Verne for once gets the actual numbers wrong. He gives the final velocity of the shell 500 m/s; which is absurdly low.[9] Concorde is about as fast; and whatever its fate may be, that beautiful aircraft stands no risk of going into orbit. This is very odd, since the man who wrote *De la Terre à la Lune* must have known that circular orbit velocity is escape velocity divided by $\sqrt{2}$, or a little less than 8000 m/sec.

Let us regard *Les 500 millions* then, as a farce. Overall, how does Verne stand in the science fiction pantheon? Obviously, he must stand very high indeed as a predictor. His major ideas—aircraft, submarines, and flight to the moon—have all been fulfilled. Certainly, he was almost always wrong in detail; and certainly, too, he wildly overestimated the future of electric storage. It must also be allowed that other men before him had thought of, and tried to construct, both submarines and aircraft; although, as has been remarked, he was the first to do serious sums on space-flight.

As a writer he had lightness of touch, sparkle and verve. If his characters often lack depth, his narrative, at its best, carries the reader along with an infectious gusto. Above all, he propagated a vibrant confidence and enthusiasm. It is impossible to guess the number of readers he inspired into, or reinforced in, a decision to devote their lives to science and technology: it must, one feels, have been a great many. We could do with a new Jules Verne today.

NOTES

1. The first by Michel Corday, *Confessions d'un enfant du siège*. The second was an honour also accorded to Lucian of Samosata, Cyrano de Bergerac, Dean Swift and Mary Shelley amongst others.

2. For example, the *Nautilus* in *Vingt Mille Lieues* is 70 m long. This is 229.6 ft, or 230 ft to the nearest unit. The first hack made this 232 ft (how?). And every edition that I have seen reproduces the same mistake. There are plenty of other instances.

3. 'Of course, he was a member of an inferior race, but a good man in his way ...': in *Adventures de trois Russes et de trois Anglais dans l'Afrique australe*, 1872 (chapter 2).

4. *Vingt mille lieues sous les mers*, Ch.XII '... dit le capitaine Nemo "Veuillez donc m'écouter ... Il est un agent puissant, obéissant, rapide, facile, qui se plie à tous les usages et qui règne en maître à mon bord. Tout

se fait pàr lui. Il m'éclaire, il me chauffe, il est l'âme de mes appareils mécaniques. Cet agent, c'est l'électricité.'''

5. I am indebted to Dr. E. Glover, of the Department of Marine Engineering, University of Newcastle upon Tyne, for computing this value.

6. *From the Earth to the Moon*, Chapter 1.

7. *Maître du Monde* (chapter 5). 'L'appareil était de structure fusiforme, l'avant plus aigu que l'arrière, la coque en aluminium, les ailes en une substance dont je ne pus déterminer la nature. Il reposait sur quatre roues . . . Leurs rayons s'élargissaient comme des palettes, et, alors que *L'Epouvante* se mouvait sur ou sous les eaux, elles devaient accélérer sa marche. Mais . . . le principal moteur . . . comprenait deux turbines Parsons, placées longitudinalement de chaque côté de la quille. Mués avec une extrême rapidité par la machine, elles provoquaient le déplacement en se vissant dans l'eau et je me demandai si elles ne s'employaient pas à la propulsion à travers les milieux atmosphériques.'

8. *Ibid* '. . . l'agent qui mettait en action ces divers mécanismes . . . ne pouvait être que l'électricité.'

9. *Les 500 millions de la Bégum*, chapters 12 and 13.

Imagining the Future: Predictive Fiction in the Nineteenth Century

BRIAN NELLIST

Keats, explaining to Reynolds why Wordsworth's thinking was profounder than Milton's, appealed to a familiar idea, 'the general and gregarious advance of intellect'. More ironically, when a local farmer's ricks were burnt by use of the newly invented *lucifer* match, Charles Lamb comments to George Dyer, 'There is a march of Science; but who shall beat the drums for its retreat?'[1] The consequence of this belief in an inevitable forward movement of the mind and its inventions is to create a consciousness of the future instead of the transcended past, as appointing the direction of the present. The assumption long pre-dates Lyell and Darwin and they are to an extent its inheritors. It must account also for the transformation of the idea of Utopia from being a remote place but contemporary with the visitor to being in a familiar place but in the writer's future, near or far. It transforms the future into a distinct world, with its own laws and language, like the past in being open for exploration, and discovered in the end to be the spot where the visitor finds out the truth about his own time. Writing about the future became for some Victorians a new aspect of the historical novel, a way of historicizing their own time.

It can affect the most familiar moments in the novel, for instance. 'What was the primitive tissue? In that way Lydgate put the question—not quite in the way required by the awaiting answer.'[2] The sense of time in this passage from *Middlemarch*, with a future as apparently as determined as the past, is typically Victorian, at once grave and vertiginous. Lydgate's puppyish enthusiasm is sickeningly at odds with the calmly patient process of time. With a calculated break in the expected logic, it is the man who is made to face the question and the Sphinx, time, which holds the solution. The novel itself is written in that future to which Lydgate so ardently wishes to contribute and the reader is invited to recognize that it is not mere accident that 'such missing of the right word befalls many seekers'.

The idealist character such as Lydgate lives not simply with a personally formulated sense of the future but thinks it is in step with the 'grand march of intellect', yet any child can now see that you do not make discoveries by asking baldly, 'What is the primitive tissue?'. Von Mohl's naming of protoplasm was one stage only in the science of histology for which Schwann and Schultze were establishing the grounds.[3] For Lydgate it is as though the excitement generated by the possible achievement, the sincerity of the ambition, the idea of the future itself, gets in the way of contributing to the future. That interest in how the future gets made is not unique to George Eliot but is a common concern of the period. The characters in *Middlemarch* belong to a history they share with the reader, which reminds us of a common impatience with limitation and the torpor of the 'march'.

In George Eliot's last work, *The Impressions of Theophrastus Such* (1879), the melancholy 'author' disputes with a German scientist, significantly called Trost, the nature of the future. The essay, 'Shadows of the Coming Race', parodies the arguments of Lytton and Butler that, by an inverted Darwinism, natural selection might produce a triumph of the machine over the organism. By one of those nightmare recoils, like that in 'The Lifted Veil', George Eliot momentarily considers her assumptions and principles from the outside, as though the future might actually be telling a different story from the one she habitually tells:

> ... every machine would be perfectly educated, that is to say, would have the suitable molecular adjustments, which would act not the less infallibly for being free from the fussy accompaniment of that consciousness to which our prejudice gives a supreme governing rank, when in truth it is an idle parasite on the grand sequence of things.

How can we know, unlike Lydgate, that we are asking the right questions when our beliefs might turn out after all to be 'prejudices' only? The machine would never 'die of that roar which lies on the other side of silence', awareness of which here becomes idly parasitic, not life but as reductive of vitality as ivy or a flea.

The imagined future is allowed, with dismaying logical absurdity, to cast doubt not on an individual piece of knowledge but on what is valued in mental process itself:

> Thus this planet may be filled with beings who will be blind and deaf as the inmost rock, yet will execute changes as delicate and complicated as those of human language and all the intricate web of what we call its effects, without sensitive impressions, without sensitive impulse: there may be, let us say, mute orations, mute rhapsodies, mute discussions, and no consciousness there even to enjoy the silence.[4]

Recurrent registers of significance in George Eliot's habitual vocabulary, 'delicate and complicated', 'intricate web', 'sensitive impressions', are uttered in order to be flouted, and with pain despite the lightness of manner. The timescale she allows for a parliament full of derivatives from Charles Babbage's 'analytical engines', which is what they sound like, is long, a thousand years; but the future is projected out of fears in the present. The intelligence demanded by the conduct of the world's affairs might turn out to be at odds with other functions of the human brain. The mismatch between future and present, for which Lydgate had been held personally responsible, might turn out to be generic.

The model for the derivation of future from the past by secret, but at least retrospectively comprehensible, ways had been the relation of New to Old Testaments. But the Pauline reading of Christian history as the fulfilling of the Prophets had been called into question by the new textual criticism of the Bible that George Eliot was so conscious of. A novel, advancing on its conclusion like a convergence on the present, should offer it as the point where its past events receive their clarification. In her late works, it is as though George Eliot wants to do without such consolations. In *Daniel Deronda* the supposed Christian future itself seems acutely in decay and it is instead the apparently superseded Jewish remnant which turns out to be more vital, in its hidden identity actually to contain more of the future. 'Israel would be acknowledged, as in some sense still a Messiah': Rowland Williams' words in *Essays and Reviews* may appear grudging but excusably so; this is a man making a discovery which alters his whole perception of history.[5] At the end of *Daniel Deronda* (1876) the future calculatedly excludes most of her Christian readers, except vicariously, and leaves them with their own futures only as uncertain as that of Gwendolen herself.

Instead of the present of the ending finding answers to the past, the present itself becomes a question that the future is asking. The characters in this conception of the novel cannot be all of a piece. The solidly observed realism will keep being displaced by strange fears, as with Gwendolen, and others, like Mordecai, will scarcely achieve realization, being the prophets of that barely specifiable future.

Even in the thousand year stretch of *Theophrastus Such*, George Eliot, like James Hutton, offers the reader 'no prospect of an end'. Her futures convict the present rather of the naivety of its calculations and its improvident insufficiency. Yet if, immediately, this seems different from earlier apocalyptic fiction, which offered a future with no future of its own, the function of the conclusion seems at least comparable: a criticism of rational prediction.

It is in this sense that Mary Shelley's *The Last Man* (1826) can be read not as a naturalizing of apocalypse but as a refusal to politicize or moralize its finality. She separates ending from its customary teleology. Thomas Campbell's poem of the same title, written two years before, had offered a Christian reply to Byron's 'Darkness'. Where ending had for Byron intensified habitual human rapacity, Campbell's last man had risen above his circumstances by his appeal to God. What would persist at the end becomes a revelation of essential identity. In Hood's grotesque ballad 'The Last Man', for instance, the hangman strings up the beggar, his only companion, for stealing the crown; behind the conventions of social morality lies a competitiveness finally self-destructive.[6] Impressively, Mary Shelley does not write last words for mankind. She is partly using the largest of all stages to replay her private drama. Lionel, the last man, is Mary, survivor of the Pisan circle. If Lord Raymond, Byron, dies of a fever at least in this case it is the plague that is to wipe out humanity itself. And Adrian, Shelley, flatteringly the son of the British royal house, indeed becomes the leader of mankind, though only when it has been reduced to a few hundred souls.

More even than *Frankenstein*, *The Last Man* is a narrative miscellany unified by its respectful detachment from rationalist predictions and imagined salvations. Mary Shelley sets the work boldly in a specified time: her first date is 2073. But excitement is subdued when we discover that so very little has changed and the conflicts of the present are only just coming to fruition so far ahead. Politically, Britain has only recently become an aristocratic republic,

though there is a large populist party, and the major international
issue is still the Greek war of independence. At the end of the
twenty-first century, tastes seem transfixed back in Mary Shelley's
own day. The poets quoted are still Goethe and the Romantics,
and music means Mozart. The only significant change is that if
you are in a hurry you abandon the stage-coach for balloon.

What is impressive in the book is that the catastrophe is so
entirely arbitrary, so remote from being any judgment on, or
motive for, human action. Where Malthus can write his own
plague prospectus within the dynamic of his theory, Mary Shelley's
is inexplicable and final:

> Were a wasting plague to sweep off two millions in
> England and six millions in France, there can be no
> doubt whatever that, after the inhabitants had recovered
> from the dreadful shock, the proportion of births to burials
> would be much above what it is in either country at
> present.[7]

As in Malthus, nothing changes much in *The Last Man*, but unlike
him Mary Shelley makes natural law include life's arbitrariness,
including the possibility that there might simply be no recovery
from the plague. In personal life for her as in the world at large,
things often happen without apparent causation. At the start of
Volume II, Lionel is watching his friend Raymond's reactions:
'Attentively perusing this animated volume, I was the less surprised at the tale I read on the new turned-page'.[8] Looking
ahead at Raymond's life is like reading; if you are surprised,
you are not surprised at your surprise, recognizing that is the
book's style. Only two paragraphs later, what the novel itself
has unexpectedly in store for the reader first enters the account as
Perdita, Raymond's wife, reads with foreboding, though she has
not been a clairvoyant character, about the plague: 'This enemy
to the human race had begun early in June to raise its serpent
head on the shores of the Nile . . . but . . . small attention was paid
to those accounts'.[9] The actual tale to be told is overlooked while
Lionel eagerly scans his friends' faces, thinking at the time that
this is a story mainly of tense and destructive domestic relations.
The reader's eye itself glosses over 'enemy to the human race' as
the merest cliché, though the book is to trace its victory over
all but the last three human beings. Raymond, Perdita and
Adrian have a mental set which sees in Asia only the enemy
of Greek independence, not a danger to public health. The real

threat comes when Raymond, refusing not to be the victor of Constantinople, rides into a dead city destroyed by his enemy's enemy.

That the novel should change direction is the point of view from which it is told then, not its weakness. There simply is no causation for the conclusion in the actions of the characters. Raymond's death does not bring the plague to England; it has no consequences, except that his solitary ride to plant the Greek flag in the Byzantine capital shields his army from contagion. On the contrary, some of the side effects of depopulation are callously misread by generous characters:

> Delight awoke in every heart, delight and exultation; for there was peace through all the world; the temple of Universal Janus was shut, and man died not that year by the hand of man.
>
> 'Let this last but twelve months,' said Adrian, 'and earth will become a Paradise.'[10]

Irony is the compulsive mode for Mary Shelley. The disparity between the local view and the universal constantly makes the over-determination of meaning from individual perception, the operation of such intelligences as Adrian-Shelley, historically futile.

She maximizes surprise by composing events into a local sequence without offering comment or explanation. In the last days, for example, history goes into reverse. Survivors from the U.S.A. land in Ireland and the Irish savagely invade England. The few English survivors muster under Adrian to seek warmer lands to die in and in effect invade Normandy. Lionel is left as solitary survivor in Rome, the place where it all started, spectator of human history, of the ruins not only of the past but of the present. The pressures of empire are put into reverse, not by the quest for glory or the expansion of population, but by the flight from an invisible enemy. The ironic comment on the history of European expansion implies less a political position in the book than a gruesome disparity between past intention and the authority of the purely accidental.

Nothing seems inevitable in the future except chance. Merrival, the astronomer, is engaged in research on the precession of the equinoxes and his prophecies of an inevitable golden future for the earth, as the axis gradually straightens, derive from an idealizing note in Shelley's *Queen Mab*.[11] While the world collapses around him, he insists on the natural laws which, in the long view, promise the return of the Golden Age:

> Man, no longer with an appetite for sympathy, clothed his thoughts in visible signs; nor were there any readers left: while each one, having thrown away his sword with opposing shield alone, awaited the plague, Merrival talked of the state of mankind six thousand years hence. He might with equal interest to us, have added a commentary to describe the unknown and unimaginable lineaments of the creatures, who would then occupy the vacated dwelling of mankind.[12]

The apparently miscellaneous contents of Mary Shelley's long sentences make their own comment. She mingles the past (sword and shield) with apocalyptic hopes about the end of warfare within a despairing present, where communication is reduced to signs, as the context for the bright chatter of Merrival, whose own imagined future now assumes the status of science fiction.

Mary Shelley is writing a kind of count-down novel but its ending has no sustaining thesis of entropy. There is no necessary collapse from causes deep within the present. Her future is the present extended and, as in true apocalypse, the last days are appointed beyond human calculations, yet remain here secular. She turns her husband's vision of history inside out; where for Shelley the foreground is dark and his imagination journeys in search of a vision beyond occlusion, Mary presents figures who achieve local victories on the way to final defeat. Her characters, like Frankenstein, like the Shelley of her edition of his poems one is tempted to add, think they are doing one thing and are really doing another.

It is less her scepticism about the future than her claim that it literally cannot be thought which makes her different from later nineteenth-century writers and *The Last Man* is in that respect alien to the premises of science fiction. That is partly because she refuses to characterize her own time, her present, as having a distinct identity. It is the consciousness of the present as critical which creates futures in the later novel. It would be difficult, for example, to imagine a journal published in 1777 that would have called itself *The Eighteenth Century*, as James Knowles was to do with his magazine a hundred years later. According to the *OED* the first use of the term 'nineteenth century' was, prophetically, by Burke in one of his anti-revolutionary writings. No book would have been published in 1794 with the title Alfred Wallace gave to his a hundred years later, *This Wonderful Century*. Though Dr. Johnson can write in his dictionary that century 'usually' means a period of a hundred years, Gibbon his contemporary does not usually use it to divide up the vast stretches of his history. He can use it to show the history of Venice as a progression; 'the twelfth century produced the first rudiments of the wise and jealous aristocracy, which has reduced the doge to a pageant and the people to a cipher', but his usual divisions of time are sovereigns or invasions or movements of ideas.[13] Numbers are part of a progressive series and tend to imply, as in his account of Venice, an evolutionary view. We could contrast with Gibbon, Morley's passing comment: 'We cannot understand the issues of the Seven Years' War, nor indeed of the eighteenth century on any of its more important sides, without tolerably distinct ideas about the ages before and behind it, about the sixteenth century and the twentieth'.[14] Morley's even 'tolerably' clear impression of the twentieth century in 1872 derives from his Liberal reading of his own time. The increasing pressure to identify the present and predict its future is evidenced by the rise of the concept of the decade. 'A decade of years' like a 'century of years' is noted in the dictionary as entering usage in the early seventeenth century and is being so specified even as late as 1869. Even the new supplement to the *OED* gives no reference for 'the decade' as the series of years with a definite but projected character within which one is now living. That sense of presentness defines time not simply by contrast (usually) with the previous decade, but specifies the character of the immediate future. The familiar term for decades (thirties, forties, fifties and so on) tends, if the *OED* is to be trusted, to come into usage during the 1870s and 1880s, not for the writers' own decades, but with a time lag and the references quoted are from journalistic sources. The reason for the usage is clear: decades catch the feet of the 'march of mind' in motion.

That very phrase, though earlier in origin, is associated particularly with the foundation of the Society for the Dissemination of Useful Knowledge by radicals like Lord Brougham in 1826. There is a satirical squib by the Tory journalist, Theodore Hook, called 'The March of Intellect' which usefully demonstrates the association of the idea with precise futures.[15] It describes the events of 31 March 1926 in the life of the family of the Duke of Bedford in terms of the radical politics of 1826. Conforming Catholics, with property repossessed by the church, they are terrorized by democratic servants, all of them obsessed with information and despising their employers for their ignorance about Siberian geography, but they themselves are to be outshone by talking horses. Where Swift, say, would have used a change of place, Hook uses a change of time, not because he believes in the inevitability of projected futures but because he does not. Yet the idea of evolution was available for its implications to be understood immediately by the casual reader of *John Bull*. It is the interiorizing of that idea which marks the difference between *The Last Man* and such a momentary extravagance as George Eliot's *Theophrastus Such* essay.

The symbolic point at which the present can be best read by a history of the future can almost be put as precisely as 1871. *The Battle of Dorking* is an argument by an army engineer, George Chesney, for British rearmament following the defeat of France by Prussia. It would be difficult to think of another work which was more influential in the formation of that sense of time crucial to the science fiction genre. Written some time in the early twentieth century by an old man for his grandchildren, it explains why Britain is a bankrupt and ruined country, surviving only by emigration. These opening assumptions are made without giving dates or explanation and must, for the initial readers, have given a sense of vertigo like that in George Eliot's sense of time. The reassuringly familiar present, lapped in suburban comfort, becomes for all its apparent inactivity the moment of crisis, dependent on concealed economic dangers:

> In our blindness we did not see that we were merely a big workshop, making up the things which came from all parts of the world; and that if other nations stopped sending us raw goods to work up, we could not produce them ourselves. True, we had in those days an advantage in our cheap coal and iron; and had we taken care not to waste the fuel, it might have lasted us longer. But even then there were signs that coal and iron would soon become cheaper in foreign parts.[16]

The phrase 'workshop of the world', coined originally by Disraeli in a speech of 1838 to remind the country of the rigours of European competition, is changed by Chesney into an older Conservative reminder about the need for national self-sufficiency and a citizen army. Free-trade capitalism, for him, only encouraged an illusion of constant growth which in turn encouraged waste. More importantly, the illusionism affects the collective political mind, producing too many overseas commitments, and finally an over-confident declaration of war on Prussia. Within a week Britain is invaded and defeated in a lightning strike, all of which is described in circumstantial detail of bungle and mess. The author serves in a volunteer regiment:

> You may fancy the scene. There seemed to be as many people as ever in London, and we could hardly move for the crowds of spectators—fellows hawking fruits and volunteers' comforts, newsboys and so forth, to say nothing of the cabs and omnibuses; while orderlies and staff-officers were constantly riding up with messages . . . The din, dirt and heat were indescribable. So the evening wore on, and all the information our officers could get from the brigadier, who appeared to be acting under another general, was that orders had come to stand fast for the present. Gradually the street became quieter and cooler. The brigadier, who, by way of setting an example, had remained for some hours without leaving his saddle, had got a chair out of a shop, and sat nodding in it. (p.24)

The narrative advantage of describing a future as an imagined past lies in the capacity to recover the present as a perplexing palimpsest of the unfamiliar imposed on the recognizable. The muster of troops becomes an opportunity for the minor free enterprise of the streets. The absence of information, so critical to the battle, is as familiar and made to seem no more important than casual office gossip. The chain of command is dubious. The brigadier sets a futile example of devotion to supposed duty and then compensates for it by a relaxation that betrays its emptiness. All the time, a simple London scene of average activity is part of a national catastrophe. Everyone half knows that the moment is crucial yet turns it into a kind of show and cannot realize its necessities.

Chesney's very title for his piece is revealing. In his day Hastings was a seaside resort so he takes a pretty picnic-spot in the Downs and turns it into as significant a field of battle as the arena of 1066. Dorking, Leatherhead, Guildford and Box Hill were all comfortable destinations for day jaunts from London.

> Thus the main part of the town of Dorking was on our right front, but the suburbs stretched away eastward nearly to our proper front, culminating in a small railway station, from which the grassy slopes of the park rose up dotted with shrubs and trees to where we were standing. (p.36)

The small-scale pleasures of a day in the country acquire a chilling glint from the cold eye of military assessment. Civilians in flight from the intended war zone are all mixed up on the local trains with soldiers and volunteers arriving on the scene. On the hot summer day the troops waiting for engagement are allowed down to the stream in the valley to drink. The descriptions and places are fitted into half-a-dozen categories of normality: commuting, day-trips, and Boys' Club outings, and the horror lies in the participants not being able to realize it.

If Chesney himself had been a more accomplished writer he would have had to struggle for effects which are, one suspects, the consequence of his literary limitations. The result is as though a man whose responses were in the past adequate for a limited range of experiences is suddenly confronted by a disaster the scale of which is registered only by the circumstantial flatness of his account. When the battle starts the utterly conventional named characters are obliterated in the midst of their undevelopment, Travers his best friend and Dick Wake, the Cockney wag: 'I heard something like the sound of metal striking metal, and at the same moment Dick Wake, who was next to me in the ranks, leaning on his elbows, sank forward on his face' (p.50). The emptiness, the suddenness of death in combat, makes a more significant language of grief seem another of the luxuries that are in the process of being lost. The author no longer knows how to feel with the usual depth, when there's so much death around and the civilian pieties depend on time and familiar rituals no longer available: 'A few paces down the lane I found Travers, sitting with his back against the bank. A ball had gone through his lungs, and blood was coming from his mouth' (p.54). At first it sounds like finding a chum resting on a hike, followed in the same flat tone by the brutality of the detail. Later, trailing back to London after the defeat, he finds Travers' house with his friend weeping in his wife's arms. He leaves the room to take Arthur, the young son, to shelter: 'I had not noticed the crash among the other noises, but a splinter of a shell must have come through the open doorway; it had carried away the back of his head. The poor child's death must have been instantaneous' (p.73). Arthur has been the conventional winsome child with golden curls. The callousness of the final consolation here becomes part of the anaesthetism of the frightful happening within the normal. The wearied observation, the writing carrying on beyond any capacity to realize adequately, belongs within the small-scale circumstances of the domestic novel but outdoes any of the events of sensation fiction.

Science fiction is a logical form bent on carrying out the surprising consequences of a dominant idea and it is often generated by the measuring of the distance between the impossible results and the circumstances of the familiar, houses, food, other people. The future is not another country but the ordinary rendered unrecognizable in *The Battle of Dorking*. It takes a gigantic fear, what it is like to be totally defeated and then to live on the sufferance of the conqueror, which the author takes to be a long way from the future expected by readers of 1871, and then makes them live it through. One tiny success the speaker achieves is to appeal to a German officer as two unarmed prisoners are about casually to be shot:

> Had the two men been dogs, their fate could not have been decided more contemptuously. They were let go simply because they were not worth keeping as prisoners, and perhaps to kill any living thing without cause went against the *hauptmann's* sense of justice. (p.79)

It is the insult he remembers, not that two lives are saved. The officer does recognize the prisoners as 'living things', but that is the only connection he recognises. The cliché 'dogs' does its work as the author begins to understand the humiliation he must now live with.

By writing an alternative history backwards Chesney hoped that he could affect present decisions, as Morris was to do later. That future depends on the status of the machine. He appeals to no secret weaponry though initial naval defeat occurs because Britain has backed the wrong technology. The fleet sails with a cable-laying ship, an adaptation of commercial invention, which leaves the admiral subject to contradictory bureaucratic control. The enemy navy relies on the military-specific science of torpedoes and, apparently, mines, 'the fatal engines which sent our ships, one after the other to the bottom . . . in a few minutes'. It is the whole German campaign, swift and efficient, which is in fact the machine. History's course is settled in moments.

By writing about a future as though it were the present, Chesney works within history's familiar determinism: 'Reasons for the Decline of Britain as a Major Power'. By setting our future in someone else's past Samuel Butler is able to imagine in *Erewhon* (which appeared the same year as *The Battle of Dorking*) a different resolution to the issue of the machine, and on Darwinian grounds. By giving the Erewhonians in the fifteenth century a technology in advance of nineteenth-century Europe, which they then chose to surrender, he makes them a kind of future transported in place instead of time. Since Higgs the traveller is a contemporary it allows Butler to question the current significance of terms like 'primitive' and 'advanced', value words which imply a response to time as technological progress. The thesis of the machine is taken for granted by Higgs so that his initial reaction to their response to watches—recognition but horror—is to find explanations from necessity:

> They were about as far advanced as Europeans of the twelfth or thirteenth century; certainly not more so. And yet they must have had at one time the fullest knowledge of our own most recent inventions. How could it have happened that having been so far in advance they were now as much behind us? . . . at last I concluded that they must have worked out their mines of coal and iron.[17]

What he mistakes for necessity is, of course, choice to disinvest the priority of the future as Higgs perceives it, the whole paraphernalia of progression. Their own mythologies of birth contain the warning story of the tribe 'who knew the future better than the past' but who died out in a single year 'from the misery which their knowledge caused them'. The logical puzzle induces the frustration, presumably, of knowing they would die of what they knew, and what they knew was that they would die.

The Erewhonians chose to live the life of the senses of the practical reason because they feared the autonomy of pure intelligence offered by the machine. In a parody of evolution by natural selection, a phrase they use for their own rational freedom to control the process, machines, as in *Theophrastus Such*, could become the supplanters of their human originators:

> 'Assume for the sake of argument that conscious beings have existed for some twenty million years: see what strides machines have made in the last thousand! May not the world last twenty million years longer? If so, what will they not in the end become?' (p.199)

The computation of time in the grand figures of evolution by the supposed fifteenth-century Erewhonian writer implies a concern with the future as progression, exactly the argument he is attacking.

Moreover, what is at issue, the difference between 'conscious life' and the machine, is taken for granted by the pronoun, 'what will *they* not become', and the verb associated with growth. Paley's argument ends by deifying the machine itself. For Butler, even minds subjected to such doubts and confusions may still assert choice. The Erewhonian medieval text must have influenced George Eliot:

> 'There was a time when it must have seemed highly improbable that machines should learn to make their wants known by sound, even through the ears of man; may we not conceive, then, that a day will come when those ears will no longer be needed, and the hearing will be done by the delicacy of the machine's own construction?—when its language shall have been developed from the cry of animals to a speech as intricate as our own? . . . Again, might not the glory of machines consist in their being without this same boasted gift of language?' (pp.203–04)

The confidence of Higgs in his terms 'primitive' and 'advanced' is the real issue here. The puzzling rationality he originally recognized in Erewhon was the ground so long before for the denial of the machine which is usually taken as the product of the rational mind. The visitor is as puzzled as Sirians are by Canopus in Doris Lessing, though the tone is different. Butler thinks of the future as Lewis Carroll thinks of Wonderland. He wants to question the attainments of contemporary heroic engineering: 'How many men at this hour are living in a state of bondage to machines?'

The future in *Erewhon*, except that we have scarcely yet reached that point, lies in thinking about the future in order to abolish its pretensions. The argument is as determinist as any Darwinian thesis in that, for the medieval Erewhonian, what is determined is the point at which human intelligence recognizes its competitor in life and moves to obliterate it:

> 'The only reason why we cannot see the future as plainly as the past, is because we know too little of the actual past and actual present; these things are too great for us, otherwise the future, in its minutest details, would lie spread out before our eyes, and we should lose our sense of time present by reason of the clearness with which we should see the past and future?' (p.216)

It is in its recognized deficiencies that the human lies; 'Could I believe that ten hundred thousand years from now a single one of my ancestors was another kind of being to myself, I should lose all self-respect'. The revolutionary Erewhonian wrote 'ancestors', not 'descendants'; in that distant future the writer would still want to recognize that he came from another such being as himself. So what happens to the 'Descent of Man'? The degree of play interferes with the straight reading of the text but it is precisely that playfulness which Butler is trying to protect from the solemnity of the machine.

Unlike *The Battle of Dorking*, *Erewhon* cannot be a narrative because where Chesney argues, with whatever misgivings, the dynamic of the future, Butler presents it as a steady state. Significantly, *Erewhon Revisited* (the 1901 sequel) is more of a novel because Higgs returns and has to eradicate the consequences of his first visit, basically a misunderstanding of his reports about revealed religion. The visitor has been an intrusion from Erewhon's past and the society he had originally thought of as stuck in the thirteenth century has advanced to the future without the benefit of stories. As such it presents a future without a future, a state beyond history. It is on such grounds that the conservatism of Butler had meaning for Socialist Shaw. Richard Jefferies wants, instead, to imagine a future with a future, where so many stories can be invented that, for a contrary reason, the book cannot find the containments of the novel. *After London* (1885) looks at first like a return to the arbitrary and apocalyptic future of *The Last Man*. The differences are instructive, however. *After London* describes an England after some terrestrial catastrophe has depopulated the earth and changed its geography. Since records have been lost, and the fight for mere existence among the degenerate remnant has been primary for many decades, the history of the collapse has been forgotten, and even legend is scanty. Did some cosmic body alter the conditions of life on earth? Does the responsibility lie with war or disease? Did the richer population simply leave? The survivors have reverted, from whatever cause, to a way of life like that in Britain after the Romans left. Since literacy is now the distinction of the aristocracy, the prestige of the old classical education means that the characters know more about ancient Rome than they do about nineteenth-century Britain, and they all have Latin names. Fitfully, the present is sardonically recognizable within this unlikely future.

What makes this version of the accidental different from Mary Shelley's is not that there are survivors, but that Jefferies renders problematic an assumed determinism about the future and writes historically, to spring on the model of progression the possibility of reversion. In place of the determinant of steadily increasing human control, the environment, so massively changed, sets the limits within which the characters live. The consequences of a reaction against progressive futures so great are instructive. Jefferies imagines a world struggling to reinvent machines and to create closer relations between separated social classes against the resistance of those who hold power and enjoy the benefits of the *status quo*. Reversion allows Jefferies to reinvent the future.

The hero Felix Aquila partly despises his father because, banished from the court of the local prince, he has made no attempt to regain his position but instead cultivates his lands with the aid of simple machines which he is constantly improving. Without any recognition of whom he owes it to, Felix is also an inventor and almost gets himself killed by another warlord to whom he offers an improved siege engine. Jefferies himself grimly accepted the increasing capitalism of farming. In an essay in a posthumous collection he also argued for co-operative enterprise to organize steam-roller convoys of produce from collaborating farms:

> It is not too much to say that three parts of England are quite as much in need of opening up as the backwoods of America. When a new railroad track is pushed over prairie and through primeval woods, settlements spring up beside it. When road trains run through remote hamlets those remote hamlets will awake to new life.[18]

By imagining in the fiction the overthrow of the wearisome advance along the known route of rational progress, Jefferies can restore the reason as friend.

After London is not a novel. The future will also reinvent romance, the adventures of the hero in a countryside so unknown and unshaped that it has to be reclaimed all over again for human intention; Felix is knight errant. It is told as though he is already a figure in the past—in Felix's own day, after all, books were not being written—but the writer feels able, with whatever gaps, to describe the origins of the natural history of Felix's England, the four varieties of wild dog, for example, and of man. The book is not a naive re-telling of *Bevis*, as is sometimes claimed. Felix is forced into adventure and its circumstances are painful, though strangely familiar to the reader. A series of petty princes maintaining a precarious truce rule the population through a hereditary nobility, the sign of which is their capacity to read and write, while large sections of the population are enslaved and devoted to servile occupations. Men remain free only by favour of the powerful and only to amass wealth for them. Merchants must have a licence to trade and pay heavily for the privilege to their noble patrons. There is a chain of mutual oppression. The diction of the writer is stately and aloof, the idiom of the scholarly chronicler, commenting with distance and distaste upon the rest of the social structure. The future has slipped back to a remote past from which the social arrangements of the nineteenth-century reader, including a critical intelligentsia, still recognizably devolve. The discomforts of social stratification are apparent when Felix shakes the hand of a man who, he then realizes, is not wearing the moustache of a free-man, and is embarrassed by his own awkwardness and that of his companion.

It is a landscape book but, unlike the *Battle of Dorking*, this is an unrecognizable version of familiar terrain. Whether because of the raising of the sea level or because of the collapse of port cities, most notably London, into massive ruins which become, in effect, dams, the valleys of the Thames and the lower Severn have flooded to form a great inland sea. Dismayed by the poverty of his family, Felix sets sail from the north-west to the south-east of it in search of his fortune to win the hand of Lady Aurora. At the easternmost end he travels through marshes and eventually lands on black soil during a westerly gale. Narcotized by the fumes and the nightmare strangeness of this wasteland, he at first does not realize where he is:

> The deserted and utterly extinct city of London was under his feet. He had penetrated into the midst of that dreadful place, of which he had heard many a tradition: how the earth was poison, the water poison, the air poison, the very light of heaven, falling through such an atmosphere, poison. There were said to be places where the earth was on fire and belched forth sulphurous fumes, supposed to be from the combustion of the enormous stores of strange and unknown chemicals collected by the wonderful people of those times. Upon the surface of the water there was a greenish-yellow oil, to touch which was death to any creature; it was the very essence of corruption.[19]

It would be perverse to resist the implication that this is the city of dreadful night where everything poisons and contaminates, but it would be naive to read the book as a simple act of revenge upon contemporary London. Where in the present everything economically looks to the metropolis, in this future London is the one place to be avoided; the achievements of the past become a burden to its descendants. It survives like the Roman ruins in Anglo-Saxon poetry, a witchcraft but a wonder. London is not simply forgotten but survives in tales that are a mixture of superstition and truth, the subject of 'many a tradition' and formulations like 'they were said to be' and 'supposed to be'. The present is still recognizable in the glass of the future. Moreover, it is in this dreadful place that Felix finds the gold on which his fortune depends. Yet the imaginative release of the book lies in the disconnection of future from present. The compelling fear that an absence of energy to sustain the complicated fabric of the contemporary world might be followed by collapse on a scale that turns the place of maximal life for 'those wonderful people' into the place of death, is not left by Jefferies as sheer apocalypse.

Immediately after his escape from the marshes of London, Felix meets a tribe of shepherds in the Downs, a peaceable people molested by gypsies, one of the four extant social groupings. His mastery of the bow, a weapon they have never met before, ensures victory and makes them choose him as prince. He sets them to build a castle and town while he goes west on foot to find Aurora:

> Felix was much taken with this spot; the beauty of the inland lake, the evident richness of the soil, the river communicating with the great Lake, the cliff commanding its entrance; never, in all his wanderings, had he seen a district so well suited for a settlement and the founding of a city.[20]

As always in romance, juxtapositions make their own point. This is not the story of idyllic country life restored after the removal of the Great Wen. The battle with the gypsies has been specific and savage and is a tribute to Felix's superior technology, bows like guns being able to kill at a distance. Time is a circular process by which the wreckage of the great city is deserted so that a new city may be founded. It is not the shepherds who convert Felix to their admirable way of life but the restless, ingenious hero who begins the organization of settled life for the nomads. The future does not lie with low-grade technology and conservation. There is an enormous amount of wasteful hacking and hewing of the land and its products in the book, a consistent contempt for the barbarians of the forest and an irritation in Felix precisely that his machines are so simple. If *After London* resists the evolutionary model of steady progression, the one good result of the lapse into barbarism is that it clarifies again the value of rational progress, the qualities of enterprise and ingenuity, no longer to sustain an overblown capital, but as the individually treasurable qualities they always might be.

For Jefferies, civilization knows only one way and if it is lost then it is found by the same route as in the past, out of conflict and tyranny, which is only sufferable because it limits the conflict. He wants to imagine a future in which its predicted ills become tolerable again. Simpler to an obvious degree, *After London* still seems to need *Thus Spake Zarathustra* as its best commentary. We know from MacKail's life that William Morris admired both *After London* and *Erewhon*, and it is as though in *News from Nowhere* (1891) he is impelled both by Jefferies' sense of the return of the past and Butler's imagining of a society that achieves a steady state. Like the other writers, he releases the reader from the weariness of predictable futures that complicate the existing machinery of progress. Yet he achieves this not by unconvincing free choice as in Butler or accident as in Jefferies, but by an idea of necessity that derives from socialist historiography. The writing of the alternative history of the future helps to distinguish true determinism from the false necessity of the machine, that the greatest pleasure imaginable is mail-order shopping as, unfairly, in Bellamy's *Looking Backwards*. Where Chesney wanted to make his imagined future unforetell itself by affecting present choices, Morris wants to make his future contribute to bringing itself about. Old Hammond, the historian in the book, comments:

> 'Who knows but I may not have been talking to many people? For perhaps our guest may some day go back to the people he has come from, and may take a message from us which may bear fruit for them, and consequently for us'.[21]

The future interferes with the past in order to help produce itself; the future will also include this very book.

The difficulty lies not just in an imaginative torpor but of thinking, as in *Erewhon*, within a different mental set. Morris's *alter ego*, William Guest, calls himself 'a being from another planet' and Hammond accepts the metaphor, 'when you were dwelling in the other planet'. Though Hammond knows Morris's time from the records and research, he knows also that minds defined by different circumstance, relationships, dominant ideas, sympathies and oppositions cannot transcend them:

> 'Looking back now, we can see that the great motive-power of the change was a longing for freedom and equality, akin if you please to the unreasonable passion of the lover; a sickness of heart that rejected with loathing the aimless solitary life of the well-to-do educated man of that time: phrases, my dear friend, which have lost their meaning to us of the present day; so far removed we are from the dreadful facts which they represent.' (p.89)

The happily integrated man of the future notionally understands alienation as a contribution to change but still responds to it with distaste as a 'sickness'. The problem is that of the historical novel. The more conscious a man is of his own times, the more its manifestations are realized at the level of consciousness, then the less able he is, though compelled to do so by curiosity and the desire for knowledge, totally to become interior to the style of thought of another period. All he can do is to present the evidence in a series of startling pictures which register the transformation. *News from Nowhere* works so much better than most future representations because so much of it is conveyed by image. Its theoretical base is constantly realized in descriptions and incident from which talk then originates.

Part of the work's persuasiveness comes from the replacing of present by the overlaid image from the future as in *The Battle of Dorking*, but to a contrary effect. It is a journey as in Jefferies, though through familiar London and a repeat of the voyage up the Thames to Kelmscott that Morris had made in 1880; but it is the present which becomes the illusion.[22] London, now a succession of villages and market towns, with Parliament turned into a dung market, is made to spring constant surprises:

> A strange sensation came over me; I shut my eyes to keep out the sight of the sun glittering on this fair abode of gardens, and for a moment there passed before them a phantasmagoria of another day. A great space surrounded by tall ugly houses, with an ugly church at the corner and a nondescript ugly cupolaed building at my back . . .
> I opened my eyes to the sunlight again and looked round me, and cried out among the whispering trees and odorous

blossoms, 'Trafalgar Square!' (pp.34–35)

The stately, slightly archaic voice ('abode') with its co-ordinated accumulations of short phrases can express the future adequately but makes the sudden realism of 'Trafalgar Square' seem alien. Yet the image involves a massive and violent demolition of the only London Morris knows. The actual despair of the present, 'sickness of heart' turns the present into a 'phantasmagoria'. But his friend, Dick Hammond, the historian's great-grandson and Guest's guide through London, can only imagine that he is exclaiming at the absurdity of commemorating an ancient battle. The social democratic riot of 1887 in which Morris took part on this very spot seems so unconvincing that their old companion thinks he is telling lies. Memories are best forgotten in this future though prospective memory is what the text is written out of.

As with the two works that influenced him, Morris sees the machine off the premises, as the engine driving that competitive over-production of the capitalist past. But the dynamic is historical rather than rational as in *Erewhon*. In the class war of the twentieth-century revolution, machines as wealth-producers are destroyed by both sides. The capitalist owners 'cared little what they did, so long as they injured the enemies who had destroyed the sweets of life for them. As to "the rebels," I have told you that the outbreak of the actual war made them careless of trying to save the wretched scraps of wealth that they had' (p.112). The machines that produced the riches also produced the wrong definition of what constitutes 'the sweets of life' or even 'wealth'. Technology is not itself the determinant but is the result of a way of life which, changing by necessity, changes its meanings along with it. As for Blake, received words become no longer received and 'rebels' needs its inverted and inverting commas. The consequences are acceptable because the old ideal argument, that machines will do the drudgery of life to free the higher human consciousness, no longer convinces when it is recognized that such language depended on social stratification. When higher and lower cease to be class distinctions all the derivative metaphors, which is what they were though they claimed otherwise, die with them. The distinction between physical and mental activity, also class conditioned, also disappears: 'the one aim of all people before our time was to avoid work, or at least they thought it was;

so of course the work which their daily life *forced* them to do, seemed more like work than that which they *seemed* to choose for themselves'. Only 'seemed' of course, because actually they were choosing it on social grounds. The argument is that to remove the pressure of such priorities frees men to recognize what they really want to do, which often involves the satisfactions of the physical. The machine does not disappear because of any evolutionary threat as in Butler or from pure catastrophe as in Jefferies but because it does not, in the end, give enough pleasure. Like most utopias, *News from Nowhere* is an epicurean argument on the priority of pleasure. The dismissal of the machine is neither archaism nor casual arts-and-crafts preference, but the major dynamic of the vision. The human consciousness that emerges when the machine has gone is not totally new since the sources of pleasure are perennial. The preferred reading of the late twentieth century, according to Morris, turns out to be Shakespeare and medieval texts, not the nineteenth-century novel, except among the few dissidents.

What changes is the relation between man and the environment as Clara, Dick Hammond's once and future wife in the rational marriage of the future, explains:

> 'Was not their mistake once more bred of the life of slavery that they had been living?—a life which was always looking upon everything, except mankind, animate and inanimate— "nature" as people used to call it—as one thing, and mankind as another. It was natural to people thinking in this way, that should they try to make "nature" their slave, since they thought "nature" was something outside them'. (p.154)

The machine is the natural result of a dualist habit of mind in which everything outside the social group to which the self belongs is there to be used. Men needed the idea of nature as that which they could dominate because the fundamental source of analogy was the distinction between master and slave. Nature becomes the equivalent of body in a body-mind split and the machine the clever ghost inside it. The problem is not the machine but the mechanical apprehension of life: 'under the guise of pleasure that was not supposed to be work, work that was pleasure began to push out the mechanical toil' (pp.154–55). The paradoxical play of that sentence is needed to force words into authentic meanings.

The period of the machine is seen as the realm of illusion, the consequence of a perception of 'nature' as separated entity. The argument is patient of Marxist analysis but it also seems close to Blake or even to Eliot's 'dissociation of sensibility'.

Significantly, it is the dissidents of the future who are most interested in nineteenth-century literature and that form of expression *News from Nowhere* is insistent on not being, the novel. It is no more a study of individual lives than any of the works under discussion here because it is the difference between collective images of present and future which generates the progression of the writing, not the interplay of individual experience. The criticism to which science fiction is habitually open, that its agents are representations not lives, is countered here by the largest and most troublesome debate in Morris's rewriting of the agenda of the imagination. Harry Johnson is a dustman who dresses extravagantly and is called Boffin, after Dickens' golden colleague in *Our Mutual Friend*. According to Hammond, Johnson writes 'reactionary novels, and is very proud of getting the local colour right as he calls it; and as he thinks you come from some forgotten corner of the earth, where people are unhappy, and consequently interesting to a story-teller, he thinks he might get some information out of you . . . Only for your own comfort beware of him!' (p.18). There are no novels in the realm of pleasure because, as Tolstoy says, 'All happy families are happy in the same way'. Comfort, no longer a suspect word, demands distance from Boffin for such as William Guest. Though everyone Guest meets is dressed colourfully (for his subdued Victorian tastes, indeed with vulgarity), Boffin's snappy dressing is in pursuit of still more 'colour', which he finds in the individuality of lives in the novel. It is the grumbler of Runnymede who most acutely feels the dissatisfaction of pleasure. He reads the novels of Morris's contemporaries because 'there is a spirit of adventure in them, and signs of a capacity to extract good out of evil which our literature quite lacks now'. The steady-state future, unlike Jefferies' primitive world, is always subject to the longing for the struggle out of which it emerged. Morris does not dodge the issue that the imagination longs also to reinstate the exceptional individual, greatly tested and greatly strong, led by the 'spirit of adventure'. Either literature, for the old man's grand-daughter, Ellen, ceases to matter so much when happiness becomes normal or it must learn to care more for the collective rather than the individual experience, in contrast to the shape of Romantic writing:

> 'Towards the end of the story we must be contented to see the hero and heroine living happily in an island of bliss on other people's troubles; and that after a long series of sham troubles (or mostly sham) of their own making, illustrated by dreary introspective nonsense about their feelings and aspirations, and all the rest of it.' (p.130)

This reads at first less as another incapacity of the future to understand its past and sounds suspiciously like Morris's own critical preference.

If the facility of the rejection irritates, an incident a few pages later serves to remind the reader that Morris is also interested in resisting a simply progressive reading of literature that would make, for example, the mode of consciousness parodied in Ellen's critique, the only model of feeling. There are valued emotions which earlier literature had expressed but which found little place in the realist novel. As the boat on which the party is travelling nears what we know as Kelmscott, the hay is being gathered and Guest notices the response of Dick Hammond as peculiar. He speaks of it as being less painful than the grain harvest and apparently feels the death of the year personally: 'I am part of it all'. It is that passionate identification with seasonal process, with the ritual of the year, that it seems to Guest his own times have lost: 'the prevailing feeling amongst intellectual persons was a kind of sour distaste for the changing drama of the year, for the life of earth and its dealings with men. Indeed, in those days it was thought poetic and imaginative to look upon life as a thing to be borne, rather than enjoyed' (p.179). *In Illo Tempore* here means the present where natural futures are occluded by a sense of living as realized pain. But within the confidence the future will possess in its own present, the cycle of recurrent winter dying is felt as sorrow by Hammond, who tells Guest that he cannot merely witness it as though he was in the theatre. The phrase 'changing drama of the year' is used by a writer who can sympathize with Hammond's point of view yet cannot quite feel within it because he inhabits his own alienated dissatisfactions, and such Shakespearean iden- tification is beyond him. *News from Nowhere* is so robustly happy because it has to face the depth of the writer's dismay about his own time or, in another way, by making a future so hugely successful he can find words for a radically bleak description of the present.

Ways of deriving the future from the present became more unusually defined in the course of the century and it is this definition of their own time which holds these books together. We should remember the wise words of Brian Stableford in resisting close definitions of what he calls Scientific Romance; it is held together by 'loose bonds of kinship which are only partly inherent in the imaginative exercises themselves and partly in the minds of authors and readers who recognise in them some degree of common cause'.[23] The taxonomy of apocalypse, utopia, futurist war and ecological prophecy matters less in the end than the expression of a common anxiety about the future and its possible redefinition of the human or of the function of intelligence. It is this perception which makes these works different from the writings of Lucian, More or Robert Paltock. Victorian literature found a new way of describing the present as a tendency with a concealed agenda rather than as a result of the past. In their concern with the machine and its consequences, the birth of technology, they stand in manifest relation to later science fiction. The machine is the expression of a hidden ideology, the visible expression of society itself as an instrument for controlling the language and the individual. Even *The Last Man* in its rejection of such an analysis is conscious of it in its resistance. This sense of time has written the programme for some of the most serious science fiction of the twentieth century.

NOTES

1. John Keats, letter of 3 May 1818; Charles Lamb, letter of 20 December 1830.

2. George Eliot, *Middlemarch* (London, 1872), p.108.

3. Charles Singer, *A Short History of Scientific Ideas* (Oxford, 1959), pp.412–13; for Von Mohl see *OED* under 'protoplasm'.

4. George Eliot, *The Impressions of Theophrastus Such* (Edinburgh, 1901), pp.250–51 and p.254.

5. 'Bunsen's Biblical Researches' in *Essays and Reviews*, 1860 (London, 1862), p.88.

6. Thomas Campbell, *The Poetical Works*, ed. W.A. Hill (London, 1890), p.88; *The Poetical Works*, ed. Walter Jerrold (Oxford, 1920), p.41.

7. Thomas Malthus, *An Essay on the Principle of Population*, 1789, ed. A. Flew (Harmondsworth, 1970), p.114.

8. Mary Shelley, *The Last Man*, introd. Brian Aldiss (London, 1985), p.126.

9. *The Last Man*, p.127.

10. *The Last Man*, p.159.

11. Note on *Queen Mab*, VI.45 – 46, in P.B. Shelley, *The Complete Poetical Works*, ed. Thomas Hutchinson (Oxford, 1952), p.808.

12. *The Last Man*, pp.209 – 10.

13. Edward Gibbon, *The Decline and Fall of the Roman Empire, 1776 – 88*, ed. W. Smith (London, 1855), vol.VII, p.292.

14. John Morley, *Voltaire* (London, 1893), p.177.

15. Theodore Hook, *Choice Humorous Works* (London, 1893), p.395.

16. *Tales from 'Blackwood'* n.s., n.d., Vol.II, pp.3 – 4.

17. Samuel Butler, *Erewhon*, 1872, ed. Peter Mudford (Harmondsworth, 1985), p.85.

18. 'Steam on Country Roads', 1881, in *Field and Hedgerow*, 1889 (London, 1916), p.238; for capital in farming, see 'The Future of Farming', 1873, in *Richard Jefferies: Landscape and Labour*, ed. John Pearson (Bradford-on-Avon, 1979), p.99.

19. Richard Jefferies, *After London* (Oxford, 1980), p.206.

20. *After London*, p.229.

21. William Morris, *News from Nowhere*, ed. James Redmond (London, 1970), p.116.

22. W. MacKail, *The Life of William Morris* (London, 1912), vol.II, p.9.

23. Brian Stableford, *Scientific Romance in Britain, 1890 – 1950* (London, 1985), p.4.

Imagination and Inversion in Nineteenth-Century Utopian Writing

SIMON DENTITH

In Chapter 17 of *Adam Bede*, 'In which the story pauses a little', George Eliot contrasts the 'wonderful facility for drawing a griffin' with the difficulty faced in trying to draw a real lion. George Eliot was a writer who was generally anti-utopian in spirit, for whom science meant not so much the possibility of emancipation as the recognition of limits, and for whom imagination was fundamentally subservient to realism; as such she can be taken as providing a strong case against the 'imaginativeness' of both science fiction and utopia. Her hostility to the 'imaginative' understood as drawing griffins is one that she retains throughout her writing; in an essay written at the end of her life she again insists on a similarly severe notion of the imagination:

> . . . powerful imagination is not false outward vision, but intense inward representation, and a creative energy constantly fed by susceptibility to the veriest minutiae of experience, which it reproduces and constructs in fresh and fresh wholes.[1]

But perhaps this begins to give us some criteria for thinking about the imaginative inversions that utopia performs upon the world. Certainly utopian writing can be of little interest if it seeks only to draw griffins, that is, if its visions are unconstrained by 'susceptibility to the veriest minutiae of experience'; but if it seeks to construct 'fresh and fresh wholes', with a creative energy that is indeed susceptible to the 'veriest minutiae of experience', then perhaps we are nearer to an imaginative transformation.

So can utopian writing ever be anything other than an *inversion* of the society from which it springs? That is the central question that I want to address in this essay. To put the question more precisely:

in what directions can those inversions be imagined? For inversion is certainly the dominant figure of the four nineteenth-century utopian texts that I wish to discuss: Edward Bulwer-Lytton's *The Coming Race* and Samuel Butler's *Erewhon* from the early 1870s, and Edward Bellamy's *Looking Backward* and William Morris's *News from Nowhere* from the late 1880s. At a fundamental level, none of these texts are even comprehensible without the constant reference that they make to the society to which the utopian place offers a contrast. This is evident from the titles alone. *The Coming Race* anticipates the future from the stand-point of the present, while *Looking Backward* and *News from Nowhere* both suggest a perspective from the outside on the contemporary world. As for *Erewhon*, this too is a literal orthographic inversion, and it is inhabited by people who bear the back-to-front names of Nosnibor and Senoj. But what does inversion achieve? Can it ever be imaginative in the way George Eliot demands, or is it doomed to be merely fanciful?—to draw on the Coleridgean distinction which lies behind Eliot's thinking. Can inversion ever achieve more than rearranging its materials without ever really transforming them? As we shall see, this is far more than a merely formal question.

E.P. Thompson approaches this question, or something like it, in his great defence of utopianism as the 'education of desire', a defence written in 1976 as the postscript to his book on William Morris. It has to be shown, he writes, 'that a utopian writer can proceed in any other way than by re-ordering the values of present or past, or by proposing antitheses to these'.[2] I take it from the context of his remarks that it cannot be shown to be otherwise: that the utopian writer is indeed obliged to proceed by 're-ordering the values of present or past', or by 'antitheses'. But this does not mean that all re-orderings are of equal value, or that antitheses can only occur in one direction. Part of Thompson's defence of the utopian imagination is precisely that it *is* subject to criticism, although this criticism has to respect the specificity of the utopian mode.

I take inversion, then, to be the dominant figure in utopian writing. This has both a formal and a historical aspect; or rather, this formal description is founded on the historical location of this writing. From a formal point of view, utopian writing is only comprehensible by means of its constant reference to the contemporary world; the imaginary is only imaginable by reference to the actual. I have described this elsewhere as the 'negative pragmatics' of utopian writing; such writing situates itself by means of its constant allusions to the world from which the utopians have escaped, and the writing takes its force from the negative contrast from that world.[3] Hence those constant lectures by 'historical experts' of the new society, explaining their present by its contrast from the past; hence also those frequent sentences which draw a contrast between the old and the new.

But though this is a preliminary *formal* description, it has to be grounded on a historical description; writers can only imagine what their own life-world permits them to imagine. The utopian imagination is arguably an agent of historical change, utopia being, in Oscar Wilde's famous phrase, 'the one country for which mankind are always setting out'; but historical change is, without argument, the agent of the utopian imagination. Ruth Levitas puts this well:

> ... whatever we think of particular utopias, we learn a lot about the experience of living under any set of conditions by reflecting upon the desires which those conditions generate and yet leave unfulfilled. For this is the space which utopia occupies.[4]

This is not, I take it, an assertion of historical determinism, which would be odd in an essay in praise of the utopian imagination. It is, rather, a recognition that the contradictory nature of historical change both generates extraordinary new possibilities and frustrates them as it does so; the utopian impulse may be universal if understood in sufficiently general terms, but it is always inflected in the particular accents that successive historical epochs make available.

These considerations apply to Samuel Butler's *Erewhon* (1872), which works via a series of inversions with respect to the high Victorian world from which it comes. It is of course arguable whether *Erewhon* should be considered a utopia at all, since the satiric element is so strong in it. Utopia and satire are closely allied, for related reasons: the imagined utopian world sheds a satiric light upon the real world, and indeed both forms spring from a dissatisfaction with the world as it is. But *Erewhon* combines utopia and satire more closely than these general considerations suggest; the text requires an especially alert reading, since it shifts so rapidly in and out of an ironic relationship to Erewhon. Does Erewhon represent a genuine utopia, a desired state that has solved some of the pressing problems of the nineteenth century? Or is it an ironic description of the world the traveller has left behind, in which some of its more ludicrous aspects are satirically redescribed? It is both of these, and readers have to be alert to nuances of tone and implication in trying to situate themselves with respect to what remains, at times, an enigmatic text.

If it is a utopia, however, it is a realization of a darwinian utopia, and this involves what is perhaps the text's most startling inversion: in Erewhon, the sick are punished while criminals are sent to the doctor's (doctors are known as 'straighteners'). This is difficult to decipher. It is clearly not sufficient to read this only in a utopian register, though such a reading will take you surprisingly far. Perhaps the most powerful statement in defence of this apparently perverse moral and social code occurs in chapter 10, 'Current opinions':

> Indeed, that dislike and even disgust should be felt by the fortunate for the unfortunate, or at any rate for those who have been discovered to have met with any of the more serious and less familiar misfortunes, is not only natural, but desirable for any society, whether of man or brute.[5]

There is a crazy darwinian logic to this, and the general results of this inversion do lead to the aspect of Erewhon which most fully exhibits utopian desire: the inhabitants are indeed physically fit and attractive, in a way that appeals to their visitor. Moreover, the appeal to the 'natural' in the foregoing quotation seems to me to be quite without irony, and certainly seeks to ground the operation of Erewhonian society upon natural law (now understood in a darwinian way), in a manner that is reminiscent of the classical utopian impulse—for, like pastoral, classical utopianism seeks to ground itself upon a profounder sense of the natural then prevalent in the artificial world of actuality.

Nevertheless, it is clearly insufficient to see this inversion, of the status of illness and crime, solely in its utopian aspect. It evidently has a strong satiric impulse, for the moral consequences of punishing the sick are at the very least unpalatable. In this respect the text moves nearer to a satiric redescription of Victorian society, in which the rhetoric which is used by those who punish the ill can be seen as a transposition of the rhetoric of those who in mid-nineteenth-century England punish the criminal—and to have as much justification. The inversion, therefore, requires a complex act of decipherment and positioning on the part of the reader, who must rely both on habitual moral responses—it is indeed outrageous to punish those who are ill—while at the same time recognizing the inadequacy of those responses.

The inversions in Erewhon have complex effects, but in general they point more in satirical than utopian directions. Thus the more straightforwardly satirical aspects of the book can readily be seen as using inversion as a way of exposing what Victorian England would like to take for granted. The satire on the church, with the tempered praise of the Ydgrunites, is a case in point. The Erewhonians have two banking systems, a real one, and one which they resort to only for show: the Musical Banks. As far as practical matters are concerned, they are ruled by the Ydgrunites. So far so straightforward. But Butler actually is not concerned with a simple satire on the Victorian church and the actual dominance of Mrs. Grundy. In fact the Erewhonians are right not to allow anything more than outward deference to the Musical Banks, and the most admirable inhabitants of Erewhon are the high Ydgrunites who bear a striking resemblance to English gentlemen.[6] So the inversion permits Butler a relatively complex series of defamiliarizations and reorderings of value.

Nevertheless, the familiar description of Butler as an iconoclast has a truth to it that perhaps finally measures his witty inversions. To revert to that Coleridgean vocabulary, this is definitely a fanciful rather than an imaginative text, for the reordering of values it proposes is to take place within the set of values already available in the mid-Victorian world. The relative importance attached to public opinion (Ydgrun), to the church (the Musical Banks), and to codes of gentlemanliness (the high Ydgrunites), is re-evaluated via the supposition of a place where these things are ordered differently. This is a kind of witty iconoclasm which takes as its object an enhanced clarity about the currently existing state of affairs, rather than any desire to transform it.

A similar point can be made about Lytton's *The Coming Race* (1871), practically contemporaneous with *Erewhon*. Like Butler's, Lytton's starting point was in part darwinian, as his title suggests; Lytton wished to imagine a race so radically superior to humanity that it might at some future point supplant it. Raymond Williams has made the point that the transformation that Lytton imagines is only made possible by a kind of magic—the wonderful force called *vril*, which permits flight and total physical control over the environment.[7] The Vril-ya, the subterranean people who have mastered this force, are then permitted a level of life, and a form of social organization, that fulfils the Whiggish fantasies of the book's author. If one of your principal anxieties is the growth of democracy, then your utopia is going to demonstrate that democracy has been banished from the society of the future. *The Coming Race* solves the pressing nineteenth-century political problem of popular power by abolishing the people.

Perhaps the most interesting aspect of the text, however, and the one that most clearly seeks to invert the order of Victorian England, is the inversion of the relative powers, and to some extent the roles, of the sexes. Both the value and the limitation of categorical inversion become apparent in this move. For part of the force of this element of the text is to provide no more than a frisson of shock, with no real investigation of the cultural determinations of gender, an investigation apparently promised by the decision to invert the roles of men and women. The nature of the inversion can be gauged from the following passage:

> Their argument for the reversal of that relationship of the sexes which the blind tyranny of man has established on the surface of the earth, appears cogent, and is advanced with a frankness which might well be commended to impartial consideration. They say, that of the two, the female is by nature of a more loving disposition than the male—that love occupies a larger space in her thoughts, and is more essential to her happiness, and that therefore she ought to be the wooing party; that otherwise the male is a shy and dubitant creature—that he has often a selfish predilection for the single state—that he often pretends to misunderstand tender glances and delicate hints—that, in short, he must be resolutely pursued and captured.[8]

The limitations of this are evident enough. Like Butler's text, it seeks something of the force of the logical *reductio*; we can imagine the opposite of our current practices—in this case the responsibility of men to initiate wooing—by pursuing a logic that is forceful if unusual. Yet the imagined inversion of the roles of the sexes is remarkably superficial, confined to women's superior strength, their better use of the *vril*, and limited intellectual superiority. None of this extends to a real investigation of the likely personal and cultural consequences of such changes, so the women remain remarkably like mid-Victorian ladies who spend a large proportion of their waking time thinking about 'love'. The courtship rituals of the nineteenth-century middle class are transposed, with the piquant difference of female rather than male initiation, into the manners of the utopian world. Small wonder then that the male reader is left reassured to discover that despite their imagined greater powers, and their abstract rights, the women of the Vril-ya 'are the most amiable, conciliatory, and submissive wives I have ever seen even in the happiest households above ground' (p.72).

Both these utopian texts from the early 1870s, then, use inversion as a way of momentarily defamiliarizing the customs of high Victorian England, but neither are seriously proposing their utopian societies as models of a future state with transformative possibilities in the present. The profoundly conservative and anti-democratic nature of Lytton's utopia only confirms this point; the dangers of Koom-Posh (democracy) are offered as a warning against the further democratic development of society, to the extent that *The Coming Race* can be seen as emerging from the debates around the Second Reform Act of 1867, in much the same way as *Culture and Anarchy*. The contrast with the two utopian texts of the late 1880s is therefore striking. Both *Looking Backward* and *News from Nowhere* do indeed propose the wholesale transformation of the social order, though in radically different ways. Both emerge from the socialist ferments of the 1880s, in America as well as Britain. The inversions proposed by both texts are far more radical than those envisaged by either Butler or Lytton; yet the same question remains: are they both bound to remain trapped by a repetition of the categories they invert?

Let me put the case against utopian writing, in rather different terms than made either by Marxists or conservatives. Utopias, it might be said, are fated to repeat by inversion the categories of the society from which they spring. It is in the nature of human history to be radically open-ended, so that it never develops wholly in the direction which might be anticipated; utopian anticipations, like all other anticipations therefore, are bound to be outstripped by reality. *News from Nowhere* famously describes 'an epoch of rest'; the social problems of the nineteenth century are solved, alienation is overcome, and the imagined utopian world is one no longer subject to historical change. Such transformations are necessarily in the direction of simplification rather than further complexity.[9] Where there was ugliness there is now beauty, but the aesthetic categories themselves remain untransformed; Morris—or anybody—is incapable of anticipating a new standard of beauty. Equally, Boston in the year 2000, the scene of *Looking Backward* (1888), is an immeasurably improved city to that of Boston in 1887; where there was poverty, there is now wealth, and where there was misery there is now happiness. But the manner of wealth and happiness remains untransformed; in this respect at least, Morris was right in saying of *Looking Backward* that it projects the standard of life of the comfortable professional classes of the late nineteenth century as the standard for all life in the socialist future.[10] In this context, the negative pragmatics of utopian writing, its necessity of describing the otherness of utopia by means of its negative difference from the familiar, is not simply a formal feature of the text, establishing the manner in which it becomes comprehensible. It becomes, in effect, a measure of the limitations of the mode itself, doomed always to repeat by inversion the social order that produces it, and always susceptible to deconstruction by hindsight.

There is real force to this objection. Yet I intend to take the remainder of this essay to propose two ways of suggesting that not all utopian writing is subject to this criticism. The first concerns those aspects of the world that utopia is proposed as inverting. After all, the world's problems vary in severity. The status of the Victorian church, or the courtship rituals of the middle class, can be inverted with no fundamental challenge to the social order, and their utopian realization is bound to be historically superseded. By contrast, the overcoming of alienation in work, the fundamental contradiction which Morris seeks, imaginatively, to resolve in *News from Nowhere*, is by no means a problem special to the late nineteenth century. In other words, some utopias are simply addressed to more profound and historically persistent aspects of life than others.

This is important even when, or especially when, utopian writing does anticipate the future successfully. The fact that Edward Bellamy invents the notion of credit cards (cardboard, not plastic, but otherwise exact) does not make *Looking Backward* a more valuable text than *News from Nowhere*, whose anticipation of a mysterious force that can move machinery and barges in a clean and quiet way has definitely not been realized. This is because *Looking Backward*, for all the real moral energy that is driving it, and for all the sincerity of its socialism, is nevertheless concerned with arrangements that do not go as far as Morris, who anticipates no less than a transformation of human relations, and with them, of human relations with the natural world.

Moreover, the question of inversion is complicated in Morris's case by the fact that he habitually imagines the utopian future by recourse to the medieval or even the barbaric past. This brings me to my second way of defending utopian writers—or Morris at least—from the charge that they are doomed to repeat their own age in inverted form. Morris's allusions to the medieval past are not merely a matter of style or aesthetic preference, though of course Morris was overwhelmingly drawn to pre-capitalist forms. More significantly, those forms offer him a way of imagining human lives unaffected by market and commodity relations. Morris himself was aware that there never can be a question of a simple *return*; in some places he adopts the metaphor of the spiral as a way of thinking how history proceeds in a manner that both transcends and includes what came before. But this means that history offers a kind of repertoire of possibilities to inform the way in which the future can be imagined.

An example may be sought in the second chapter of *News from Nowhere*, when the narrator is describing in an astonished fashion the new surroundings, and the new people, of the London he has woken into. This is his description of a transformed Hammersmith bridge:

> Then the bridge! I had perhaps dreamed of such a bridge, but never seen such an one out of an illuminated manuscript; for not even the Ponte Vecchio at Florence came anywhere near it. It was of stone arches, splendidly solid, and as graceful as they were strong; high enough also to let ordinary river traffic through easily. Over the parapet showed quaint and fanciful little buildings, which I supposed to be booths or shops, beset with painted and gilded vanes and spirelets. The stone was a little weathered, but showed no marks of the grimy sootiness which I was used to on every London building more than a year old. In short, to me a wonder of a bridge.[11]

The negative pragmatics of this are important; the bridge is partly imagined by means of its difference from the distinguishing characteristics of the nineteenth-century bridge it replaces. In discussing this passage, one architectural reader of *News from Nowhere* has rightly pointed to the values of 'permanence, usage, performance and cleanliness' that are informing its description.[12] It is just these qualities that made Nikolaus Pevsner claim Morris as one of the pioneers of the modern movement in architecture.[13] But another look at the description will make both the force and the perversity of this judgment apparent; Morris invokes the Ponte Vecchio as the crucial analogue for the bridge he has imagined, decorates it with 'gilded vanes and spirelets', and erects 'fanciful little buildings' upon it—all architectural details which are the reverse of the functionalism characteristic of the modern movement. In ascribing these details to the bridge, Morris repeats the move made by Ruskin in 'The Nature of Gothic'; he brings forward decoration and the fanciful, as practised in Gothic architecture, as antidotes to the oppressive uniformity and finish of work under capitalism. Thus the reference to the Ponte Vecchio expresses far more than an aesthetic preference; it marks an allusion to conditions of labour that permit the full development of human powers, partially achieved under feudalism but to be fully achieved in the society of the future.

However, there are evident pitfalls in such an attempt to point forwards by means of the past. One danger is that the specific gravity of those past aesthetic forms will persist into the present. This is just what has happened, in fact, with this description of the new Hammersmith bridge. Mark Pearson, in addition to enumerating the quasi-modernist values that inform the way Morris has imagined the bridge, also points out that there are historic reasons why the Ponte Vecchio should take the form that it does, in particular the extreme population density of its urban site in Florence. These reasons are absent in Nowhere, one of whose features, precisely, is that the distinction between town and country has been abolished, leaving no centres of high density population. Morris, misled by his aesthetic enthusiasm, has in effect failed to follow one of the aesthetic principles that he inherited from Ruskin, that the art of a period springs directly from its form of life.

In general, though, it can be asserted that Morris effects a genuine dialectical inversion of the present; that is, that his desired anticipation of the future becomes fuller and more persuasive because it can draw on the aesthetic and hence the social riches of the past. Thus when Guest visits old Hammond in the British Museum, he enters

> a fair-sized room of the old type, as plain as the rest of the house, with a few necessary pieces of furniture, and those very simple and even rude, but solid and with a good deal of carving about them, well designed but rather crudely executed. At the furthest corner of the room, at a desk near the window, sat a little old man in a roomy oak chair, well be-cushioned.[14]

This is persuasive, and not merely because it recognizes the possibility of imperfection in Nowhere—indeed, it is later explained that the crudeness of the furniture is a result of it being one of the first efforts at handicraft after the change away from machine production. In this Morris is following one of Ruskin's central principles; that allowing workers to produce their own work will not necessarily produce fine work, but it will be the essential condition for free, and distinctively human, work. But the force of passages such as this depends, not on the subliminal presence of these Ruskinian arguments, but on Morris's ability to draw on the residual impact of the aesthetic and cultural forms of the past, which now have a defamiliarizing impact in the present.

I recognize that this has not been the usual view of *News from Nowhere*, which has been to see it as hampered by its medievalism. But a good comparison in this context is with Bellamy's effort to realize the future of Boston, where he is forced to draw on an especially vapid aesthetic vocabulary. Let us stick with an architectural example:

> There was nothing in the exterior aspect of the edifice to suggest a store to a representative of the nineteenth century. There was no display of goods in the great windows, or any devices to advertise wares or attract custom. Nor was there any sort of sign or legend on the front of the building to indicate the character of the business carried on there; but instead, above the portal, standing out from the front of the building, a majestic life-size group of statuary, the central figure of which was a female ideal of Plenty, with her cornucopia.[15]

I think it is to understate the contrast between this and Morris's writing to assert that this is informed by a classical aesthetic while *News from Nowhere* is pre-Raphaelite. In fact, this 'majestic' statuary has no historic weight behind it at all, and can only be a gesture towards an unspecific notion of the beautiful. And Bellamy's inversions, his negative pragmatics, are still more pronounced than those of Morris; this shop is principally realized by its difference from the stores of the nineteenth century. It may be old Hammond, in Nowhere, who tells William Guest that 'It is true that I can better tell you what we don't do, than what we do do' (p.67), but actually it is Bellamy rather than Morris who is most handicapped by this principle. Morris, while not always entirely persuasive in giving a sense of the life of Nowhere, is enabled to achieve what success he does because of that dialectical loop back to the past; Bellamy's lengthy dissertations on life in the Boston of the year 2000 are handicapped by consisting almost entirely of his critique of the nineteenth century. The critique is real, and sometimes powerful; but as a utopian gesture his text is imaginatively stillborn.

It is not difficult to see how extensively *Looking Backward* is constructed from the trope of inversion. Every detail of life in the future is introduced by its contrast with the life of the nineteenth century, be it the organization of labour, the position of women (though here some of the same problems apply that we saw with *The Coming Race*), or architecture. Even the organization of sport is explained by its difference from nineteenth-century professional sportsmen, 'such a curious feature of your day'.[16] This last instance is worth pursuing, for it provides a further interesting contrast with *News from Nowhere*. This is how Dr. Leete explains the attitude of the new Boston to recreation:

> 'The demand for "panem et circenses" preferred by the Roman populace is recognized nowadays as a wholly reasonable one. If bread is the first necessity of life, recreation is a close second, and the nation caters for both. Americans of the nineteenth century were as unfortunate in lacking for the one sort of need as for the other. Even if the people of that period had enjoyed larger leisure, they would, I fancy, have often been at loss how to pass it agreeably. We are never in that predicament'.[17]

The reference back to the social organization of the past, in the allusion to *panem et circenses*, works in quite a different way from Morris's persistent allusions to pre-capitalist forms. It has the force of a historical comparison or explanation; there is no effort to mobilize the specific historical gravity of an alternative mode of life; indeed, Bellamy would be horrified by the implications of attempting anything like the actual Roman circus. On the contrary, the allusion to bread and circuses functions as a moderately attractive way of making a point about the difference between *then* and *now*.

A further comparison can be made between Dr. Leete's complacency about the inability of the citizens of Boston in the year 2000 to be bored, and the sad moment in *News from Nowhere* when Ellen informs Guest that 'even our happiness would weary you'. Once again, it is Morris's text that turns out to be making the more interesting and complex use of the trope of inversion. For Bellamy, there is no difficulty involved: once you solve the problem of overwork, and provide appropriate ('majestic') entertainment (like music on the radio), then the problem of leisure will be solved.

But in Morris's case, the recognition that the utopian future might prove wearying to an inhabitant of the nineteenth century is part of the complex relationship between his utopian vision and the fraught actuality of the late nineteenth century. Overwhelmingly, the vision of the future is a locus of longing for Morris: a longing figured most acutely in the figure of Ellen. This longing is partly qualified by the recognition that a figure from the nineteenth century might be wearied by the happiness of the twenty-first. This is not a recognition on Morris's part that utopia is boring, for the text does not invite that kind of reading, though of course it cannot exclude it. Rather at this point Morris recognizes Guest's (that is to say, his own) formation in the unresolved contradictions of the nineteenth century, and his inability to inhabit comfortably a world in which those contradictions have been resolved.

But this takes us back to our starting point. Isn't it ultimately fatuous to imagine a world in which the substantial contradictions of human history have been resolved?; for that, finally, is what is performed by the trope of inversion, if it is addressed to problems which are sufficiently deep-seated. To answer this question we need to make one further comparison between *Looking Backward* and *News from Nowhere*. The former text is much closer to a political programme than the latter—which is not to say that Morris's writing did not emerge from, and speak directly to, people engaged in the most immediate and day-to-day political struggles, as its initial publication in *Commonweal*, the paper of the Socialist League, sufficiently indicates.[18] But E.P. Thompson's formulation—that utopia is concerned with the 'education of desire'—is illuminating in this context. *News from Nowhere* does not offer a blueprint of the desired place, but an indication of the kind of place it is worth desiring. *Looking Backward*, by contrast, certainly does offer a blueprint of the desired place, and in part falls subject to the fate of all such anticipations, to be outstripped by historical developments, by the very creativity of human praxis which they celebrate in utopian form.

The negative pragmatics of all these utopian stories are finally realized in the various protagonists' return to the societies from which they first adventured. The narrative return poses most acutely the question of the use to which utopian knowledge may be put. In Morris's case the political context of his writing is clear, though somewhat complicated in later editions of *News from Nowhere* when the text no longer appears in an agitational paper, but becomes instead the highly-wrought art object produced on a fine art press. At all events, the relation of the imagined world to the real world is mediated by desire; if that desire can become sufficiently widespread it can help in 'making socialists' and thus bring about the very utopia of which it writes. Guest's return to the London of the late nineteenth century may be personally distressing—as who should wrench their sight from a lovely but unattainable vision—but the very dissatisfaction it provokes furthers the text's own political project.

In *Looking Backward*, by contrast, the narrative plays with a false ending in which the reader is led to believe that the protagonist has been returned to the nineteenth century, only to discover that he has been dreaming and that he really is to stay in the Boston of the year 2000. This allows a genuinely shocking sense of despair at the apparent return to the horrors of Boston in 1887, while simultaneously allowing readers the gratification of romance fulfilment. And again, this association—of the resolution of social contradiction with the romantic resolution of the narrative of the protagonist—is not as necessarily damaging as it may appear. Utopian longings have the force of desire, and this desire is often figured in utopian writing by an actual romance. But Fredric Jameson is surely right to invert the seemingly damaging association of Marxism in its utopian aspect with romance:

> Romance now and again seems to offer the possibility of sensing other historical rhythms, and of demonic or Utopian transformations of a real now unshakably set in place; and Frye is surely not wrong to assimilate the salvational perspective of romance to a reexpression of Utopian feelings, a renewed meditation on the Utopian community, a reconquest (but at what price?) of some feeling for a salvational future.[19]

News from Nowhere: 'Chapters from a utopian romance'. Once again Morris's generic archaism can be seen as a resource rather than a hindrance.

If we take the trope of inversion as our starting point, then, we are led in a number of directions in considering nineteenth-century utopian writing. On the one hand there is a relatively straightforward but important formal point; the imaginary place can only be imagined by reference to the actual, even if this is only in inverted form. When considering *Erewhon*, this reference to the actual turns out to be the crucial motivating point of the book; to imagine Erewhon is a witty means to shed a defamiliarizing light on the actualities of high Victorian England. There is a similar point to much of the other utopian writing that I have discussed—utopia is a way of shining a different light on a social landscape with which we have become too familiar. This defamiliarization needs to be recognized as operating in a specifically utopian mode; *Gulliver's Travels* also works by a series of defamiliarizations but these redescriptions work to debunk human pretensions, not to suggest that things might be otherwise. Nineteenth-century utopian anticipations, like many of their late twentieth-century descendants (Ursula Le Guin's *The Dispossessed*, or Joanna Russ's *The Female Man*) make the present seem strange in the light of a hitherto unrealized social potential.

Thus, it is not sufficient simply to recognize a series of merely formal defamiliarizations when considering the later utopian texts of Morris and Bellamy, because their formal inversions are only possible given a history that makes them imaginable. But this consideration takes us in turn to considering the value of the utopian imagination, at least insofar as it is realized in extended pieces of writing. I have suggested that *News from Nowhere* at least escapes from being trapped in the inverted categories of the present because Morris can mobilize the weight of pre-capitalist forms. This does not take us altogether away from the more limited objectives of defamiliarization, since those forms have the force and meaning that they do because of their difference from the present. But it means that Morris can imagine the future in ways that are both persuasive—though not to everybody—and properly dialectical. In this respect at least, the trope of inversion has been overcome.

NOTES

1. George Eliot, *Impressions of Theophrastus Such* (London, 1879), p.197.

2. E.P. Thompson, *William Morris: Romantic to Revolutionary* (London, 1977), p.797.

3. Simon Dentith, *A Rhetoric of the Real* (Hemel Hempstead, 1990), pp.119–47.

4. Ruth Levitas, *The Concept of Utopia* (Hemel Hempstead, 1990), p.8.

5. Samuel Butler, *Erewhon, or Over the Range*, (Harmondsworth, 1985), p.104. Penguin reprints the revised edition of 1901.

6. Butler carries his satire of nineteenth-century religion much further in *Erewhon Revisited* (1901), in which the protagonist of the earlier book

returns to Erewhon to discover that since his disappearance in a balloon at the end of his previous visit, he has become the centre of a new religious cult. This is much more in the satiric than the utopian mode.

7. Raymond Williams, 'Utopia and Science Fiction', in *Problems in Materialism and Culture* (London, 1980), p.201.

8. Edward Bulwer-Lytton, *The Coming Race* (London, n.d.), chapter 10, p.71.

9. Raymond Williams has made this point very powerfully, in the essay referred to in note 7 above. Yet the emergence of an ecological politics has made this whole area of argument more ambivalent.

10. See William Morris, *'Looking Backward'*, in *Commonweal*, 22 June 1889, pp.194–95.

11. William Morris, *News from Nowhere*, ed. James Redmond (London, 1970), p.6.

12. Mark Pearson, 'The Hammersmith Guest House again: William Morris and the Architecture of Nowhere', in Stephen Coleman and Paddy O'Sullivan, *William Morris and News from Nowhere: A Vision for Our Time* (Bideford, 1990), p.139.

13. Nikolaus Pevsner, *Pioneers of Modern Design: From William Morris to Walter Gropius* (Harmondsworth, 1975).

14. *News from Nowhere*, p.44.

15. Edward Bellamy, *Looking Backward* (London, twenty-first edition, n.d.) p.76.

16. *Looking Backward*, p.148.

17. *Looking Backward*, p.148.

18. I have discussed this aspect of *News from Nowhere* more fully in *A Rhetoric of the Real*, referred to in note 3 above.

19. Fredric Jameson, *The Political Unconscious: Narrative as a Socially Symbolic Act* (London, 1981), pp.104–05.

Prediction, Programme and Fantasy in Jack London's *The Iron Heel*

TONY BARLEY

Citing the strain of socialist-influenced, speculative writing produced in Britain and the USA between the late 1880s and the
1920s, the entry under 'Politics' in the new edition of *The Encyclopedia of Science Fiction* observes: 'Most of the works which we
can characterize with hindsight as "Proto Science Fiction" are
political fantasies'.[1] So far as it goes, this designation is helpful,
but it prompts more questions than it settles. These concern the
quality of the relationship between SF and social reality, and
between political prediction and fictional fantasy. What, if anything, distinguishes the real from the imaginative in those utopian
recommendations, dystopian warnings, and prophetic extrapolations from the present, which occupy alike the politician and the SF
hypothesist? If imagined futures are the business of SF, prefiguring
the future is also the provenance of politics—what kinds of value
attach to each? And what line, if any, separates the political parable
or programme which deduces from the present in order to discount
the fanciful, from those visions of the future which glory in the
imaginative freedom of a fictional potential?

Jack London's *The Iron Heel*, written in 1906 and published the
following year, poses just such questions head-on. The work of
a revolutionary socialist, the novel employs a far-future frame,
within which its principal near-future action is set. The far-
future conjures a utopian socialist commonwealth in the year
'409 B.O.M.' (Brotherhood of Man), seven centuries hence. An
editor from the city of Ardis, built on the ruins of twentieth-century
Chicago, introduces and annotates the near-future dystopian narrative (1910–1932) which constitutes the body of the novel. This
is purportedly the long-lost biography of the American revolu-

tionary Ernest Everhard, written as a personal memoir by his comrade and wife Avis just prior to the ill-fated Second Revolt, one of four insurrections by the proletariat of the United States against the dictatorial oligarchy known as the 'Iron Heel'. The Everhard manuscript begins in the reality of turn-of-the-century America; its first third or so offers a thinly-veiled, but assured, crash-course in Marxist theory.

The Iron Heel is compulsively inter-textual, which is perhaps only to say that in it London alludes both directly and indirectly to his immediate predecessors in the 'sub-genre' of utopian-dystopian fantasy, as well as to a fairly wide range of specifically political writing and reportage from his own era. To understand the novel adequately is to understand something of the (literary and historical) contexts and conditions which occasioned its production, and to distinguish it from London's more easily identifiable proto-SF in which he adopted wholesale what is best described as the 'Wellsian' manner.[2]

London wrote over a dozen fictions in the Wellsian vein, relying therein on a variety of quasi-scientific motifs: invisibility experiments, the development of world-destructive weaponry, the discovery of extra-terrestrial energy and suchlike. His primeval fantasy *Before Adam* (1907) explores the dual 'reality' experienced by its dreamer-hero, for instance, while *The Star Rover* (1915) improvises on the theme of metempsychosis. 'The Unparalleled Invasion' envisages a racist-Malthusian catastrophe; in 'Goliah', London imagines a 'socialist' utopia imposed by the superhuman powers of a hero-genius. *The Scarlet Plague*'s (1912) apocalyptic scenario sees civilization degenerate as a depleted humanity reverts to primitivism.[3]

From his mixed bag of Social Darwinism, Fabianism and pseudo-scientific mysticism, Wells produced a corpus of utopias and anti-utopias which are full of narrative interest but in which he is unable to project a coherent authorial position with regard to the positives and negatives of 'the state', of centralized world organization, and the benefits or failings of technological innovation.[4] Wells's rejection of class struggle as the motive force of historical change and his belief in the constancy of a socially-transcendent 'human nature' leads to visions of the future in which alternately benevolent or malevolent castes of the élite instigate or prevent change, and govern by virtue of their superior intellect or sensibility. In only one of his futuristic fictions, *When the Sleeper Wakes* (1899), does Wells allow 'the people' an active revolutionary role, but even there the 'Tramp, tramp, tramp, tramp' of the masses on the march disturbs and frightens the hero of the tale who, carried helplessly along with them, 'did not know whither he went' and 'did not want to know'.[5] And when those same 'multitudes' have defeated 'the old order', their roared chants for 'The Master, the Master! For God and the Master!' repel Graham, and he looks away to 'the familiar quiet stars' to escape his distaste and disappointment.[6]

Uncommitted to a view of society as developing through the play of its own internal contradictions, Wells prefigures new worlds which have arisen from external or autonomous catastrophes, each with their own independent dynamic. As Kumar shows, the successive 'stages' that result in the Wellsian utopia ultimately reflect a religious (salvationist) scheme.[7] On reaching one such stage at the end of 'A Story of the Days to Come', Wells's protagonist remarks:

> 'It has been chance', he said, 'it has been luck. We have come through. It happens we have come through. Not by any strength of our own . . .'[8]

Whenever London departs from Marxism in his speculative social fiction, he proves himself a Wellsian copyist. A sense of the arbitrary predominates, the sense of process diminishes. The vision of the future is experienced as alien and unfamiliar, yet also as total, substantial and discrete, categorically separate from the (real) present rather than its implicit extension. Present reality is made to seem notional, not vice versa. Both *The Iron Heel* and London's related fantasy on the effects of a future general strike, 'The Dream of Debs' from 1908, contain their Wellsian traces too; indeed *The Iron Heel* includes an approving footnote referring the reader to Wells's utopian tracts *Anticipations* and *Mankind in the Making*: 'two of his greatest achievements' which 'have come down to us intact'.[9] But throughout London's novel, Wells's method is consistently held at bay, or is qualitatively transformed.

The Iron Heel eschews quasi-scientific/technological paraphernalia, omits virtually all signs of mystical psychology, and refrains from privileging the mirror-image ideologies of Social Darwinism and Nietzsche-esque individualism which crop up depressingly throughout much of London's popular fiction, and which animate, in one form or another, scores of SF narratives. Nonetheless, the novel exposes (and again partly via Wells) what was a larger set of SF antecedents, namely those political fantasies which emerged towards the end of the nineteenth century in response to the rapid rise of monopoly capitalism, and which reflected to a greater or lesser extent a growing popular interest in 'socialist' analyses of the same phenomenon.

Edward Bellamy's *Looking Backward* (1888) inaugurated the modern utopian sub-genre. Using a minimum of novelistic resources, Bellamy has his nineteenth-century dreamer awaken from (or is it within?) a hypnotic sleep into the United States of the year 2000. Bewildered but curious, the dreamer learns through prolonged discussion with patient instructors that 'now' all industry is nationalized, and that government exists simply to supervise each citizen's fifteen-year term in 'the industrial army', and to distribute the social product equitably. This strange, new stable-static order has evolved democratically and peacefully. The dreamer hears how the old industrial monopolies ceased to compete with each other and gradually merged to form one national organization. When 'public opinion had become fully ripe', industry and commerce were passed into the hands of a 'syndicate' of the entire populace, a stateless state.[10]

In Bellamy's future, capitalism has disappeared, along with its waste of labour and resources, and its periodic crises of overproduction, unemployment and inflation. The militant labour struggles of the past, which for so long obstructed rational social evolution, are now extinct, as are social classes themselves. The much-edified dreamer returns to his own 'cruel, insensate' reality (or is *this* the dream world?) to recommend 'with fervency' the golden age to come, only to exhaust his unheeded self in despair.[11]

The Iron Heel was one of the last critiques of Bellamy's astonishingly popular fantasy. By 1900 over 60 Bellamy-inspired titles had been published in the United States, and the novel had also achieved international status. The vision of the future offered in *Looking Backward* had from the start prompted several refutations: for example, Ignatius Donnelly's *Caesar's Column* (1890), William Morris's *News from Nowhere* (1891), and Wells's aforementioned *When the Sleeper Wakes*. Bellamy was also debated in 'straight' political tracts such as W.J. Ghent's ironically titled *Our Benevolent Feudalism* (1901), London's principal source.[12]

Donnelly found nothing benevolent in the rise of the Trusts. In *Caesar's Column*, he prophesied an epidemic of corporate corruption causing mass immiseration and stimulating a world-wide revolt. Led by the nihilist 'Brotherhood of Destruction', the bloody rebellion of the downtrodden results only in an even bloodier counter-revolution. Donnelly's proposed solution found its embodiment in his agrarian (African) haven of classless individualism. In his turn, Morris polemicized against Bellamy's 'unhistoric' disappearance of militant class struggle, and disparaged his gradualist reformism as 'misleading' and 'futile'. Judging Bellamy's conception and advocacy of centralized 'state communism' 'mechanistic' in every sense of that term, Morris dismissed the proposed new order as 'working by a kind of magic'.[13] In *News from Nowhere*, he turned Bellamy's speculations inside out, depicting his own vision of utopian communism where a humane, cultured fellowship is enabled to realize individual potential and exercise its creative freedom in the decentralized, semi-rural commonwealth of the far future. Characteristically, Wells couldn't quite decide whether *his* world state (in whichever of its numerous incarnations), built on new technological improvement and old class divisions, was more for the better or more for the worse. Ghent forecast a widening divide and an increasingly vicious struggle between the economically and politically integrated Trust plutocracy and the fracturing labouring classes, ending in the long-term 'feudal' victory of corporate capitalism. London found Ghent's scenario the most persuasive.

The foregoing sketch of this futuristic debate has paid attention to the political attitudes of their respective authors rather than to the artistic/formal similarities of the texts themselves. But it was in the political as much as in the literary domain that most of these works enjoyed most effect. Wells's Fabian, then anti-Fabian, fictions and pamphlets were, of course, standard fare for early twentieth-century socialists, while the appeal of *Looking Backward* in the United States had been such as to generate the country-wide formation of Bellamy Clubs and Nationalist Clubs, which propagated the author's theories in a new political movement with Bellamy at its helm. Significant sections of the Clubs allied with the Populist Party which, while not for nationalization, also stood on an anti-Trust platform. The Populists expressed the interests of small farmers and businessmen who were being 'squeezed' by the banks and the railroad monopolies, and were deserting the Democrats in considerable numbers. The 'Grange' organizations of the 1870s through to the 1890s represented the same farmer constituency, seeking protective state legislation against the banks and company tariffs. Ignatius Donnelly was an early 'Granger', and *Caesar's Column* was published during his term as the leading

Populist in the State Senate of Minnesota. Ghent too was a member of the Populist party; and both Granger and Populist policies and fortunes figure prominently in *The Iron Heel*.

As a political (i.e. programmatic) text, *Looking Backward* offers no more than a sprinkling of flimsy wishfulness; it is the achieved social scheme in and of itself that really interests Bellamy and which overridingly engages his speculative temperament. But the critique of capitalist competition offered in the work ensured its impact not only in petit-bourgeois circles but also in the socialist movement as a whole. William Morris was a leading member of the (Marxist) Socialist League when he reviewed *Looking Backward* in the League's journal *Commonweal; News from Nowhere* was originally published in instalments in the same organ. Morris's attempt there to inoculate fellow revolutionaries against Bellamy's views was largely unsuccessful. Both books became central texts in the libraries of British and American working-class parties during the decades spanning the century's divide. Describing James Connolly's introduction to socialism, and the reading material on offer in the Edinburgh branch of the Scottish Socialist Federation, C. Desmond Greaves explains that with Socialist literature 'still in its infancy', and with Marx's *Capital* and *The Communist Manifesto* 'available, but above the heads of some of the members', Bellamy and Morris helped meet demands for 'a mental picture of the new society'.[14] Such demands for images of future socialism, it should be said, were repeatedly opposed by the two founders of 'scientific socialism', not least in Engels's introduction to the English translation of *Socialism, Utopian and Scientific*, in 1892.

If in the United States Bellamy was a far more influential figure than Marx in the popularization of socialistic notions, in some important cases he opened a route towards Marxism. Daniel De Leon, who was to become the foremost American Marxist of his day, began his political career in Bellamy's Nationalist groupings. De Leon subsequently led the Socialist Labor Party of America, recruiting a significant membership from the Nationalist Clubs. Jack London joined the Oakland branch of the SLP in 1895; its library too contained the obligatory copy of *Looking Backward*.[15] In 1906, John Spargo, voice of the reformist wing of the American Socialist Party (which party London joined in 1901) segued together 'Saint-Simon and Owen, Marx and Engels, Morris and Bellamy' in the same 'prophetic line' of 'those whose eyes have seen the . . . glorious vision of a love-welded world'.[16] On a fund-raising trip to the States for the victims of St. Petersburg's

'Bloody Sunday', the then Bolshevik Maxim Gorky told audiences of American workers that Bellamy's work, though banned by the Czarist censors, was even better known there than in its country of origin. In 1913, another Bolshevik was to write in less sanguine terms of the 'advanced' (Bellamy-derived) doctrines peddled by the American Vice-Chairman of the International Congress of Chambers of Commerce:

> 'We are experiencing a great historic movement', he proclaims, 'that will end in the transfer of all power over the modern world to representatives of commercial capital . . . Power over the whole world must pass into the hands of the masses, that is, into *the hands of our employees* . . . The natural leaders of the masses should be the *industrialists and merchants*, who are learning more and more to understand the community of their interests and those of the masses'. He called upon the commercial world of Paris, Berlin etc.,. . . to unite the merchants and industrialists *of all* civilised countries in a single, mighty organisation.
>
> Such are the ideas of an 'advanced' capitalist.

The Bolshevik critic was V.I. Lenin.[17]

The 'single mighty organization' envisaged in *The Iron Heel* as the creature of corporate finance capital is a totalitarian state. Where Bellamy refuses to conceive of the state as such, seeing government as a classless, administrative function, London shows the state as the repressive instrument by which the dominant social class enforces its rule over others. Where Bellamy predicts and recommends the gradual, peaceful merging of social classes, London sees class struggle as inescapable, informing all aspects of social existence. Where Bellamy advocates reform, pinning his faith on a 'magical', fatalistic emergence of 'common sense', London campaigns for revolution, showing the future as 'inevitable' only in terms of the operation of specific historical contingencies, the crux of which is political will. And where Bellamy solemnly details the life of his far-future utopia, complete with its 'side-walk coverings', 'pneumatic communication tubes' and 'credit-cards', London ironizes his socialist paradise—the 'wonder city' of Ardis, 'one of the most wonderful' of the Oligarchy's constructions, and the blueprint for the 'still more wonderful wonder cities' from the era of the Brotherhood of Man (p.143).

In the fictional 'Foreword' to the novel, the Ardis editor introduces Avis Everhard's memoir to readers of his own time as an obscure and flawed text from the dark, turbulent age of the now-remote twentieth century. From the start, wry, knowing chords sound:

> It cannot be said that the Everhard Manuscript is an important historical document. To the historian it bristles with errors—not errors of fact, but errors of interpretation. Looking back across the seven centuries that have lapsed since Avis Everhard completed her manuscript, events, and the bearings of events, that were confused and veiled to her, are clear to us. She lacked perspective. She was too close to the events she writes about . . . (p.1)

With the clarity of hindsight and the benefit of the heightened consciousness of his own higher civilization, the future editor looks charitably upon the memoir, pleasantly excusing its 'vitiation due to the bias of love', and its defective phraseology: Ernest's terms 'proletarian science' and 'proletarian philosophy', we are told, express an unavoidable 'provincialism of mind' characteristic of the hero and of his day. 'Especially valuable in communicating to us the *feel* of those terrible times', the manuscript conveys something of the mistakes, the ignorance, the 'ethical delusions', the 'inconceivable sordidness and selfishness' of the period: 'things that are so hard for us of this enlightened age to understand'. The future understands more, but at the expense of understanding less.

Few commentators mention the humour of *The Iron Heel*'s editorial matter: its Foreword and its footnoted sub-text. Both bemused and amused by the past, the editor-annotator is alternately informative, authoritative, helpful, complacent, serene, coy, naive, quirky and pedantic. Frequently London allows the mask of his futurist persona to slip its position in those obviously authorial footnotes offering (say) a sharp summary biography of W.R. Hearst, a brief history of the Rockefeller corporation, tables of census and voting figures from 1900–1906, an account of the role of the Black Hundreds in the (first) Russian Revolution, and the like. But these notes appear together with bizarrely interruptive definitions of extinct slang vocabulary, and with a peppering of tangential inconsequential comment. Ostensibly reinforcing the illusion of a far-future world, the gloss in fact maintains the sense of disbelief. Often breaking moments of considerable dramatic tension, the Ardis footnotes explicate (for instance) 'ripped', 'grub', 'lobby', 'fake', or 'Tamales'—'A Mexican dish', we are told; 'It is supposed that it was warmly seasoned' (p.128). With an offhand flourish, one footnote dismisses Nietzsche: 'who caught wild glimpses of the truth, but who, before he was done, reasoned himself around the great circle of human thought and off into madness' (p.8). Another is whimsically devoted to the ancient practice of filling living rooms with bric-à-brac, and the endless labour of domestic cleanliness: 'There were a myriad devices for catching dust, and only a few devices for getting rid of it' (p.49). The compulsion, rawness, compression and crude passion of the main narrative are indeed inconceivable to the unimaginable Ardis editor, who, though 'correct' in most of his explanations, seems as often as not to miss the point, being detached in his nowhere world, where the Everhards' urgency can only seem mildly puzzling, archaically quaint.

London's playful irony in his presentation of the far-future world and its spokesman has no intention of undercutting the goal of a future communist commonwealth. It is utilized instead to express an orthodox Marxist disinclination to dream-up the socialist future, to forecast the fabric of its social relations and to anticipate the experience of its inhabitants. The communist goal can only be figured in algebraic terms; fanciful speculation diverts the socialist movement from present tasks and tactics. So the distant future of London's B.O.M. communism remains a barely characterized sketch. From it we learn only that the 'wonder' future is urban, that its children still filch from their parents, and that its rational social organization is as alien to us, as our present is alien to it. The vagueness and self-reflexive jokiness inscribed in London's presentation of the far-future make for a deliberate estrangement device which spurns the genre—and politics—of utopian fantasy to induce its readers to acknowledge that today and tomorrow matter, and the complexities of the historical process which links them, not the fabulous leap-year to come.

The utopian attitude London undercuts typically exhibits a paradoxical form. In the work of Bellamy and his successors, the far-future world is separated from the present by a substantial time-gap and its economic/social organization is described and accounted for in substantial detail. However much the self-contained future induces a critical re-examination of the present, the fantasy society is always given sufficient embodiment to be credible and experienceable in its own right. Initially, the fantasy far-future is so alien, so divorced from the present that the dreamer (reader) who awakens into it perceives it at first as a dream, and so must be taught step by step to accept its reality. Typically the crossing of the time-gap is a mysterious, automatic and unconscious passage which apparently occurs instantaneously. This is so even though the future is assumed to have 'evolved' gradually and 'naturally'. In the generic examples, the process of transformation from now to then (or occasionally, from here to there) is either underplayed or entirely absent. Only *News from Nowhere* offers a variation within the type, in its one 'near-future' chapter, 'How the Change Came', which charts meticulously the development of pre-revolutionary conditions within the social process.

In *The Iron Heel*, the sleep/dream transition device is dispensed with altogether, and the conventional magically crossable 'gap' between the present and an alternative, 'credible' far-future is quite absent. Departing from SF and utopian-dystopian norms, London looks at the far-future through a reversed telescope, whilst making the near-future telescopically imminent. Glaringly transmuted allusions to recent (real) labour struggles in the USA, and to the crackdown following the Russian Revolution, make the action of '1910–1925' and '1932' exaggeratedly present. The working-class readers London wishes to win to a revolutionary programme with the aid of this novel are to be offered awakening visions rather than fabulous daydreams. Yet *The Iron Heel* is still part fantasy. The compression of its epic sequence of events and their accelerated pace from chapter 10 ('The Vortex') onwards produce an action which is often hypnotically compelling. The apocalyptic final third of the novel, with its scenes of clandestine preparation, night-time mayhem and massacre, dehumanized riot and terrorist assassination build a nightmarish atmosphere as the oligarchy's totalitarian state is shown anticipating 'the First Revolt' and drowning it in blood. Broadly speaking, the narrative moves from theory to practice, from discussion and debate to dramatized example, and from character to action—while at the same time stressing the lived fusion of these formal opposites.

The first nine chapters have given the reader, alongside Avis Everhard, an initiation into a Marxist world-view. In successive debates, Ernest presses home the superiority of historical materialism over religious idealism, introducing the labour theory of value, the doctrine of class struggle, and the class nature of society en route. In one lecture, Everhard censures the great capitalist class for its 'criminal' mismanagement of society, for having made 'a shambles of civilisation' (p.57), and predicts that capitalism will be swept away as defunct. A spokesman of the plutocracy responds:

'We have no words to waste on you. When you reach out
your vaunted strong hands for our palaces and purpled ease,
we will show you what strength is. In roar of shell and
shrapnel and in whine of machine guns will our answer be
couched. We will grind you revolutionists down under our
heel, and we shall walk upon your faces. The world is ours,
we are its lords, and ours it shall remain. As for the host of
labour, it has been in the dirt since history began, and I read
history aright. And in the dirt it shall remain so long as I and
mine and those that come after us have the power. There is
the word—Power. It is the king of words—Power. Not God,
not Mammon, but Power . . .'

'I am answered', Ernest said quietly. 'It is the only answer
that could be given. Power. It is what we of the working class
preach . . .' (pp.63 – 64)

With further discussion redundant, the novel opens its second
movement and the pressure of what is to prove an increasingly
amplified chain of events begins to dominate. London's often raw
and garish descriptions of action are offset by his comparatively
sophisticated treatment of time. Setting the opening action of the
Avis memoir in the real historical present, London slides imperceptibly into the immediate near-future to depict occurrences and
tendencies which recast and compress factual materials from the
same reality. Analogy-drawing historical footnotes serve to make
the world of the '1910s' a seamlessly contiguous reformulation of
the known record of the two preceding decades. Always conscious
of history as process, London not only attends to the continuing
pressure of the past on the present, but also invokes the imminent
future which is already inherent and potential as an immanent tendency within the current of present-day events.

Modern readers, particularly those unfamiliar with US labour
history, may well suspect that from here onwards London has
stepped blindfold into the free realm of speculation. Yet in both the
second and the last movements of the narrative, London deploys his
extensive knowledge of two decades of US Labour-Socialist history,
combining it with lessons drawn from the defeated 1905 revolution
in Russia.[18] Most of the events in the following summary of the Iron
Heel tyranny, pattern what is in large measure (and particularly
up to '1915') distilled history masquerading as a projected future.
London's approach successfully avoids expository heaviness: his

concern is to show issues in action.

After an unprecedented period of industrial expansion in the US economy, a crisis of accumulation has arisen. With the markets glutted, the social surplus cannot be consumed. The ensuing slump has forced the most powerful owners of national capital, the Trust 'plutocracy' or 'oligarchy', on to the offensive against a newly combative proletariat. Socialist propaganda is refused distribution, mobs of 'Black Hundred' thugs smash the all-union presses as, on their owners' secret instructions, non-profitable factories are burned to the ground. Police riot clubs and machine-guns defeat the defensive strikes of streetcar workers, teamsters, and water-front unions. Pitched battles with gangs of strike-breakers, backed by state militia conscripts and Federal regulars, 'ingloriously' crush the machinists and the metal-workers. With the sole exception of Everhard, the undeterred leadership of the Socialist Party places its hopes in 'the end of capitalism' on continuing election successes, as workers turn from the industrial front to the political, adopting revolutionary objectives.

The year is '1912'. The great industrialists and financiers, firmly consolidated in giant Trust corporations, now turn on their former allies in the middle-class employers' associations. Credits are recalled, wrecked business plundered. Squeezed between labour and capital, the remnants of the middle classes re-group around the 'pseudo-socialism' of the weakening Democratic Party and the Hearst Press. The withdrawal of advertising revenue quickly silences the latter. Meanwhile, waylaid into their own sectoral alliance (the Grange), the nation's independent farmers line up as the oligarchy's next victims. Again the banks foreclose on mortgages and call in notes, ruining tenant-farmer and land-owner alike. The few survivors gain employment as salaried managers on the giant Trust farms. The Grangers win a dozen state legislatures but are prevented by force from sitting.

The stringency of such measures fails to revive the national economy; on the contrary, the social surplus increases still more as rising unemployment and wage-cuts drive down domestic consumption further still. Prevented from disposing of sufficient goods on a world market already cornered by its European rivals, the oligarchy whips up a war against Germany. The socialists successfully plan and execute an international general strike which paralyses both countries and stops dead the drive to war.[19] The German socialists rise up to depose the 'war-lord Emperor', but their US comrades remain passive. The Iron Heel regains the initiative, annexing vacated German markets abroad and determined at home that no general strike 'should [ever] occur again' (p.135).

It is '1913'. Now with electoral majorities in a dozen states, the Grange belatedly joins forces with the Socialists to transform each state into a 'co-operative commonwealth', heedless of Everhard's warning that the oligarchy will again react with force. Ernest appeals to the union leaders for a second general strike which, this time, might initiate the seizure of political power. But the Iron Heel has pre-empted him: O'Connor's machinists' union has already accepted increased wages and shortened hours in return for its guaranteed co-operation with the oligarchy. The rail and metal-working unions follow O'Connor's lead, aborting the planned strike. News of the betrayals results in violent clashes between 'the favoured unions' and their erstwhile brothers.

The final movement of the novel switches between stretches of hyper-acceleration and moments of intensified arrest as the Iron Heel instigates a war of state terror, suppressing opposition in brutal divide-and-rule operations. Oligarchy agents and provocateurs incite rebellions which the military ruthlessly defeat and punish. A fore-doomed Peasants' Revolt splits the Socialist-Farmer alliance and ends with the ravaged Granger States under martial law in what is London's recapitulation of the recent peasant uprisings in Russia, and the suppression of their agrarian communes. Next, the defeat of the coal miners' rebellion marks 'the expiring effort of organised labour' (p.154). Everhard covertly forms 'Fighting Groups' ('modelled somewhat after the Fighting Organisation of the Russian Revolution').[20] A stage-managed explosion in Congress signals the arrest of the Socialist Representatives; a further 300 leaders are imprisoned with them.

It is '1915'. Effecting the release of the jailed Socialists, the Fighting Groups stimulate the emergence of a bizarre array of clandestine terrorist societies, their fanatical members pledged to execute labour traitors and assassinate the worst of the oligarchy's butchers. Women revolutionaries, such as the 'slender girl' Madeline Provence and 'The Red Virgin' Anna Roylston, prove the most dauntless avengers. (Here, London hails the youthful Socialist Revolutionary executrix Maria Spiridonova, and Louise Michel—the famed 'Red Virgin' of the Paris Commune.[21]) Social fragmentation increases. The oligarchy evolves into a disciplined social élite, backed by shock troops and secret police drawn from a privileged, hereditary caste of Mercenaries, per-

manently barracked in sealed cities. The labour-caste develops a
near-autonomous existence. Giant slum districts house the ever-
increasing and near-bestial 'people of the abyss'.

It is '1917'. Social tensions exacerbate, discontent emerging even
within the protected castes. Everhard plans a revolution spear-
headed by Chicago's class-conscious proletariat. Yet again the Iron
Heel is a step ahead: its agents precipitate 'the First Revolt'. The
heroic three-day defence and defeat of the Chicago Commune, and
the slaughter of the city's ghetto masses provide the novel with
its grotesque climax, echoing both the fate of the Paris Commune
and the counter-revolutionary aftermath of Russia's 1905. The
novel ends abruptly with Avis Everhard's account of the mer-
ciless persecution which ensued and an unfinished statement on
the 'magnitude of the task' ahead.

If some of *The Iron Heel*'s allusions to international events bypassed
London's target readership, those dealing with domestic labour
disputes would certainly have found their mark. Such references
far exceed the explanatory information in the footnotes. The
generalized and brutal attacks on the working class by the conglom-
erates during this period utilized all the methods London describes
in the novel's second movement. The Chicago general strike of
1886, the Homestead Steel Lockout of 1892, the 1894 Pullman
Strike, the 1902 Anthracite Strike and the San Francisco streetcar
strike are just a few cases in point.[22] And what from London's class
standpoint seems to be an ever-intensifying mechanism of state
terror in the present, suggested its implicit extension as envisaged
in the third movement of the novel.

Two pivotal and interrelated incidents from chapter 14, 'The
Beginning of the End', and chapter 17, 'The Scarlet Livery',
illustrate clearly London's compacted allusive technique in what
is often a narrative *à clef*. The first, concerning union leader
O'Connor's betrayal on the eve of a general strike, condenses
the then notorious defections of Sam Gompers (President of the
American Federation of Labor) in 1900 and Charles Sherman
(President of the Industrial Workers of the World) in 1906. By
establishing with the employers the 'National Civic Federation',
and by agreeing to maintain peaceful labour-management relations, Gompers had taken a class-collaborationist line on behalf
of the craft unions. In return for limited union recognition, the
American Federation of Labor would desist from attempting to
unionize the unskilled, while labour activity would be restricted
to industrial disputes.[23]

Six years later, and as London was writing *The Iron Heel*, the Industrial Workers of the World (IWW) held its Second Convention in Chicago. Here, Sherman, leader of the metal workers, earned himself the unique badge of being 'the first, and so far the only, union president on record to get dumped because he was *not* a revolutionist'.[24] But when Sherman departed the IWW, he took with him the officials of its strongest delegation, the Western Federation of Miners (WFM). With the aid of armed police, Sherman and the WFM hierarchy seized and held the IWW headquarters and appropriated its funds, soon herding the metal workers and miners back into the reformist fold of the American Federation of Labor.[25]

Recasting Gompers and Sherman in *The Iron Heel* as the shady negotiator O'Connor, London paints a sulkily self-defensive, reticently guilty character, and the machinists' leader is exposed as the definitive 'labor-faker', lamely justifying the 'grab-sharing' terms he had made 'with the enemy': 'I guess we know our business best' (p.139). London has no need explicitly to identify O'Connor's antecedents but the significance he attaches to the role of the union bureaucracy is pointed in the chapter's title, 'The Beginning of the End', and underscored by an Ardis footnote:

> Everhard's social foresight was remarkable. As clearly as in the light of past events, he saw the defection of the favoured unions, the rise and slow decay of the labour castes, and the struggle between the decaying oligarchs and labour castes for control of the great governmental machine. (p.142)

In 'The Scarlet Livery', the scene shifts to Congress to satirize the façade of formal democracy and the powerlessness of electoral reformism. Drawing on the (real-life) doubling of socialist votes in the 1900 and 1904 elections, London predicts the return of some fifty Socialist Representatives. During Ernest's defiant speech a bomb explodes, cueing the intervention of waiting Federal troops to arrest the Socialist fraction on charges of High Treason. Allusions here to the recent headline news of the arrest, trial and execution of (some of) the Workers' Deputies of the Petersburg Soviet in 1906 are self-evident; London's other sources lie nearer at hand.

Much of the long footnote offered by the Ardis editor in London's compressed version is devoted (tongue-in-cheek) to secret Vatican records unearthed centuries later, which prove Everhard innocent of the bombing, and identify the perpetrator as an Oligarchy agent. London then lists the principal analogies: the 'ferocious and wanton judicial murder of the innocent and so-called Haymarket Anarchists in Chicago' (p.165), and 'the case of Moyer and Haywood', the framed-up organizers of the WFM, and left-wing leaders of the IWW. Illegally kidnapped by the Idaho authorities late in 1905, the abducted militants stood trial on perjured evidence for the bomb-blast killing of a former State governor. Their imprisonment facilitated the split and near-fatal weakening of the IWW. London recasts these events to mark a qualitative strengthening of the oligarchy's regime. In so doing, he was repeating points he had already made in 'Something Rotten in Idaho', an article from November 1906 for the *Chicago Daily Socialist* on 'the conspiracy against Moyer, Pettibone and Haywood':

> The capitalist organization is trying to hang the labor leaders. It has tried to do this before, but its evidence and its 'confessions' were always too rotten and corrupt . . . The capitalist organization has been incendiary in speech, and by unlawful acts has lived up to its speech. It will profit by exterminating the labor organization.[26]

The inauguration of the IWW of 1905 had expressed the flowering of revolutionary social democracy in the United States. London draws most of his programmatic conclusions and prognostic warnings from its swift rise and equally swift fracture. Uniting virtually the entire left leadership of the workers' movement, the IWW aimed to recruit in 'one big union' the mass of unrepresented workers, together with the rank-and-file majority of the American Federation of Labor. More a revolutionary party than a mass trade union, the organization advocated the seizure of political power by insurrectionary general strike. Haywood defined its goal as 'a Republic of Labor', and anticipated a future proletarian government modelled on the 1905 soviets.[27] Such are Everhard's policies in *The Iron Heel*, just as the figure of Everhard is consciously modelled on the charismatic co-founder of the IWW, Gene Debs: proletarian strike-leader, editor of *The Appeal to Reason*, translator of Marx, spokesman of the anti-reformist base of the Socialist Party of America, and the already acknowledged figurehead of indigenous American socialism.[28]

If *The Iron Heel* is science fiction, its science is that of 'scientific socialism'; if it is speculative fantasy, it is speculative in so far as it concerns itself with that future which is implied in putting into action a defined political programme, and with those alternative futures such a programme campaigns against. In the later chapters of the novel, London does betray signs of gleeful, extravagant fascination with disguise and terrorism, but in general he avoids 'purely' inventive colouring and fantastic musing. The sheer weight of historical allusion and of programmatic example are sufficient to make the relationship between this novel's tactical, functional 'futurism' and the imaginative licence characteristic of SF mainly one of coincidental form. The pressure of politics *per se*, the concentration on present-day tendencies, and the continual reminders of the real, combine to such a degree as to remove *The Iron Heel* from the regular generic orbits of SF. What seems to be presented as a separate future world cannot be read as such because the reader's topical awareness is enlisted precisely to prevent that. The imaginative shift London strives for involves eschewing a mere sense of 'what might happen' in favour of that which is both actually and potentially happening *now*.

By adopting a hypothetical long-view of a near-future which simply compacts and amplifies extant factual material, London attempts to re-orient his worker-readers, to shake from their respective standpoints the proponents of trade-union sectoralism and those socialists seduced by the blithe reformism newly informing the current policies of the SPA. *The Iron Heel* thus aims to test what are algebraic predictions of the tempo and direction of the class struggle in a manner which is both pedagogic and polemical; the result is an exemplary piece of revolutionary propaganda.

Where SF fantasies tend in the main to seduce their readers into their fictional worlds, and to inculcate a sense of the future as an inevitable given, *The Iron Heel* elicits only a partial suspension of disbelief, and refuses to fall back upon a mechanical historical determinism. The 'inevitability' of London's future is emphatically denied—what is to come will be dependent upon programmatic choices. Albeit in a passage saturated with irony, London's Ardis editor drives that point home:

> The rise of the Oligarchy will always remain a cause of secret wonder to the historian and the philosopher. Other great historical events have their place in social evolution. They were inevitable ... Not so, however, with the Iron Heel ... It

was not necessary and it was not inevitable. It must always remain the great curiosity of history—a whim, an apparition, a thing unexpected and undreamed; and it should serve as a warning to those rash political theorists of today who speak with certitude of social processes. (pp.2–3).

Not necessary and not inevitable—if Everhard's revolutionary programme is adopted and enacted. But if reform is preferred to revolution, and if the latter either fails to develop, or subsequently fails, the 'unexpected' and 'undreamed' tyranny may well materialize after all. Reading *The Iron Heel* for the first time in 1938, Trotsky wrote privately to Joan London on the quality of her father's anticipations:

> One can say with assurance that in 1907 not one of the revolutionary marxists, not excluding Lenin and Rosa Luxemburg, imagined so fully the ominous perspective of the alliance between finance capital and the labour aristocracy . . . The fact is incontestable: in 1907 Jack London already foresaw and described the fascist regime as the inevitable result of the defeat of the proletarian revolution.[29]

NOTES

1. John Clute and Peter Nicholls (eds), *The Encyclopedia of Science Fiction* (London, 1993), p.945.

2. Arthur Calder Marshall (ed.), *The Pan Jack London* (London, 1963), *Introduction*, p.8.

3. For a survey and bibliography of London's SF writings see: Gordon Beauchamp, *Jack London*, Starmont Reader's Guide 15 (Washington, 1984); Clute and Nicholls credit London with 'about 20 works of sf', judging *The Iron Heel* his 'finest achievement in sf, and perhaps his masterpiece', *Encyclopedia*, pp.729–30.

4. Examples of Wells's utopianism include *Anticipations* (1901) and *A Modern Utopia* (1905). *The Time Machine* (1895), *The First Men in the Moon* (1901), and *The War in the Air* (1908) exemplify his dystopian or anti-utopian fiction. *When the Sleeper Wakes* and 'A Story of the Days to Come', both from 1899, combine both attitudes. Useful appraisals of the Wellsian project can be found in A.L. Morton, *The English Utopia* (London, 1952), pp.183–85, and Krishan Kumar, *Utopia and Anti-Utopia in Modern Times* (Oxford, 1987), pp.168–223.

5. *Three Prophetic Science Fiction Novels of H. G. Wells*, ed. E.F. Bleiler (New York, 1960), p.60.

6. Bleiler, p.91.

7. Kumar, pp.220–22.

8. Bleiler, p.261.

9. Jack London, *The Iron Heel* (London, 1984), p.159. Subsequent references in the text are taken from this edition.

10. Edward Bellamy, *Looking Backward: 2000 – 1887* (Boston, 1926), p.57.

11. Bellamy, pp.331 – 32.

12. Kumar, p.133; Philip S. Foner, *Jack London—American Rebel* (Berlin, 1958), p.111; Joan London, *Jack London and his Times: An Unconventional Biography*, rev. ed. (Washington, 1968), p.304.

13. Quoted from Morris's review of *Looking Backward* in *The Commonweal* in Kumar, p.166.

14. C. Desmond Greaves, *The Life and Times of James Connolly* (London, 1972), p.45.

15. Foner, pp.40 – 41, 43.

16. John Spargo, *Socialism: A Summary and Interpretation of Socialist Principles* (New York, 1906), p.7.

17. V.I. Lenin, 'The Ideas of an Advanced Capitalist', *Collected Works*, Vol. 19 (Moscow, 1963), pp.275 – 76.

18. London raised funds for, and lectured in support of, 'the revolutionists of Russia', Foner, pp.459 – 60, 459.

19. Joan London (p.306) notes the reference to a minority motion for a general strike against war mobilizations at the 1907 International Socialist Congress in Stuttgart.

20. *The Iron Heel*, pp.156 – 57; in his 1906 lecture 'Revolution' (in Foner, pp.461 – 62), London defended the assassinations of Czarist Ministers of the Interior, Spiaguin and von Phleve, by the S.R.s' (Socialist Revolutionaries') combat groups.

21. Spiridonova shot Governor Lubjenovsky in 1905; Louise Michel's *Mémoires* were first published in 1886.

22. See, for example, Samuel Yelen, *American Labor Struggles 1877 – 1934* (New York, 1980), chs.2 – 6.

23. Farrell Dobbs, *Revolutionary Continuity: The Early Years 1848 – 1917* (New York, 1980), pp.89 – 91.

24. James P. Cannon, *The First Ten Years of American Communism: Report of a Participant* (New York, 1973), p.284.

25. Dobbs, pp.105 – 06.

26. Foner, p.403. 'Something Rotten in Idaho' is reprinted in full in Foner's selection (pp.400 – 04), and discussed in pp.109 – 11.

27. Cannon, pp.281 – 84.

28. Cannon, pp.267 – 71.

29. Leon Trotsky, *On Literature and Art* (New York, 1970), pp.223 – 24; Joan London, p.313.

Alien Dreams: Kipling

STEPHEN R.L. CLARK

I. A STRANGE COMPARISON

Once upon a time there was an orphan boy called Kimball, known as Kim, whose special gift was to impersonate and communicate with peoples of all kinds. He was also exceptionally skilled in map-making and mathematics. He worked undercover to maintain the peace against powers who wished to impose despotic rule upon a thronging multitude of different trades, cults and races, many of them addicted to vile drugs that bring bad dreams. A high point of his career was the day he first put on the uniform prepared for him, even though he often had to put it aside. As identification (in or out of uniform) he carried a gem, obtained only from a master of illusion (to whose powers he was himself immune, or nearly so).

This boy, whom I have described with careful ambiguity, might either be the chief hero of E.E. Smith's space opera (namely Kimball Kinnison), first encountered in *Galactic Patrol* (1937), or else Kipling's Kim O'Hara, Friend of all the World.[1] The comparison, of course, is ludicrous: the Lensman series of which *Galactic Patrol* is a part is pulp fiction, ill-written and poorly characterized. Its sole merit (or at least its sole claim to fame) is that it expounds an ancient myth in scientific (and pseudo-scientific) imagery: namely the perennial war between 'Good' and 'Evil' (each epitomized in an alien race that struggles over human, and galactic, destiny). Kipling's *Kim* (1901) is probably his single greatest work, and one of the profoundest studies of human affection, religious sensibility, and India, in the English language. There are also detailed differences between the two. Smith's Kim is unselfconsciously dedicated to the active maintenance of the law, and ready to kill any number of enemies (as long as they aren't female). Kipling's Kim may carry a revolver (a gift from the Afghan horse-dealer and secret agent, Mahbub Ali), but uses it only once, and not to kill. The bond of affection between boy and Tibetan lama has no parallel in Smith, nor yet the lama himself. A structuralist comparison uncovers yet more illuminating differences. Smith's Kim is nursed through convalescence (in *Galactic Patrol*, and in *Grey Lensman*, 1951) by his predestined bride; Kipling's by a mother-figure, the talkative Sahiba, whom he had charmed into supporting his adoptive (grand)father, the lama, years before. Kim O'Hara's red hair and Irish ancestry is transferred to Kim Kinnison's bride, Clarrissa (sic). There are also hidden identities: consider Kim's colleague and occasional companion, who constantly professes his own cowardice in literary periods (namely Hurree Chunder Mookerjee, on the one hand, and Nadreck the Palainian on the other). Or Mahbub Ali the horse-dealer, with his blood feuds and feigned hostility to all idolaters, and Worsel the Velantian (a flying snake). It may even be that Smith intended his Kim's third companion, Tregonsee the Rigelian, as an echo of the lama: Rigelians can sense the world in the round, and themselves, their particular identities, as of no greater significance than any other's. If that comparison was intended, it falls flat, since the Rigelian is as much an active soldier as the rest, and there is no special or illuminating bond between Smith's Kim and this image of four-square enlightenment. Kipling knew more about affection, and more about the realities of soldiering, than Smith.

It falls flat, perhaps because—along with other critics—Smith misunderstood Kipling's Kim: or else Smith really intended to convey a message. Maybe Smith really thought that *Kim* was an adventure story, set in a strange land, where the young hero rises to high office in a decent empire. Maybe he actually meant to contrast his Kim with Kipling's more pacific hero. Kipling's Kim acknowledges the attraction of Mahbub Ali and the Game, but his heart is given to the lama, and the novel ends with their joint enlightenment, their release from the Wheel exactly in the moment that 'the wheels of [Kim's] being lock up anew on the world without', and the lama returns from 'the Threshold of Freedom'. This is not, by the way, a sign of 'Christian' or 'Western' influence: it is standard doctrine in the 'Greater Vehicle' of Buddhism, the Mahayana (of which the lama is a devotee). Although it is absurd to ask 'what Kim did next', there are plenty of clues within the text to suggest that Kipling thought he vanished into the wide world: at the very least the records of his secret service, mentioned in the text, are said to have been thoroughly confused, and Kim is greatly relieved to hand the Russian documents he has captured on to Mookerjee. Smith's Kim rejects the possibility of enlightenment, to ally himself instead with the flying snake, and rise to be (in all but name) a king. 'I will teach thee other and better desires upon the road', the lama said.[2]

Does the comparison still seem ludicrous? The fact is that Smith, like other writers of science fiction, knew Kipling's work, and often quotes it (most notably the Ballad of Boh Da Thone), even if he misses much of Kipling's irony.[3] He may even have believed that he too sought to reproduce the common speech and understanding of common soldiers and unlearned multitudes, who deserved to be protected from the imperial ambitions of those who aim only at dominion. Even his occasional references to 'the Supreme Witness' may be a deliberate echo of 'the Great Soul which is beyond [and contains] all things' (on which more hereafter). That he was a far less able writer and thinker than Kipling is obvious; likewise that he sought to honour Kipling by echo, commentary and imitation.

II. KIPLING'S SCIENTIFIC ROMANCES

Some of Kipling's stories are unambiguously of a kind with stories later written in the genre known as science fiction. In the future he imagines in 'With the Night Mail' (*Actions and Reactions*) and 'As Easy as A.B.C.' (*A Diversity of Creatures*) the Aerial Board of Control has unquestioned responsibility for the transport system 'and all that it implies', and is thereby saddled with the whole burden of planetary administration. 'Theoretically we do what we please, so long as we do not interfere with the traffic *and all it implies*. Practically, the A.B.C. confirms or annuls all international arrangements.'[4] In *Kim* the one admitted gift of the Government to all India is the train; in the later stories the train and its equivalents (especially the dirigibles that carry almost all the traffic of the Planet) are the sole but sufficient business of all the Government our descendants can endure. 'In *Kim*, the rulers carry out their lonely arduous task in order that the *diversity* of the Great Trunk Road shall flourish.'[5] That condition—anarchism tempered by despotism—lies on the far side of a world-wide rebellion against 'whatsoever for any cause, /seeketh to take or give /power above or beyond the Laws'.[6] It is especially a rebellion against mobs: 'the Planet, she has had her dose of popular government . . . She has no—ah—use for crowds.'[7] In the second story of the pair Kipling imagines a statue of a negro in flames, bitterly inscribed 'to the Eternal Memory of the Justice of the People'. He did not live to witness what India now remembers as 'the Holocaust'—the ten million murdered in the Partition Riots—but might justly have remarked that this was what he feared. Those who would bind us to do all and only what 'the People' say (especially as this is given voice by 'the word-drunk') are as much the enemies of personal liberty, and responsibility, as any literal kings. Kipling's principled, and often misunderstood, antagonism to democracy and to a rhetoric of 'human dignity', will concern me later. His particular imagined future has echoes in the alternate world imagined by L. Neil Smith in *The Probability Broach:*[8] there too people insist upon their privacy, detest politicians and travel by enormous dirigible.[9]

Others of Kipling's stories employ devices that might easily be science-fictional. Investigation of circadian rhythms, and the impact of external tides, lies behind a study of the relationship of millionaire patron, medical researcher, and patient, in 'Unprofessional' (*Limits and Renewals*). Angus Wilson suggests that the story might be contrived more convincingly 'now that science fantasy has been so much developed', to make its central point about the importance of imagination in scientific theorizing.[10] A similar point, that new discoveries may rest on *false* hypotheses, is made in 'A Doctor of Medicine' (*Rewards and Fairies*), whose hero finds an answer to the plague because he believes 'Divine Astrology'.

> Dare sound Authority confess
> That one can err his way to riches,
> Win glory by mistake, his dear
> Through sheer wrong-headedness?[11]

For Kipling, the answer (to which I shall return) is yes. The useful and the true are not quite the same—and some truths, perhaps, are deadly: witness the premature discovery of the microscope, celebrated in one of his most brilliant stories, 'The Eye of Allah' (*Debits and Credits*).

In 'The Ship that Found Herself' and '.007' (a newly commissioned railway engine!) machinery is given a voice (both in *The Day's Work*), and allowed to work through folly to mature responsibility. In very many stories non-human animals act out the same progression from childishness to adulthood, or else secure a place for themselves within an uncomprehending human world: for example, in 'The Maltese Cat' (*The Day's Work*), 'The Bull that Thought' (*Debits and Credits*), and the stories of *The Jungle Books*.[12]

There is a pair of monsters from the deep in 'A Matter of Fact' (*Many Inventions*). Ghost stories, tales of magic amulets, and his satires on the heavenly bureaucracy ('On the Gate', in *Debits and Credits*, and 'Uncovenanted Mercies', in *Limits and Renewals*) could all be given science fictional readings—especially with respect to the Galaxy created without the knowledge of Death, or mention of the wondering sigh of new-born suns a universe of universes away. All these stories, that is, could have been provided with a richer background in real or imaginary science—and many of their devices have been used since Kipling's day by less able, but slightly better equipped, 'science fantasists'.

But though the devices have been more adeptly used, Kipling's work is richer in ideas, as well as in human insight, than most. 'The Brushwood Boy' (in *The Day's Work*), for example, imagines how an ordinarily decent young head of school, and soldier, can also be a figure in another world. Kipling quite deliberately makes his hero innocent beyond belief: the perfect head of school, and subaltern, moved by different sorts of dream. On the one hand, 'his training had set the public-school mask upon his face, and had taught him how many were the things no fellow can do' (it may be that Smith's Kim owes something to this paragon). On the other, he inhabits a dream world, 'beyond the brushwood pile', whose geography he shares with a woman he met, once only, when they were children. The mask cannot ever have been all he was, any more than Kim can ever *be* a sahib. But better wear that mask than the one worn by too many of Kipling's parsons (the Reverend Bennett, for example, in *Kim*), just because it does represent a truth about obedience and decency.

In all these stories (and many others that lie quite outside the broadest limits of the nascent genre), is the sense of a world beyond, a world with different meanings, a world that does not bend to the wishes of the undisciplined, those of whom the Muslim Shafiz Ullah Khan is made to write 'If they desire a thing they declare that it is true. If they desire it not, though that were Death itself, they cry aloud, "It has never been"' ('One View of the Question', in *Many Inventions*). Those afflicted by this condition can perhaps be cured only by dreadful experience, like the bumptious atheist McGoggin ('The Conversion of Aurelian McGoggin', in *Plain Tales from the Hills*), who found that 'something had wiped his lips of speech, as a mother wipes the milky lips of her child'. 'By the time you have put in my length of service', said the Doctor, 'you'll know exactly how much a man dare call his own in this world.'

That sort of experience, by Kipling's account, was especially to be found in India, where 'the climate and the work are against playing bricks with words'. In Town, he suggests, a man may naturally suppose that there is no one higher than himself, and that the Metropolitan Board of Works made everything. In India, full of 'a raw, brown, naked humanity' between the blazing sky and 'the used-up, over-handled earth', it is all too obvious that everyone is under orders, from the Deputy to the Empress.[13] And 'if the Empress be not responsible to her Maker—if there is no Maker for her to be responsible to—the entire system of Our administration must be wrong; which is manifestly impossible'. Critics often fail to hear the multiple ironies in this bland remark, because they have convinced themselves, by careful inattention, that Kipling was 'a bully, and a defender of bullies'. The fact is that he was certainly no uncritical admirer of the Raj and of its officers: what he did admire was obedience, truthfulness and mercy. The Protestant chaplain and his wife who betray Lispeth (to return in *Kim*, as the Woman of Shamlegh) deserve Kipling's censure (*Plain Tales from the Hills*), but we might also acknowledge that 'by some mysterious rule-of-thumb magic, [the English] *did* establish and maintain reasonable security and peace among simple folk in very many parts of the world, and that too, without overmuch murder, robbery, oppression, or torture'.[14] That they are now attacked (not quite unjustly) for the sins they did commit (especially in the aftermath of the Mutiny) is a sign that they set higher standards for imperial control than any earlier empire.

That we lie under orders, and dare call very little even of our mind and memory 'our own', does not imply that we are helpless. On the contrary, by learning humbly how the world works we can work with it: machinery, which Kipling loved, did not exist to dominate or control the natural world, but to take a careful advantage of it. What social changes new machines will bring cannot always be predicted: optimistic liberals expect, for example, that the train will help to break down caste boundaries, since 'there is not one rule of right living which these *te-rains* do not cause us to break'.[15] But it is equally true that trains allow a stricter segregation than the older ways, since 'well-educated natives are of opinion that when their womenfolk travel . . . it is better to take them quickly by rail in a sealed compartment'.[16] What happens does not depend on what 'we' say, or want—but there is no security in refusing change. It is that intense interest in how things work, the recognition that there are no secure boundaries in space or time, that marks Kipling as a true pre-cursor of the genre.

III. RETURN TO INDIA

In *Kim*, and in the other Indian stories, there is a sub-continent of varied and conflicting cultures, an alien and dangerous climate, secret societies, forgotten histories and unexpected powers. The habits of its natives constantly outrage the etiquette and ethics of its British visitors, who find their own behaviour judged to be cowardly, mean-spirited, hypocritical, unclean or pretentious, even while they find native behaviour treacherous or homicidal.

> And if you cross over the sea,
> Instead of over the way,
> You may end by (think of it!) looking on We
> As only a sort of They![17]

What is significant in this is that there are, after all, shared standards in Kipling's India: despite the manifold conflicts, courage and hospitality and oath-keeping are to be praised by all. Smith's heroes (and those of many other science fiction writers) must also respect almost entirely alien moral codes, while still maintaining their allegiance to deeper, would-be universal standards. The frequent failures of the British (and perhaps especially of Protestant pastors) derive from their conviction that the natives are *merely* heathen, and could neither appreciate nor deserve fair dealing. Their occasional successes turn on their realization that caste, race and creed are simultaneously real and finally unimportant. The English, Kipling thought, had been made 'akin to all the universe' by their mixed origin, 'and sympathetic in their dumb way with remote Gods and strange people'.[18] Kim is Irish by descent, but no-one would be able to tell this from his habits: he is an English type, and therefore ready to believe that 'to those who follow the Way there is neither black nor white, Hind nor Bhotiyal'.[19] Not only to those who follow the lama's Way: those who 'go looking for *tarkeean*' (which is the password of the secret service) also lie beyond all castes. Kim even transcends the grand division between European and Asiatic (though it seems he remains afraid of snakes and sometimes requires fleshfoods – neither of which failings strike modern readers as either European or admirable).[20] The deeper division in Kipling's world is between those who know and those who don't, those who see the true significance of action and those misled by appearances.

Some of the peoples encountered in India—the Hill-folk of Shamlegh for example—know almost nothing beyond their own locale, and speak of elsewhere as a mystery: 'the hot terrible Plains where the cattle run as big as elephants, unfit to plough on a hillside'.[21] Others travel between these places on foot, on horseback or by train. The last, in particular, functions as a place outside all places, moving outside ordinary time between locations, lifting Kim and the lama from Lahore to Benares to Delhi. Travel around India, whether it is the lama's search around the holy places for his River or Kim's holidays, lays the foundation for that vision of the whole that the lama at last experiences, and that regularly appears in science fiction. Consider, for example, Valentine's visions in Robert Silverberg's Majipoor trilogy: Valentine sees all the lands of Majipoor in the world-mind, as the lama sees everything in the Great Soul.

So Kipling:

> As a drop draws to water, so my soul drew near to that Great Soul which is beyond all things. At this point, exalted in contemplation, I saw all Hind, from Ceylon in the sea to the Hills, and my own Painted Rocks at Suchzen; I saw every camp and village, to the least, where we have ever rested. I saw them at one time and in one place; for they were within the Soul.[22]

And Silverberg:

> The water-king carried him effortlessly, serenely, as a giant might carry a kitten in the palm of his hand. Onward, onward over the world, which was altogether open to him as he coursed above it. He felt that he and the planet were one, that he embodied in himself the twenty billion people of Majipoor . . . He was everywhere at once; he was all the sorrow in the world, and all the joy, and all the yearning, and all the need. He was everything . . . Everything enfolded itself into That Which Is. Everything was part of a vast seamless harmony.[23]

Edward Said's comment on the passage from Kipling, that 'some of this is mumbo jumbo, *of course*', would better apply to Silverberg's.[24] The problem with invoking science fictional

representations of familiar philosophy is that it invites scientific enquiry. What sort of energies are involved in Majipoor's
telepathy and dream manipulation? What sort of species are the
water-kings, enormous sea/mammals who think of themselves
as gods (and must remind all Kipling-readers of Small Porgies, risen
to shame Solomon)?[25] Kipling's more familiar version allows his
readers to suppose either that the lama is describing a personal,
psychological event which needs to be transcended, or that he
really is attuned to the Soul which lies beyond the realm of
physical science. That metaphysical vision (which is not certainly
ridiculous) is also Silverberg's, but genre conventions require him
to imagine that there might be mechanical aids for its attainment,
and manipulation of the Underlying World. The dream-world of
the Brushwood Boy, with its sudden terrors, may have formed part
of the background to Majipoor's economy of dreams. There too,
Silverberg gives the appearance of an explanation for what, in
Kipling, needs no gloss.

Silverberg's sequence of stories, indeed, offers another gloss and
transformation. They begin, like *Kim*, with a meeting between
a childlike older man fallen from high office and a street-wise
boy, within a vast world of many races called Majipoor. But the
older man, radiant with goodwill though he is, must at last climb
back into the Hills to power, and the boy remains peripheral. The
pattern is at once repeated: later in the sequence another orphan
child, encountered as a guide in the underground Labyrinth that
is the seat of power, is befriended, educated through immersion
in the lives of others, and transformed at last into another king,
and Valentine's successor when the older man does what he most
hates, but what he sees he must—namely to use force against the
world's enemy (a challenge or temptation that the lama refused).
The identity and differences here are evident, but it is Majipoor
itself that re-embodies Kipling's vision of open country. The one
thing missing from Kipling's India is Ocean, and that is lovingly
restored in Majipoor, in the shape of an unnavigable hemisphere
of water.

'Big Worlds' offer the greatest opportunities and dangers for
science fiction writers: opportunities because as many races, cultures, places as they wish can be encountered there; dangers
because the opportunity may sometimes reveal the weakness
of the author's imagination. Big Worlds can be literal globes, or
some imaginable artificial world (ringworlds or Dyson spheres),
or else a galactic milieu traversed by interstellar magic (like

Kipling's train). They can also be expanses of alternate histories: movement between the myriad possibilities of human history (what if Alexander lived, or the Battle of Tours was won by Muslims, or Babbage's computer worked?) allows that sense of open country, and of possibility, that Kipling offered. Kipling's India (and India itself) is densely populated: for the other aspect of Big Worlds we look instead to Kipling's Africa, as it is described in 'The Explorer' (1898):

> 'There's no sense in going further—it's the edge of cultivation'.
> So they said, and I believed it – broke my land and sowed my crop—
> Built my barns and strung my fences in the little border station
> Tucked away below the foothills where the trails run out and stop:
> Till a voice, as bad as Conscience, rang interminable changes
> On one everlasting Whisper day and night repeated—so:
> 'Something hidden. Go and find it. Go and look behind the Ranges—
> 'Something lost behind the Ranges. Lost and waiting for you. Go!'[26]

Just out of sight, behind the Ranges, there is a new world waiting, which the later comers will enjoy and till, but never really see as the explorer does.

IV. POLITICAL IDEOLOGIES

Kipling, of course, needed less creative imagination (in a sense) than later writers: he had only to represent the actual castes, cults and races of the real India, and the actual experience of exploration. The probability is that he really did just that: certainly those critics who declare that he knew and understood much less than he pretended, that he only voiced the British prejudices of his day, themselves know very little, and mostly voice the prejudices of a later day. But it is obvious that Kipling cannot be regarded as 'politically correct'. His crimes are manifold: he believed, or seemed to have believed, that British rule was beneficial, even if it was often

foolish; he believed that its follies rested with the word-drunk politicians or parochial pastors who could not understand the honour
of an alien culture; he mocked Democracy and Human Dignity;
he doubted, with good reason, that 'natural humanity' could be
expected to be kind. That he also mocked imperial pretensions, and
prophesied the fall of empires, always seems to escape the notice of
his modern critics. Also that he could hear—and voice—what the
poor thought of patronage.

> God bless the Squire
> And all his rich relations
> Who teach us poor people
> We eat our proper rations—
> We eat our proper rations,
> In spite of inundations,
> Malarial exhalations,
> And casual starvations,
> We have, we have, they say we have—
> We *have* our proper rations![27]

He seems to have believed—like almost everyone until late in
this century—that there were some hereditary virtues, that it
was possible to breed and educate honest and intelligent officials, so long as we also recognized the underlying natures of
particular lines, and the possibility of going bad. Good breeding
is a value, but far less than good education, and the effects of dangerous responsibility. Greatness could emerge from humble origins
(as Kim emerged). But those who now deny that breeding counts
apparently believe that human beings are not animals, even though
they usually also mock the suggestion that they are therefore real
souls. If we are animals, then it is irrational to suppose that there
are no distinctive lineages; if any lineage can produce any human
character or talent (as though Great Danes could be bred together
to produce chihuahuas), then our character and talent cannot rest
entirely on our physical inheritance, nor even on our early education. Kipling believed (if 'belief' is what we should attribute to
creative writers) both that we were animals and that there was
something else in us than nature and nurture could provide. He
was prepared to suggest, as he does in 'With the Night Mail', that
we are our fathers (a fable given slightly different form in stories
about reincarnation). He also insisted that each successive incar-
nation of the lineal type must find its own way in the world, and
might transcend its ancestry.

This image, of a soul embodied in a body that carried its own character and value, is what many Indians (then and now) believed. Such a belief, notoriously, helps people to endure what otherwise would be unbearable: by bearing this life, whatever it is like, and doing the duties of my line and station, I may secure a better life hereafter. If I 'am' a sweeper (and should act as such), it is still true that I, the abiding Self, 'am not a sweeper'. When Kim asks 'Who is Kim?' the answer cannot be that he is a sahib (even if, in another sense, he is): that is, perhaps, *what* but not *who* he is. One conclusion, of course, might be politically correct. Any one of us is the equal, essentially, of any other, for all alike are 'souls seeking escape'. Difference and inequality lie in the realm of appearance. But precisely because all such are mere appearances, we do not need to be troubled by them. 'India is the only democratic land in the world', for riches and political station give no special kudos.[28] Holy men, and even spurious holy men, have kudos, because they have no riches or political station. We all have duties to perform, the 'highest' as well as the 'lowest', and acquire merit by recalling who essentially we are, and who we deal with. Asking that those not bred and trained, in this life, for high office should be trusted with those duties is absurd; forgetting that those bred and trained for lower offices can be our spiritual superiors is sillier by far.

Critics are right to say that Kipling and other British writers of the time sensed an affinity between Indian castes and British breeding. We have forgotten that hierarchies, with stable lineages, have been the norm in civilized societies. The idea (that we hardly act on) that there should be absolute identity of opportunity, and absolute equality of respect, would have been wholly strange in every century but this, except perhaps for bands of hunter-gatherers (at any rate while they are prosperous). 'Inequality and wretchedness were then to be found in society; but the souls of neither rank of men [noble or serf] were degraded.'[29] Kipling was orthodox in this, as he was in his dislike (which now seems dangerous) of Germans, Russians and such other 'breeds without the Law' who fail to acknowledge their fragility, or put their trust in weaponry. Science fiction writers now may be more self-conscious in their political imaginings, but they are often like Kipling in being 'politically incorrect'. Hierarchical societies, perhaps with kings, and ones that lay great stress on personal and family honour manifested in martial arts, are common in the genre. One of the most completely realized of those societies is that of C.J. Cherryh's 'mri', but Poul Anderson's stories constantly repeat the same idea, often with explicit reference to Kipling.[30]

Liberal democracies live in uneasy balance: correct ideology requires that any human individual (or every 'rationally responsible individual') be the equal in dignity and opportunity of any other, but no substantive effort is made to break down the ties of family, talent and association which impede the realization of this vision. Such efforts would, most probably, create their own gross inequalities (occasionally imagined in such dystopias as *1984* or 'ambiguous utopias' as Anarres).[31] The best we can manage, we could say, must be to imagine some loathly opposites of our preferred society. We cannot wholly create the liberal ideal, but we can at least imagine what 'illiberal' societies would be, and find occasional antidotes. Or perhaps we might decide instead that 'liberal' societies are not an absolute ideal. It is understandable that serious representations of illiberal societies are found more often in science fiction than in 'mainstream' writing. Seeming to approve (even for debating purposes) of caste-bound, hierarchical arrangements is a scandal best avoided by representing different castes (of the kind that Kipling's India contains, and India) by different species. Whereas it is politically incorrect to wonder whether there are human sub-species having different talents, characters and dignity, no-one need deny that there are, or might be, really different species. Species do not interbreed, and generally breed true: that is why they are species. Pretending or believing that there might be distinct human species (castes or classes or races) is too dangerous to conceive, except in metaphor. Correspondingly, it may be possible to give a sympathetic ear to really horrendous ideologies, if they are conceived to be the thoughts of other species. Any number of imagined enemies of a Terran empire, or the Federation, are depicted as calmly genocidal, callous and yet admirable, as we might admire (but not approve of) a cat. We can imagine beings, that is, who cannot transcend their species, and who do have natural virtues: they may be elegant and honourable in all their dealings with each other, while openly contemptuous of all other kinds. Klingons (from *Star Trek*), Merseians (from Poul Anderson's future history) and Larry Niven's Kzin are all embodiments of the spirit Kipling saw in Shafiz Ullah Khan.

That picture of a Muslim warrior prepared to feign a common cause with Hindus for as long as was needed to confuse an ignorant Britain no doubt seemed shocking to those who believed that all men of goodwill must love each other (a dangerously ambiguous dictat). Even now, after much evidence to the contrary, it still seems clear to some of Kipling's critics (who are also critics of the British Raj) that the insurrection of 1857—'the Mutiny'— must obviously have been the action of an Indian Nation which (others might reasonably hold) did not at the time exist. Perhaps the loyal soldier Kim encounters was correct to say that the mutineers were moved to carve out little holdings for themselves now that, they thought, the British were defeated. What justified 'rebellion' against government? Modern nationalists (who cannot easily pretend that the British Raj was uniformly harsher or more violent than present Indian governments) insist that it matters that the Raj was British, and not 'Indian'. In one sense, Kipling agreed: he dreamed instead of a native European élite, with some Eurasian backing, who would preserve the peace of an independent India, a marvellous Dominion, precisely because they were not parties to ancestral feuds between castes, races and religions. 'The English' held Zam-Zammah, the great bronze gun of Lahore, and the Punjab, as Muslims and Hindus had before them, by conquest and present responsibility. But the subjects of that Dominion would have as little to do with government as most subjects of the British Isles themselves: the consent of the governed matters for the legitimacy of government, but not necessarily their 'participation', by symbolic vote or by official duties. Consent might actually be withheld if there were any prospect of our immediate rivals participating in the rituals of government.

It may be that these political ideas are dangerous, or foolish. But it is not obvious that we should therefore sweep them aside, or castigate an author brave enough to hold them to the light. If they are dreams we choose to reckon nightmares, we should still examine them—and think it possible that we are ourselves mistaken. Two dreams stand opposite to Kipling in this matter. The first requires us all to participate in government rather than to be content with managing our own affairs in an order preserved by government. But why should we surrender our control of our own lives to get a trifling share in the control of all? Older liberals felt less affection for government, and wished not to give it any power beyond what would be needed to keep the peace, to keep traffic moving and 'all that this implies'. Modern liberals may attack the government, but only because they wish themselves to govern, and will interfere far sooner while denying that they have any authority to do so. If government controls all our lives we had better get our word in; if it tries to control very little, we might prefer to get on with our lives, and not interfere with others. The Prime Directive, according to Nadreck the Palainian, is 'Ignore and Be Ignored'! In 'As Easy as A.B.C.' those throwbacks who profess allegiance to Democracy are almost lynched (and eventually saved to become a comic turn).

The second dream is nationalism itself, and it is one that sits a little oddly with the other liberal dogmas, even though in origin Democracy and Nationalism are one in demanding that 'the People' rule. With one voice liberals insist that there are no sub-species of humanity, that every individual is to be judged interchangeable in law with any other; with a second voice, they insist that people are defined by nationhood, that it is an offence to be governed, even if well-governed, by any but our fellow-nationals. Kipling, more realistically, acknowledged the importance of national (and other) groupings, but for that very reason denied that we should trust our lives entirely to one government. Good government is to pre- serve the peace within which different groups can live their lives. Not everything that they might wish to do can be permitted, but if they will accept those limits they will have the chance to live much as they please.

V. TRUTH OR DARE

'What should they know of England who only England know?'[32] Kipling's question rests upon his deep understanding of the odd- ities, in space and time, of English, British and European attitudes. Not knowing what the other options are we fail to understand or to appreciate our own. The liberties we now enjoy, the demands we make upon each other and the world, are not 'natural' to humanity.

> Ancient Right unnoticed as the breath we draw—
> Leave to live by no man's leave, underneath the Law—
> Lance and torch and tumult, steel and grey-goose wing,
> Wrenched it, inch and ell and all, slowly from the King.[33]

Kipling detested those without the Law, the irresponsible and greedy. He also detested, and with sharper venom, those com- placently convinced that they *deserved* their lawful liberties, that they need not honour anyone. The song of an 'English Irregular, discharged', Chant-Pagan:

> Me that 'ave been what I've been—
> Me that 'ave gone where I've gone—
> Me that 'ave seen what I've seen—
> 'Ow can I ever take on
> With awful old England again,
> An' 'ouses both sides of the street,
> And 'edges two sides of the lane,
> And the parson an' gentry between,
> An' touchin' my 'at when we meet—
> Me that 'ave been what I've been?[34]

That irregular remembers open country, 'an' the silence, the shine an' the size /of the 'igh, unexpressible skies'. There is something greater than 'awful old England'—even if that same England, properly appreciated, is also 'Merlin's Isle of Gramarye'.[35] It is that latter because, to the discerning eye, it is full of strange, remembered histories as alien and exciting as any contemporary land 'beyond the Ranges'. Imagining or rediscovering different times and places, we can identify the principles we choose to act upon, and understand our own place better. That was why, so Kipling said, Rhodes arranged his 'game' so 'that each man, bringing with him that side of his head which belonged to the important land of his birth, was put in the way of getting another side to his head by men belonging to other not unimportant countries'.[36] Kipling's grasp of which other countries *were* important was somewhat broader than Rhodes's.

It was also rather broader than that of many modern writers who think that their 'modernity' is obvious and universal (and so think nothing of insulting those whom they can identify as 'fundamentalists'). The commonest ideological stance in contemporary science fiction is an atheistic humanism, although its devices are often those of a more ancient metaphysics.[37] By this account there is no overarching Providence, nor any difference that is not physical. At the same time, there is a residual conviction that there is, within the human species, something quite distinctive, that will triumph over every possible disaster. Why we should imagine that this might be true is difficult to see, unless that the occasional denials of it make depressing reading.

Consider 'The Bridge Builders' (*The Day's Work*): British engineers, much hampered by corruption, incompetence and disease, have constructed a great bridge across the Ganges. A flood comes down, and one engineer, marooned upon a sandbank with his Lascar subordinate, beholds, as in a dream, the conversation of the gods of India about his bridge. Mother Ganges and Kali demand that the bridge be broken; Hanuman and Ganesh explain that those humans who admire machinery and riches are, unknowingly, their worshippers, and therefore wish the bridge to stand; Bhairon speaks for the Common Man, and Krishna persuades Ganges that the bridge, in any case, will stand only for a while. Krishna then predicts that all the gods, save he, will end their days as 'rag-Gods, pot Godlings of the tree, and the village-mark', as Wayland Smith had ended in *Puck of Pook's Hill*. Shiva concludes by reassuring all the gods that they will exist as long as Brahm dreams (a remark the Lascar interprets to mean that they are the engineer's dream).

There can be many readings of this text. Are bridges, trains and all the rest attempts to dominate the world of nature, or ways of enabling nature? Are all the achievements of the engineers bound, in the end, to pass? Will the bridges, if they fail, be constantly rebuilt, to higher standards? Are the engineers in service, unknowingly, to Hanuman the Ape? Or is it that the people are at last to deny such godlings as are only the priests' excuse for begging? Who is Brahm, who will one day awake? There is no absolute conclusion. On the one hand, Kipling insists in many stories on the virtue of curing and preventing pestilence, famine and war. On the other, there is little chance of any final victory (which might, if it occurred, be a disaster). Maybe we must do honour to the little gods, but the gods whose presence we desire are those of forgiveness, order and affection. Many of his stories do suggest that there will, in the end, be mercy, even if we have no adequate account of what the world must be to provide for it, and even if events here and now often seem incalculably cruel.

> The Ocean demands truth:
> Ye shall not clear by Greekly speech, nor cozen from your path
> The twinkling shoal, the leeward beach, or Hadria's white-lipped wrath.[38]

The same is true of machinery, which is 'not built to comprehend a lie'. Machines may be 'nothing but the children of [our] brain', but they work by courtesy of natural law, a law that does not allow them to 'love or pity or forgive'.[39] The other law of our being, which is to forgive, demands something more than trust in our machines. For despite Kipling's insistence upon truth, there is something to be said for fiction. 'Splendaciously mendacious rolled the Brass-bound Man ashore . . .'. Language, indeed, begins with lies. 'No one in the world knew what truth was till someone had told a story.'[40] Kipling identifies the 'pride, the awestricken admiration of himself' that the First Liar experienced 'when he saw that, by mere word of mouth, he could send his simpler companions shinning up trees in search of fruit that he knew was not there'.[41] All we know of Truth comes down to 'That that is, is'—

> But it is just this Truth that Man most bitterly resents being brought to his notice . . . He desires that the waters which he has digged and canalised should run up hill by themselves when it suits him. He desires that the numerals which he has himself counted on his fingers and christened 'two and two' should make three and five according to his varying needs and moods . . . In other words, we want to be independent of the facts; and the younger we are the more intolerant we are of those who tell us that this is impossible.[42]

Most of us, indeed, will find that it *is* impossible. Some (and who can tell beforehand who they will be?) will follow their dream, their fiction, their God away from what was imagined to be unchangeably the case, and find a new world waiting. 'These were men who intended to own themselves, in obedience to some dream, teaching or word which had come to them'—and we had best not fight against them![43]

> I'll not fight with the Herald of God
> (I know what his Master can do!)
> Open the gate, he must enter in state,
> 'Tis the Dreamer whose dreams come true![44]

That dreaming and demanding presence refuses to accept Things as They Are, or as they are seen to be. Kipling, he said, 'visualised [the Empire], as [he did] most ideas, in the shape of a semicircle of buildings and temples projecting into a sea—of dreams'.[45] On the one hand, this is folly: 'for every dreamer whose dreams have been good . . . there are thousands who have been a hindrance to themselves, an expense to their families and a nuisance to mankind'.[46] On the other hand, it is the source of all improvements, and all mercy. So the lama pursues his entirely fictional River, till the world invents it for him. So science pursues

'the dream of an essential unity of all created things, . . .
the boldest dream of all, that eventually Man might surprise
the ultimate secret of his being where Brahm had hidden
it, in the body of Man'.[47] So the explorer follows God's
Whisper:

> Then I knew, the while I doubted—knew His Hand was
> certain o'er me.
> Still—it might be self-delusion—scores of better men had
> died—
> I could reach the township living, but . . . He knows what
> terror tore me . . .
> But I didn't . . . but I didn't. I went down the other
> side . . .
> I remember going crazy. I remember that I knew
> it
> When I heard myself hallooing to the funny folk I
> saw.
> *Very full of dreams that desert*, but my two legs took me
> through it . . .
> And I used to watch 'em moving with the toes all black and
> raw.[48]

Truth matters, but so does Fiction. And Kipling had reason to
suspect that many who mocked fiction were themselves deluded.
A grimy realism, 'a ram-you-damn-you-liner with a brace of
bucking screws' will never reach the Islands of the Blest that
are achieved by 'the old three-decker', the romantic three-volume
novel.[49]

Science fictional devices, I suggested, often flow from a
more ancient metaphysics, which reflects this demanding
dream, that we can lay our hands upon the engines of
the world, or pray down the gods. Telepathy and interstellar travel alike are often referred to some Other Place,
where all places are coincident. If only we could enter
that Place, in thought or body, we could exit it wherever
we might please. All minds, and times, and places are a
step away.[50] Again, the pattern of stars and human history are caused by the acts of fire-folk overhead: galactic
empires, Elder Races, gods. Machinery itself can speak the
thoughts of greater intellects than ours. We ourselves will
one day speak the thoughts of greater intellects. All these
dreams give shape to the demand that things be Different,

and to the conviction that How They Are depends upon a dream.

> Read here the story of Evarra—man—
> Maker of Gods in lands beyond the sea.

Evarra makes 'four wondrous Gods', declaiming on each occasion 'Thus Gods are made, /and whoso makes them otherwise shall die'.

> Yet at the last he came to Paradise,
> And found his own four Gods, and that he wrote,
> And marvelled, being very near to God,
> What oaf on earth had made his toil God's law,
> Till God said mocking: 'Mock not. These be thine.'
> Then cried Evarra: 'I have sinned!' 'Not so.
> If thou hadst written otherwise, thy Gods
> Had rested in the mountain and the mire,
> And I were poorer by four wondrous Gods,
> And thy more wondrous law, Evarra. Thine,
> Servant of shouting crowds and lowing kine!'
> Thereat, with laughing mouth, but tear-wet eyes,
> Evarra cast his Gods from Paradise.[51]

The 'two sides to [Kipling's] head' ensure that he always gives due weight to both convictions: that we cannot stand against the Truth, and that we sometimes must.[52] There is perhaps a possible resolution of the conflict, in the notion that there is indeed a God who calls us out from former certainties, but also requires a proper reverence for ordinary life. The lust for something New and Different, something that the Squire and Parson will not understand, is an important force in science fiction, and in Kipling: the lust for something new, and the knowledge that it will happen whether we lust for it or not. Those old before their time, 'the Old Men' of Kipling's poem, may forget the obvious:

> We shall not acknowledge that old stars fade or brighter planets arise
> (That the sere bush buds or the desert blooms or the ancient well-head dries),
> Or any new compass wherewith new men adventure 'neath new skies.[53]

Science fiction is a genre that has chosen not to forget the obvious. Kipling is a precursor of that genre, in the devices and plot-lines he contrives, in the pleasure he takes in alien worlds and new machinery, in the political ideas he uses India and elsewhere to explore, and in the philosophical concerns his fantasies reveal. Some authors of Kipling's day employed their talents to express a fear that there were things 'we were not meant to know'. 'Kim laughed. "He is new. Run to your mothers' laps, and be safe."'[54] Others closer to our own have chosen to despise those small and ordinary people, those too tired, or dull, or timid to escape. Kipling, as far as I can see, did neither. He did not despise the ordinary (only the complacent), and ensures that Kim at last returns to his (and our) Mother's lap, 'the good clean . . . dust the hopeful dust that holds the seed of all life'.[55] It is the oldest things that are always new: Krishna and Mother Earth. And they are to be found at last in our familiar places, won back from despair, as Kim wins back the world.

NOTES

1. I know only one other science fictional Kim, in David Wingrove's epic, *Chung Kuo: The Middle Kingdom* (London, 1989), and its sequels: the reference is explicit, but that Kim is more like a debased Mowgli.

2. *Kim* (London, 1901), p.24.

3. *Rudyard Kipling's Verse 1885–1926* (London, 1927), pp.252ff.

4. *Actions and Reactions* (London, 1951), p.138.

5. Angus Wilson, *The Strange Ride of Rudyard Kipling* (London, 1977), p.247.

6. 'McDonough's Song', *Verse*, pp.546ff.

7. *A Diversity of Creatures* (London, 1917), p.5.

8. L. Neil Smith, *The Probability Broach* (New York, 1980).

9. Edgar Allan Poe had imagined a similar system, in 'Mellonta Tauta' (1849).

10. Wilson, p.333.

11. W.H. Auden, 'The History of Science', *Collected Shorter Poems 1927–57* (London, 1966), p.306.

12. See also 'In the Rukh', in *Many Inventions* (1893). This story entirely refutes C. Scheerer's suggestion that 'Mowgli at the end is a tortured youth', unable to conceive of a happy adult life ('The Lost Paradise of Rudyard Kipling', in *Rudyard Kipling's 'Kim'*, ed. Harold

Bloom (New York, 1987), pp.75—85, 76. On the contrary, he is a good husband, father and forest ranger, and is depicted thus by Lockwood Kipling even in *The Jungle Book*.

13. 'The earth is iron and the skies are brass': 'The Masque of Plenty', in *Verse*, p.36.

14. 'England and the English', *A Book of Words* (London, 1928), p.181.

15. *Kim*, p.40: this fear was one of the factors in the Mutiny, which was therefore as much *in favour* of oppression, as against it.

16. *Kim*, p.91.

17. 'We and They', *Verse*, pp.709ff.

18. *A Book of Words*, p.181.

19. *Kim*, p.303: this is not, of course, the *only* English type.

20. In the earliest known version he had other ingrained European habits, which Kipling fortunately eliminated, along with far too many patronizing comments on the lama: see M.P. Feeley, 'The *Kim* that Nobody Reads', in Bloom, pp.57—74.

21. *Kim*, p.369.

22. *Kim*, p.411.

23. Robert Silverberg, *Valentine Pontifex* (London, 1984), pp.339ff.

24. Edward Said, *Culture and Imperialism* (London, 1993), p.172 (my italics).

25. *Just So Stories* (London, 1908), pp.208ff. The sea monsters of 'A Matter of Fact' are sadder creatures.

26. *Verse*, pp.103ff.

27. 'The Masque of Plenty', *Verse*, pp.35ff.

28. *Kim*, p.5.

29. Alexis de Tocqueville, *Democracy in America*, ed. H.S. Commager (London, 1946), p.9.

30. *The Faded Sun* (1978–79), published in three parts, subtitled *Kesrith*, *Shon'jir* and *Kutath*. On Anderson see, for example, *The Enemy Stars* (1968), *No Truce with Kings* (1963).

31. The latter in Ursula Le Guin, *The Dispossessed* (1974).

32. 'The English Flag' (1891), *Verse*, p.218.

33. 'The Old Issue', *Verse*, p.294.

34. *Verse*, p.453.

35. 'Puck's Song', *Verse*, p.481.

36. 'Work in the Future', *A Book of Words*, p.259.

37. Cf. S.R.L. Clark, 'Olaf Stapledon (1886–1950)', *Interdisciplinary Science Reviews*, 18 (1993), pp.112–19.

38. 'Poseidon's Law', *Verse*, pp.631ff.

39. 'The Secret of the Machines', *Verse*, pp.675ff.

40. 'Fiction', *A Book of Words*, p.282.

41. 'Independence', *A Book of Words*, p.234.

42. *A Book of Words*, p.235.

43. *A Book of Words*, p.243.

44. 'The Fairies' Siege', *Verse*, p.508.

45. Cited, without reference, by James Morris, *Pax Britannica* (London, 1986), p.255.

46. 'The Uses of Reading', *A Book of Words*, p.93.

47. 'Surgeons and the Soul', *A Book of Words*, p.227.

48. *Verse*, pp.104ff. (my italics).

49. 'The Three Decker' (1894), *Verse*, pp.327ff.; an image splendidly realized in Michael Scott Rohan's *Chase the Morning* (London, 1990) and its two sequels.

50. See Poul Anderson, *World Without Stars* (1966); Orson Scott Card, *Xenocide* (1992); Melissa Scott, *Five Twelfths of Heaven* (1986), and its sequels.

51. 'Evarra and his Gods', *Verse*, pp.335ff.

52. *Verse*, p.568.

53. *Verse*, p.318.

54. *Kim*, p.8.

55. *Kim*, p.404.

Lesbians and Virgins: The New Motherhood in *Herland*

VAL GOUGH

> We will be the New Mothers of a New World
> *Charlotte Perkins Gilman*

In her autobiography, Charlotte Perkins Gilman relates the significance that the realm of the imagination and fantasy had to her as a child: 'Of all those childish years the most important step was this, I learned the use of a constructive imagination'.[1] Not only did her 'brain-building' provide her with a sense of control which she lacked in her everyday life, closely regulated as it was by her mother, but it afforded an imaginary space for her 'scheming to improve the world', reflecting her precocious sense of social responsibility. But Gilman's utopian envisioning, which she shared with all who would listen, suffered an abrupt suppression at the age of thirteen when her mother decreed that she give it up:

> Just thirteen. This had been my chief happiness for five years. It was by far the largest, most active part of my mind. I was called upon to close off the main building as it were and live in the 'L'. No one could tell if I did it or not, it was an inner fortress, open only to me . . .
> But obedience was Right, the thing had to be done, and I did it. Night after night to shut the door on happiness, and hold it shut. Never, when dear, bright, glittering dreams pushed hard, to let them in. Just thirteen . . .[2]

Gilman did not relinquish her fantasies, but transformed their medium, developing an urgent desire for access to written discourse, symbolized by a coveted pen 'of unparalleled beauty'.[3] Her mother's command spurred her more determinedly towards her goal of writing and speaking for the public good, a realm of language associated with her absent and literary father (and with her father's family line, the Beechers), with whom she often explicitly identified.[4] Years later, by now a prolific writer and lecturer on feminism and Nationalism,[5] Gilman wrote the utopian novel *Herland* (1915), a text inscribed with the effects of the ambivalence she felt throughout her life towards her (present yet unsatisfactory) mother and her (absent yet idealized) father, and the mythic associations of these two figures. Attracted by the realm of the mother *and* the father, Gilman had utopian hopes for both, and *Herland* is a fictional negotiation of two parallel utopian impulses: her private lesbian fantasies of female nurturance, and her public belief in the potential transformation of heterosexual social structures. *Herland* is thus both a fictional fantasy of utopian lesbian motherhood, and a stunning critique of the hetero-patriarchal social structure used in the service of her other utopian ideal, the 'fully human' heterosexual subject.

Herland's critique is achieved by exploiting the typical utopian technique of estrangement:[6] hearing tales of a mysterious hidden land inhabited only by women, three young would-be explorers, Terry, Jeff and Van, arrive in a previously undiscovered all-female community which they dub 'Herland', to find all their most precious sexist assumptions reversed and subverted by its evident superiority. All three characters function as male-chauvinist types: Terry is a wealthy exploitative womanizer, aggressive and predatory in his sexual objectification of women. Jeff also stereotypes women through romantic adulation and idealization,[7] and Van, a sociologist who likes to think of himself as an objective man of reason, functions as the narrator flawed by his residual sexism. Roles are reversed as the men find themselves disempowered, and treated like (Herlander) children, mirroring the way women are treated in patriarchy. Gilman appropriates for feminist ends the trope of role reversal found in early science fictions (which tended to reinforce gender stereotypes), and in this she anticipates its use by later feminist writers such as Esmé Dodderidge, whose novel *The New Gulliver, or The Adventures of Lemuel Gulliver Jr. in Capavolta*[8] reveals the absurdities and iniquities of contemporary sexist society. The Herlanders set to work to 'educate' the men by teaching them their language and explaining their culture and social system, in the hope that the men will reciprocate with details of their own 'bi-sexual' world: ' . . . we soon found from their earnest questions that they were prepared to believe our world must be better than theirs. They

were not sure; they wanted to know; but there was no such arrogance about them as might have been expected.'[9]

A dialogue characteristic of the utopian genre destabilizes and
deconstructs the men's (and the reader's) patriarchal assumptions,
whose attitudes are transformed by varying degrees according to
the extent of their male chauvinism. Terry's sexism proves recal-
citrant and he never ceases to interpret Herland in sexist terms,
finally being expelled from Herland for attempted rape.[10] Jeff's
attitude to the women remains one of courtly love, and his
worship of them indicates a residual sexism despite his thorough
assimilation to their world. Van's transformation parallels that of
the implied reader, and when the men fall in love with three
Herlanders, it is Van and Ellador's relationship which confronts
most extensively the patriarchal nature of heterosexuality.

Herland is not a feminist blueprint for the future, but a fantasy
of what would happen if motherhood was conceived otherwise
than in hetero-patriarchal terms; it is a lesbian-feminist vision of
the nurturing and collective capacities of women:

> 'Here we have Human Motherhood—in full working use,'
> she went on.
> 'Nothing else except the literal sisterhood of our origin, and
> the far higher and deeper union of our social growth.
> 'The children in this country are the one center and focus
> of all our thoughts.
> Every step of our advance is always considered in its
> effect on them—on the race. You see, we are *Mothers*,' she
> repeated, as if in that she had said it all. (p.66)

The Herlanders are clearly lesbians as conceived by the utopian
separatist lesbianism of the late 1970s, which stressed the col-
lectivity of lesbian identity and perceived women's needs as
nurturance and interrelatedness, articulated in terms of the desire
for the pre-oedipal mother.[11] Sonya Andermahr says: 'Many
utopian separatist writings speak in mythical terms about female
identity, invoking myths of re-birth and mutual self-creation'.[12]
The intense and communitarian emotional bonds of the Herlander
women also anticipate Adrienne Rich's notion of the lesbian continuum.[13] It is, however, important to note that Gilman's vision
manifests the racism and classism which also characterized the
kind of unified lesbian identity conceptualized by the largely
white, middle-class lesbian feminism of the late 1970s. Gilman
never challenged conventional notions of the stable, monolithic

subject, and in *Herland* the utopian subject is both unified and
Aryan. Quick to question many of the gender assumptions
of her day, Gilman never questioned class and race hierarchies:
her vision of domestic freedom for middle-class women depended
upon working-class women taking over their domestic tasks, and
throughout her life she was a firm believer in theories of race evolution, whereby some races were thought to be less well-developed
towards full civilization than others. Nevertheless, *Herland*'s vision
of lesbian motherhood enabled Gilman to extrapolate the utopian
potentials of what she saw as innate female traits of nurturance,
and to imagine female identity untainted by internalized hetero-
patriarchal values.[14] It is also a feminist critique of the masculinist
fictions of the Amazon as feared and loathed Other, as castrating
mother.

In its vision of a motherhood conceived otherwise, Gilman's
Herland was continuing a tradition of feminist utopian writers who
explored alternative child-rearing and reproductive arrangements,
and proposed ethical value-systems associated with mothering as
the force empowering social amelioration.[15] In *A Sex Revolution*,
published in 1894, Lois Nichols Waisbrooker depicts the dream
vision of a female narrator in which women revolt against men,
seize control by pacifist means and work to establish a new utopian
social order, free from poverty, war and oppression: ' . . . things
that have resulted from the lack of the mother element'.[16] Mother
love is idealized in religious terms as a spiritual and ethical force
for social improvement:

> 'Man's forte is force, woman's love: suppose that force
> yields the reins of love?'
> 'Love is a syren: her dalliance leads to death if followed
> too far,' he said contemptuously.
> 'Alas,' she replied, 'how little you men understand love!
> With woman in the lead, love's true law will be learned, and
> man will cease to grovel in the dust of passion, unsanctified
> either by moral purpose or spiritual life. Then the central,
> the creative love, out of which all other loves spring, will
> become a refining instead of a consuming fire. It will then
> be like the bush that Moses saw, which burned and was not
> consumed, a glorifying fire, an uplifting power, a quickener
> in our search after truth.'[17]

A Sex Revolution manifests the feminist development of the spiritual
associations of mother-love which Gilman continues and refines

in *Herland*. Another feminist utopian novel, *Reinstern* (1900) by Eloise O. Randall Richberg, is centrally concerned with alternative child care arrangements, and it mirrors Gilman's notion of professionalized child care which she developed in numerous lectures, and in her book *Concerning Children* (1900). *Reinstern* portrays a utopian planet where parenting skills are developed through training viewed as a prerequisite to marriage. Both sexes are trained (whereas Gilman never advocated male mothering), and biological parents are not solely responsible for their children but receive support from other trained parents, enabling them to continue work outside the home as well. In a similar vein, *Other Worlds* by Lena Jane Fry (1905) depicts a communitarian society called 'The Colony' which also develops the notion of professionalized child care. Members of The Colony make use of its nursery where professionally trained staff care for the children, ensuring that childrearing is competent and allowing women a measure of economic independence by freeing them for work.

Gilman's first utopian novel, *Moving The Mountain* (1911), includes detailed nursery and child garden arrangements, but it is in *Herland* that a fusion of these two strands of feminist thinking on motherhood—the spiritual ideal of mother-love and notions of collectivized and professionalized child care—most effectively occurs. *Herland* is a forerunner[18] of later feminist utopian fiction and feminist fiction, particularly in its concentration on motherhood as a key feminist issue. Novels such as *Motherlines* (1974) by Suzy McKee Charnas, *The Wanderground* (1979) by Sally Miller Gearhart, and *Woman on the Edge of Time* (1976) by Marge Piercy, all examine collective mothering practices and the spirituality of motherhood. And in its utopian affirmation and celebration of female bonding, *Herland* is the precursor of later depictions of lesbian-separatist worlds, most notably Gearhart's *The Wanderground*, Katherine V. Forrest's *Daughters of a Coral Dawn* (1984), Joanna Russ's *The Female Man* (1976), Rochelle Singer's *The Demeter Flower* (1980), Monique Wittig's *Les Guérillères* (1979), and Donna J. Young's *Retreat! As It Was* (1979).

Gilman's treatment of motherhood in *Herland* reflects her own experiences of motherhood, both as a daughter and as a mother. Her own mother was paradigmatic of all that Gilman was later in her life to reject, '... femininely attractive in the highest degree',[19] yet according to Gilman, her life '... was one of the most painfully thwarted I have ever known'.[20] Deserted by her husband when medical advice prevented him from having sex

with her and forced to move nineteen times in eighteen years,
Mary Perkins responded to this emotional neglect by evolving a
method of parenting which involved repressing all outward manifestations of tenderness to her daughter:

> . . . suffering for the lack of a husband's love, she hero-
> ically determined that her baby daughter should not so
> suffer if she could help it. Her method was to deny the
> child all expression of affection as far as possible, so that
> she should not be used to it or long for it. 'I used to put
> away your little hand from my cheek when you were a
> nursing baby,' she told me in later years; 'I did not want
> you to suffer as I had suffered.' She would not let me caress
> her, and would not caress me, unless I was asleep. This I
> discovered at last, and then did my best to keep awake
> till she came to bed, even using pins to prevent dropping
> off, and sometimes succeeding. Then how carefully I pre-
> tended to be sound asleep, and how rapturously I enjoyed
> being gathered into her arms, held close and kissed.[21]

This emotional deprivation led Gilman to conclude that however
well-meaning, however devoted a mother may be, good intentions are not always sufficient: 'If love, devotion to duty,
sublime self-sacrifice, were enough in child-culture, mothers
would achieve better results; but there is another requisite
too often lacking—knowledge'.[22] Gilman's own experiences as
a mother reinforced this view. Gilman gave birth to Katharine
Stetson in 1885 but was unable to care for her due to mental
breakdown caused by the impossible constraints of conventional
marriage and motherhood. A few years later, when Gilman was
living alone with Katharine and supporting herself through writing
and lecturing, she decided that her daughter would be better raised
by her ex-husband Walter and his new wife Grace Channing (a
life-long friend of Gilman). The press and public reviled her as
an 'unnatural mother' who had 'deserted her child', but Gilman
never wavered in her belief that merely to love the child does
not serve the child, and that conceptions of motherhood should
be enlarged beyond individual concerns.[23]

For Gilman, the mother was 'that eternal amateur',[24] entrusted
with the most important human work, yet given no training to
help her accomplish it effectively. Aptitude for child care she
believed not to be innate: 'the special genius for child care is not
common to all women'.[25] So she advocated the professionalization

of 'baby culture' and the setting up of 'baby gardens', where women with special aptitude for the 'science' and trained for the task would during working hours care for and educate children.[26] She criticized society for confining women to the home and motherhood, and forcing women to specialize in 'sex-functions' alone: 'The more absolutely woman is segregated to sex-functions only, cut off from all economic use and made wholly dependent on the sex-relation as a means of livelihood, the more pathological does her motherhood become'.[27] Gilman eschewed assumptions of innate maternal instincts only to the extent that she believed not all women have an aptitude for the task of responsible child care. Unlike later, more radical feminist theorists of motherhood, such as Dorothy Dinnerstein, Nancy Chodorow, Mary O'Brien and Sarah Ruddick,[28] Gilman never advocated male participation in child care. And she frequently asserted that motherhood was the 'normal' role for all women, the 'common duty and the common glory of womanhood'. So although she did not reinforce the stereotype of mothers as natural nurturers, she did reinforce the traditional sexual division of labour. This separatism in the sphere of child care sprang from her belief in an innate female principle, one which she believed needed to be harnessed and developed for the improvement of the race as a whole. For Gilman did not simply seek the professionalization and collectivization of motherhood; she sought to revolutionize its fundamental purpose. She saw mothers as a potential collective political and social force: 'the union of motherhood'[29] would work together 'for a higher human type'.[30] Like Edward Bellamy and the Nationalists, Gilman drew on the key premises of progressive Darwinism: that people are rational and social; that environment determines character; that societies evolve progressively; and that violent revolution is not necessary. She collected together her ideas on child care and its utopian purposes in *Concerning Children* (1900), where she delivered her most extensive critique of traditional forms of raising children, by discipline and obedience, and called for the creation of a process and an environment that encouraged independent thought. She brought together her evolutionary and religious theories to formulate an ethical motherhood—'the New Motherhood'—and she made strong statements for transmitted traits. Refuting August Weismann, who argued in his *Essays Upon Heredity* (1889) that the determinant of character was a germ plasm, basically immortal and inviolable, sealed off from the effects of experience, she posited that new and improved traits inculcated in the child would then be transmitted to succeeding generations. 'New' mothers would enact a conscious eugenics, selecting only suitable men to reproduce: 'We will breed a better stock on earth by proper selection—that is a mother's duty!'.[31] Eschewing the free-love movement, she advocated birth control through conscious sexual restraint. Disseminating her theories of the hetero-sexual New Motherhood through public speaking, social theory and non-fiction, Gilman also chose to concretize and literalize her theories most extensively in fictional form, most notably in *Herland*.[32]

The all-female community which Terry, Van and Jeff dub 'Herland' is described as 'a land in a state of perfect cultivation', 'an enormous park', 'an enormous garden' (p.11). Thus Herland draws on associations with the Edenic, paradisal mother's body, and is the utopic literalization of Gilman's metaphor of cultivation which she frequently used to describe child care or 'baby culture'.[33] It is the concretization of her theories of inherited traits and selective breeding, for the Herlanders have eliminated many undesirable masculine and feminine characteristics through selective breeding and education:

> . . . very early they recognized the need of improvement as well as of mere repetition, and devoted their combined intelligence to that problem—how to make the best kind of people. First this was merely the hope of bearing better ones, and then they recognized that however the children differed at birth, the real growth lay later—through education.
> Then things began to hum. (p.59)

Herlander reproduction is by parthenogenesis, which has been described as a cliché of separatist fiction,[34] but Gilman uses it more specifically as a fictional exemplification of the way individual will and environment can change what is considered as biological fact and 'human nature'[35]: the Herlanders are described as '. . . developing unknown powers in the stress of new necessity' (p.56). Their practice of 'negative eugenics' to restrict population numbers is also based on individual will used for the common good:

> . . . before a child comes to one of us there is a period of utter exaltation—the whole being is uplifted and filled with a concentrated desire for that child. We learned to look forward to that period with the greatest caution. Often our

young women, those to whom motherhood had not yet come, would voluntarily defer it. (p.70)

Gilman depicts mothers devoid of active sexuality in any conventional sense, reflecting her belief in humanity's over-sexed stage of development. But she hints at the erotic potential of a transformed motherhood: an 'utter exaltation', a 'deep inner demand' (p.70). Such a 'sexuality otherwise' anticipates later feminist redefinitions of female sexuality and the body. Both conventional motherhood and its conventional locale, the home, are redefined and extended so that the race is viewed as the family and the whole of Herland viewed as its home. Children are raised by their biological mothers and their co-mothers: women whose special vocation is the education and nurturance of children. And motherhood has become a religion, a sacred vocation which parallels the processes of nature:

> Here was Mother Earth, bearing fruit. All that they ate was fruit of motherhood, from seed or egg or their product. By motherhood they were born and by motherhood they lived—life was, to them, just the long cycle of motherhood. (p.59)

Gilman's interest in the spirituality of motherhood derives partly from Edward Bellamy's Nationalism with its emphasis on spiritual as well as social development, partly from her own personal self-evolved religion, partly from her vision of a female-oriented 'religion' which she discusses in *His Religion and Hers* (1923), and partly from her feminist utopianism. She can be seen as part of a tradition of feminist utopian writers for whom envisioning alternatives is a political and spiritual imperative, for whom, as Adelaide Proctor says: 'Dreams grow holy when put in action'.[36] Several analyses of utopias by women consider these to be intrinsically spiritual,[37] and it has been argued that the quest for women's liberation is a spiritual quest.[38] Sandra Gilbert has proposed a feminist tradition of 'revisionary theology' in which women writers 'reappropriate and valorize metaphors of uniquely female creativity and primacy'.[39] In Gilman's celebration of spiritual motherhood and the uniquely female powers associated with it there are the seeds of the feminist spirituality movement which developed in the late 1960s, and which finds fictional form in feminist science fiction and utopian fiction such as Sally Miller Gearhart's *The Wanderground* (1979) and Penny Casdagli's 'Mab' (1985).[40]

In 'Coming Home: Four Feminist Utopias and Patriarchal Experience',[41] Carol Pearson views feminist utopias, including *Herland*, Mary Bradley Lane's *Mizora: A Prophecy*, Dorothy Bryant's *The Kin of Ata are Waiting for You*, and Mary Staton's *From The Legend of Biel*, as exploring a process of 'coming home', which she argues 'signifies both coming home to the self and coming home to mother, finding unity and integration, and a respect for the individual. . . .'.[42] In *Herland* we can also see in its nascent form this feminist appropriation of the utopian myth of the return to the mother which Hélène Cixous has also so strikingly explored.[43] Van, who becomes almost an honorary Herlander, describes his gradually developing ability to feel and appreciate the special 'love' the Herlanders can give, which can be interpreted in terms of the original closeness of the mother-child dyad:

> It was like—coming home to mother. I don't mean the underflannels-and-doughnuts mother, the fussy person that waits on you and doesn't really know you. I mean the feeling that a very little child would have, who had been lost—for ever so long. It was a sense of getting home; of being clean and rested; of safety and yet freedom; of love that was always there, warm like sunshine in May, not hot like a stove or a featherbed—a love that didn't irritate and didn't smother. (p.142)

In its redefinition of love, *Herland* looks forward to the feminist utopias of the 1970s, which depict alternatives to patriarchal concepts of love. Similarly, Cixous seeks to redefine love and she relates it to the pre-oedipal mother, advocating a return to the paradise or utopia of the mother in writing.[44] Gilman does not fully explore the utopian potentials of the distinctly female language which the Herlanders speak and write, apart from portraying it as the perfect medium for communication and growth. Nevertheless, Gilman's novel is a 'mother-text' in that it fulfils all the functions of her idealized mothering, as well as depicting them. The text itself enacts a mothering process upon its implied reader, who must 'grow' ideologically in the same way that Jeff, and particularly Van, as narrator, 'grow'.[45] In this sense the novel 'calls' its readers in a similar way to Cixous's view of 'feminine' texts which call their readers to construct themselves as 'feminine'/feminist subjects. Like the child in Gilman's proposed baby-garden, the reader is constructed or 'nurtured' as an active and transforming subject. Herland's history mirrors this process, for it is one of character development: 'We are at work, slowly and carefully, developing out whole people along these lines' (p.105). Just as the trained mother is adaptable to change, the novel avoids the danger of stasis (which as Northrop Frye notes, is a tendency of many utopias)[46] by making Herland open to change. The Herlanders have a history of social change which challenges the conservative ideological assumption that the social status quo is natural and inevitable, and they are open to social change if they consider it beneficial: they risk dialogue with the men and consider the future potentials of a return to 'bi-sexuality'.

In its enactment of a textual 'mothering' process, *Herland* functions as a lesbian narrative space, for the depiction of women's bonding functions as a powerful tool for subverting hetero-patriarchal narrative codes: as Rachel Blau DuPlessis says ' . . . the erotic and emotional intensity of women's friendship cuts the Gordian knots of both heterosexuality and narrative convention'.[47] Such patriarchal narrative structures as the heroic quest and the romance are structured by gender difference and predicated upon the ultimately heterosexual dichotomies which structure Western thought: active/passive, mind/body, presence/absence, male/female.[48] Notions of a lesbian discursive space which would deconstruct such hetero-patriarchal structures function as the utopian 'other' in much recent feminist theory and writing. Nicole Brossard, for example, deploys the term 'lesbian' to denote the visionary potential of hitherto unexplored female desire.[49] Nancy K. Miller says: ' . . . [it] may also be that the difference of another coming to writing requires an outside to hetero-sexual economies'.[50] And Monique Wittig argues that 'Lesbian' is that space which is 'not-woman', a space not dependent on gendered binary oppositions.[51] Gilman's novel and its utopian world both function as lesbian narrative spaces. Terry, Jeff and Van see themselves as the masculine heroes of a conventional ('not unnatural') quest for female prey. Their entry into the lesbian space of Herland, however, deconstructs their heroic and romantic fictions of the male self. Herland makes them feel effeminate, feminized. Yet femininity is also deconstructed, and the men—to varying degrees—must construct a sense of identity beyond traditional hetero-patriarchal gender roles.[52]

The novel itself functions as a lesbian narrative space for it provides a critique of hetero-patriarchal institutions, undercutting the structure of gender difference and evacuating the hetero-patriarchal meanings from conventional gender-terms such as 'mother', 'woman' and 'feminine'. Through its structure it destabilizes hetero-patriarchal narrative conventions such as the authoritative male narrator, and heterosexual romantic closure. Gilman's narrator draws attention right from the start to the inadequacies of his (overtly subjective) narrative: 'This is written from memory, unfortunately' (p.1). We are reminded that whatever does not correspond to the patriarchal gender category 'Woman' will exceed discourse: 'Descriptions are never any good when it comes to women' (p.1). Yet Gilman does not dispense with the authoritative male narrator; she preserves the role only to place it under erasure by revealing the sexism of Van's supposed 'objectivity'. In her own life Gilman seized the authoritative male speaking role (disseminating her ideas through extensive lecture tours) in order to deconstruct the patriarchal structure. In *Herland* she manipulates the authoritative male voice so that reflection upon its narrative use is incorporated into the text. Gilman places the conventional romantic narrative structure under erasure by leaving the outcome of the couples' struggles to achieve traditional romantic heterosexual harmony open and uncertain. The reader is forced to accept the provisionality both of the closure of utopian narrative itself, and of the heterosexual romantic coupling that occurs. By ending the novel with the imminent departure of Van and Ellador from Herland, Gilman avoids containment of the narrative within the utopian world, which would situate the reader passively in relation to the utopian text. Whereas most contemporary utopias were located in the future, Gilman locates hers in a geographically other space. By depicting the aggressive penetration of the separatist space of Herland by three male 'explorers', Gilman dramatizes the way in which female space is always under threat from masculinist colonization. Terry's quasi-sexual desire to penetrate Herland—'He was hot about it' (p.6)—parallels his later attempted rape of Alima, revealing the violent basis of male heterosexual desire. Thus *Herland* functions as an ironic revision of narratives of exploration (exemplified by those of Conan Doyle and H.G. Wells) which, by privileging male physical prowess and action, reinforced heterosexist gender stereotypes. Gilman contrasts the abortive attempts at action of the three men with the highly effective communal and non-aggressive action of the women.

The geographical rather than temporal displacement of the utopian state in *Herland* reflects Gilman's interest in the idea of female space: influenced by the architectural determinism of Fourier and his followers, she proposed the feminist apartment hotel, with private suites without kitchens, served by professionalized cooking facilities, as the ideal spatial setting for feminist motherhood. In her short story 'The Cottagette', Gilman portrays the influence of architecture and space on women. The geographical location of Herland also reflects Gilman's desire to highlight the immediate social relevance of her vision. She had earlier criticized Bellamy's utopian novel *Looking Backward*[53] for encouraging readers to read its utopia as a blueprint rather than as a critique of contemporary society, contrasting his '. . . kind of laborious detailed explanation of exactly how things are going to be . . .'[54] with her preferred technique: 'I like a few salient and relevant facts—and then far seeing generalization. Safe but swift and light in touch'.[55] Gilman's purpose was always social improvement through social critique, and the reader of *Herland* is never tempted to read Herland as a blueprint, partly because of the narrator's unreliability and obvious subjectivity, and partly because of the gaps and omissions in the account. Herland is not a blueprint, but 'a strategy in this engagement with the real . . .'.[56]

If *Herland* functions as a lesbian narrative space, it can also be said that Gilman's exploration of the New Motherhood in the novel reflects her ambivalence towards what in her own life functioned as the separate realms of lesbianism and hetero-sexuality. She was attracted by the nurturance of a separate female sphere, which she enjoyed through lesbian relationships and a series of mother-substitutes which she found in strong, older women, but she also felt trapped by its domesticity. Despite her feminism, Gilman denigrated women's domestic achievements and frequently criticized women for being less-than-fully adult and less-than-fully human. Despite her lesbianism, it was her second marriage which she described as 'the happy ending',[57] and she seized the tools of authority of the male sphere, entering the male-dominated field of economics and disseminating her views through public speaking, although her entry into this realm was precisely in order to criticize it. Her ambivalence, both sexual and social, and her attraction to both realms without any ability to reconcile the two, is reflected in the contradictory logic of her theories: on the one hand she believed that 'mas-culine' traits are human traits, on the other she argued for a need to restore the 'original balance' by re-emphasizing what she saw as female values of nurturance and co-operation. In *Herland*, Gilman's utopian fantasy of lesbian-separatism coexists with a further utopian vision, of heterosexual coexistence with men. She portrays women whose lesbian separatism has enabled them to develop total independence in all spheres, and who then face the challenge of maintaining that independence as heterosexuals. Does this mean that, finally, *Herland* retreats from a subversive lesbianism into the romantic closure of heterosexuality, reinforcing those very gendered binaries which Gilman sought to deconstruct? A more profitable reading is to acknowledge that Gilman posits the possibility of a radicalized female heterosexual indentity. The novel portrays women in the process of becoming what Marilyn Frye has termed 'Willful Virgins'.

Raising the question, 'do you have to be a lesbian to be a feminist?', Marilyn Frye posits an imaginary possibility: wholly independent yet heterosexual women, 'wild, undomesticated females'.[58] Frye reminds us that '[t]he word "virgin" did not originally mean a woman whose vagina was untouched by any penis, but a free woman, one not betrothed, not married, not bound to, not possessed by any man. It meant a female who is sexually and hence socially her own person'.[59] 'Willful Virgins' are free heterosexual women, almost a contradiction in terms, or what Frye calls 'impossible beings'. They are imaginary, utopian women whose answer to Frye's question 'Can you fuck without losing your virginity?'[60] would be an emphatic yes! In her own life, and despite her lesbian desires, Gilman also tried to be a Willful Virgin. Her fundamental belief was in female economic independence as the essential basis of women's liberation and consequent improvement of the race as a whole. This is the overarching concept of *Women and Economics* (1898), and it is a theme which she returned to again and again in her shorter fiction, most notably in 'What Diantha Did' (1909–10), which portrays a woman struggling to win and then keep her economic independence in marriage. In her own life, economic independence was the foundation upon which all that she achieved rested. When approaching (with some ambivalent reluctance) her first marriage, she asked her husband whether he would mind if she worked. Walter Stetson *did* mind, and the constraints of marriage and motherhood, which Stetson subtly imposed and which Gilman thought her duty to embrace, finally led to Gilman's mental breakdown and their separation. But throughout her life, Gilman strove for independence, and one of the fundamental tenets of her philosophy of child education was the encouragement of independent thought. Gilman's first attempt to 'fuck without losing her virginity' nearly cost her her sanity (her struggle with mental breakdown is fictionally portrayed in *The Yellow Wallpaper* (1892)). Despite this, and despite her lesbianism, she also strove after this heterosexual feminist utopian ideal, which she finally achieved to some extent in her second, unconventional marriage. In this heterosexual relationship she finally fully relinquished the internalized patriarchal expectations of wifely duty and confronted the fact that '. . . to uncompromisingly embody and enact a radical feminism. . . you. . . cannot be heterosexual in the standard meaning of the word—you cannot be any version of a patriarchal wife. Lesbian or not, to embody and enact a consistent and all-the-way feminism you have to be a heretic, a deviant, an undomesticated female, an impossible being. You have to be a Virgin.'[61] And in *Herland*, Gilman portrays lesbian women in the process of becoming Willful Virgins.

The question that Gilman poses to the society of her time (and to herself) at the end of the novel—a question which remains unanswered—is this: can women keep their Virginity after they have lost their virginity? By leaving the question unanswered, the narrative structure of *Herland* militates against reading the novel as a retreat into heterosexual romantic closure. *Herland*'s radicalized heterosexual ideal remains textually 'impossible', deferred beyond the end of the text.[62] It is the as yet unattained ideal for which the couples must continue to strive. In her own narrative of her life, her autobiography, Gilman portrayed heterosexuality as its romantic closure: '. . . we were married—and lived happily ever after. If this were a novel, now, here's the happy ending.'[63] But in *Herland*, Gilman refuses the mythic resolution of lesbian-separatism or the romantic closure of heterosexuality. The question is left open, and the two utopian possibilities coexist. In this way, *Herland* corresponds to Michèle Causse's notion of the project of subversive feminist writing: a 'psychic parthenogenesis' in which women give birth to themselves, coupled with an 'ontogenesis' which would grant women genuine access to 'human' being.[64] Although in her life, Gilman was forced to finally choose between lesbianism and heterosexuality, she was able to refuse this closure in *Herland*.

NOTES

1. Charlotte Perkins Gilman, *The Living of Charlotte Perkins Gilman. An Autobiography*, intro. Ann J. Lane (Madison, Wisconsin, 1990), p.19.

2. *Ibid.*, pp.23–24.

3. *Ibid.*, p.21.

4. Ann J. Lane, in *To Herland and Beyond. The Life and Work of Charlotte Perkins Gilman* (New York, 1990), says: 'Choosing not to enter the world of boys and sexuality, which could be expected to end in marriage and motherhood, she selected instead the life of the mind, which she identified with [her father]' (pp.57–58.)

5. Gilman came to view herself as a socialist, although she eschewed Marxism because of its focus on revolution and class conflict. Instead, she was drawn to a variant of native radicalism, combining Protestant morality with collectivist utopianism stressing reason and individual will. She was influenced (although not uncritical of) Edward Bellamy's utopian novel *Looking Backward* (1888), and by the Nationalist movement and British Fabian social philosophy (see Larry Ceplair (ed.), *Charlotte Perkins Gilman: A Nonfiction Reader* (New York, 1991)).

6. Darko Suvin claims estrangement is a crucial device for science fiction in general.

7. Jeff may have been modelled on Gilman's first husband, Walter Stetson, who appears to have idolized her. Ann J. Lane, in *To Herland and Beyond*, quotes Stetson thus: 'She was innocent, beautiful, frank. I grasped at her with the instincts of a drowning heart—was saved for the time. I loved all I saw pure in her . . . She was cleanliness to long for. Yes. I loved her purity of innocence, or perhaps, ignorance of the world. I told her so' (p.82). Gilman was to find out to her cost that such romantic stereotyping of women has its sinister side, a desire for domination.

8. Esmé Dodderidge, *The New Gulliver, or The Adventures of Lemuel Gulliver Jr. in Capavolta* (London, 1988).

9. Charlotte Perkins Gilman, *Herland* (1st pub. 1915), intro. Ann J. Lane (London, 1992), p.60. All further references are to this edition and appear in the body of my text.

10. Terry's hetero-patriarchal interpretation of the all-female world he calls 'Herland' is emblematized by his objectification and perjoration of the women through language: Herland is 'Feminisia', 'Ladyland', and 'Ma-land', and the women are 'old Colonels', 'Grandmas', 'Maiden Aunts', 'Morbid one-sided cripples', and 'sexless, epicene, undeveloped neuters'.

11. See Nancy Chodorow, *The Reproduction of Mothering. Psychoanalysis and the Sociology of Gender* (London, 1978). Chodorow argues that the girl's pre-Oedipal relation to the mother is closer than that of the boy's, because girls identify with their mothers more than boys due to their shared sex, and hence do not so fully separate from them to form an 'independent' identity.

12. Sonya Andermahr, 'The Politics of Separatism and Lesbian Utopian

Fiction', in *New Lesbian Criticism. Literary and Cultural Readings*, ed. Sally Munt (London, 1992), p.134.

13. Adrienne Rich, 'Compulsory Heterosexuality and Lesbian Existence', *Signs*, Vol.5, No.4, 1980, p.648.

14. Judith Kegan Gardiner in 'On Female Identity and Writing by Women' in *Writing and Sexual Difference*, ed. Elizabeth Abel (Brighton, 1982), has argued that often, 'the female author is engaged in a process of testing and defining various aspects of identity chosen from many imaginative possibilities', and she proposes that '. . . the text and its female hero begin as narcissistic extensions of the author' (p.187).

15. Laura E. Donaldson, in 'The eve of de-struction: Charlotte Perkins Gilman and the feminist re-creation of paradise', *Women's Studies*, Vol.16, 1989, highlights 'the flourishing health of women's utopian vision' in the late nineteenth century, which, she argues, provides a counter-tradition to the dystopian pessimism of many male writers of the time (pp.373–74).

16. See Carol Farley Kessler (ed.), *Daring To Dream. Utopian Stories by United States Women: 1836–1919* (Boston, Mass., 1984), p.189.

17. *Ibid.*, p.182.

18. From 1909 to 1916 Gilman wrote, edited and published her own monthly magazine, *The Forerunner*. Its title reflects her conception of her work as the envisioning of future possibilities.

19. Charlotte Perkins Gilman, *The Living of Charlotte Perkins Gilman. An Autobiography*, p.7.

20. *Ibid.*, p.8.

21. *Ibid.*, p.11.

22. *Ibid.*, p.11.

23. Gilman's short story 'The Unnatural Mother' (1916) propounds her ideal of an ethically expanded motherhood, by portraying a mother who saves an entire village and all its children when a dam bursts, by waiving her concerns for the safety of her own child.

24. Larry Ceplair (ed.), *Charlotte Perkins Gilman: A Nonfiction Reader*, p.247.

25. *Ibid.*, p.246.

26. She visualized such practices fictionally in short stories such as 'Making A Change' (1911).

27. Quoted in Dolores Hayden, *The Grand Domestic: A History of Feminist Designs for American Homes, Neighborhoods and Cities* (Cambridge, Mass. and London, 1981), p.189.

28. See Dorothy Dinnerstein, *The Rocking of the Cradle and the Ruling of the World* (London, 1987); Nancy Chodorow, *The Reproduction of Mothering*; Mary O'Brien, *The Politics of Reproduction* (London, 1981); Sarah Ruddick, 'Maternal Thinking', *Feminist Studies*, Vol.6, No.2, 1980. Gilman's theories of motherhood particularly anticipate Sarah Ruddick, who argues in 'Maternal Thinking' that motherhood involves conscious intellectual

processes which have all the characteristics of thought as defined by Jurgen Habermas. But she distinguishes 'maternal thinking' from scientific thought in three respects. First, because the object of maternal thought—the child—is in a constant state of growth, maternal thinking tends to be undogmatic and provisional. Secondly, because the child can only imperfectly articulate its needs, the mother has a highly developed capacity to observe gestures, expression and behaviour and to infer psychological states from these. Thirdly, whereas scientific thinking is largely motivated by the need to control the environment, maternal thinking is motivated by care of human beings, and the different priorities involved can result in mothers having a different set of ethical values. Gilman departs from Ruddick in that she sees these skills as acquirable through training, whereas Ruddick seems to imply that they are acquired 'naturally' through the experience of mothering itself. Nevertheless, Gilman's ideal of mothering practice corresponds closely to Ruddick's description, and the Herlanders manifest all the essential features of 'maternal thinking'. They are 'inconveniently reasonable' and have 'devoted their combined intelligence' to the issue of how best to mother. Their methods are always temporary, and open to constant improvement in response to the changing needs of their offspring; few of their laws, for example, are more than twenty years old. Their science of psychology has been developed to the highest and subtlest degree to enable the more effective and efficient education of their children, and their ethical system is fundamentally collective in nature; everything is, in Laura Donaldson's words, done for the good of the race as a whole, and morality is perceived as 'a web of relationship that extends over time' (Laura Donaldson, 'The eve of de-struction', p.378).

29. Larry Ceplair (ed.), *Charlotte Perkins Gilman: A Nonfiction Reader*, p.248.

30. *Ibid.*, p.249.

31. *Ibid.*, p.248.

32. Gilman wrote, in all, three utopian novels, *Moving the Mountain* (1911), *Herland* (1915), and *With Her in Ourland* (1916).

33. This was a metaphor frequently used by Edward Bellamy, in *Looking Backward 2000–1887*, ed. John L. Thomas (Cambridge, Mass., 1967; 1st pub. 1888), reflecting progressive Darwinist theories of society as an organism: 'So it came about that the rosebush of humanity was transplanted, and set in sweet, warm, dry earth, where the sun bathed it, the stars wooed it, and the south wind caressed it. Then it appeared that it was indeed a rosebush. The vermin and the mildew disappeared, and the bush was covered with the most beautiful red roses, whose fragrance filled the world' (p.284).

34. Margaret Miller, 'The Ideal Woman in Two Feminist Science-Fiction Utopias', *Science Fiction Studies*, Vol.10, 1983, p.191.

35. Gilman explored this theme in her poem 'Similar Cases', published in *The Nationalist* in 1890, a satiric comment on the belief in immutable 'human nature'.

36. Quoted in Carol Farley Kessler (ed.), *Daring to Dream*, p.19.

37. See Lee Cullen Khanna, 'Women's Worlds: New Directions in Utopian Fiction', *Alternative Futures* Vol.4 (2–3), 1981; and Carol Pearson and Katherine Pope, *The Female Hero in British and American Fiction* (New York, 1981).

38. See Carol Christ, *Diving Deep and Surfacing: Women Writers on Spiritual Quest* (Boston, 1980); and Carol Christ and Judith Plaskow (eds), *Womanspirit Rising: A Feminist Reader in Religion* (San Francisco, 1979).

39. Sandra Gilbert, '"The Blank Page" and Issues of Female Creativity', in *The New Feminist Criticism. Essays on Women, Literature and Theory*, ed. Elaine Showalter (London, 1986), p.308.

40. Drawing on an essentialist strand of feminist spirituality, Casdagli uses parthenogenesis as a metaphorical and literal image of innate female reproductive capacity. The story revises and transforms the myth of Zeus and Athene, and the Christian myth of virgin birth, as narratives which co-opt female reproductive capacities for the male. These patriarchal narratives are transformed into metaphors of female creativity and into examples of actual female reproduction based on the spiritual bonding of women: 'The union or yoga of women in one-gender relationships is felt by those involved to be a profoundly creative act and resultant in metaphorical, if not actual, birth' (see Penny Casdagli, 'Mab' in *Despatches From the Frontiers of the Female Mind*, eds. Jen Green and Sarah Lefanu (London, 1985), p.204).

41. See Carol Pearson and Katherine Pope, *The Female Hero*.

42. Quoted in Sarah Lefanu, *In the Chinks of the World Machine. Feminism and Science Fiction* (London, 1988), p.54. Lefanu describes the all-female community depicted in Sally Miller Gearhart's *The Wanderground* in similar terms of 'coming home': 'In many ways the novel represents an imaginative recreation of an unthreatening childhood world, one that exists before the complexities and dangers of language and sexuality come into being' (*ibid.*, p.69).

43. Hélène Cixous, 'The Laugh of the Medusa', in *New French Feminisms. An Anthology*, eds. Elaine Marks and Isabelle de Courtivron (London, 1981).

44. See Hélène Cixous 'The Laugh of the Medusa'; and Hélène Cixous and Catherine Clément, *The Newly Born Woman* (Minneapolis, 1986). For Cixous, women's marginal position in patriarchal society and in relation to the symbolic order means that they have privileged access to the mother's body, because women do not repress their libidinal desires as much as men.

45. See Judith Kegan Gardiner, 'On Female Identity and Writing by

Women', for an account of the way that, for many women writers, constructing the subject position of the reader resembles a process of mothering: 'Through the relationship between the narrator and the reader, such fictions re-create the ambivalent experiences of ego violation and mutual identification that occur between mother and daughter' (p.188).

46. Northrop Frye says in 'Varieties of Literary Utopias', in *Utopias and Utopian Thought*, ed. Frank E. Manual (Boston, 1966): '. . . considered as a final or definitive social ideal, the utopia is a static society; and most utopias have built-in safeguards against radical alteration of the structure' (p.31).

47. Quoted in Marilyn R. Farwell, 'Heterosexual Plots and Lesbian Subtexts: Toward a Theory of Lesbian Narrative Space', in *Lesbian Texts and Contexts. Radical Revisions,* eds. Karla Jay and Joanne Glasgow (London, 1992), p.93.

48. *Ibid.,* p.94.

49. See Alice Parker, 'Nicole Brossard: A Differential Equation of Lesbian Love', in *Lesbian Texts and Contexts,* p.307.

50. Nancy K. Miller, *Subject to Change: Reading Feminist Writing* (New York, 1988), p.10.

51. Monique Wittig, 'One is Not Born a Woman', in *For Lesbians Only. A Separatist Anthology,* eds. Sarah Lucia-Hoagland and Julia Penelope (London, 1988), p.441.

52. Terry, of course, fails to reconstruct his gender identity and is ultimately excluded from Herland.

53. After reading *Looking Backward* in 1889 or early 1890, Gilman wrote to Martha Lane, her lover, that Nationalism had struck at the business system but had missed the 'possibly deeper' issue of 'the struggle between man and woman' (quoted in Larry Ceplair (ed.), *Charlotte Perkins Gilman. A Nonfiction Reader,* p.34).

54. *Ibid.,* p.28.

55. *Ibid.,* p.28.

56. Anne Cranny-Francis, *Feminist Fiction. Uses of Generic Fiction* (Cambridge, 1990), p.124.

57. Charlotte Perkins Gilman, *The Living of Charlotte Perkins Gilman. An Autobiography,* p.281.

58. Marilyn Frye, *Willful Virgin. Essays in Feminism* (Freedom, Ca., 1992), p.132.

59. *Ibid.,* p.133.

60. *Ibid.,* p.136.

61. *Ibid.,* p.136.

62. Unlike *Moving the Mountain* (1911), Gilman's first and less successful utopian novel, where her heterosexual 'humanist' ideal is textually depicted in great detail.

63. Charlotte Perkins Gilman, *The Living of Charlotte Perkins Gilman. An Autobiography*, p.281.

64. See Alice Parker, 'Nicole Brossard: A Differential Equation of Lesbian Love', p.305.

Index